BOSS
OF THE
GRIPS

OTHER BOOKS BY ERIC K. WASHINGTON

Manhattanville: Old Heart of West Harlem

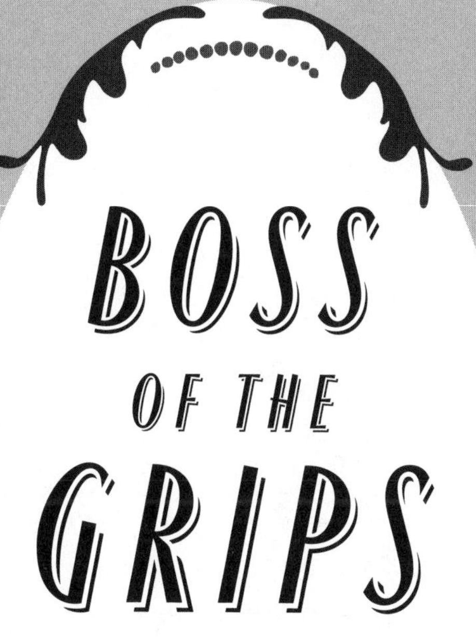

BOSS OF THE GRIPS

THE LIFE OF JAMES H. WILLIAMS AND THE RED CAPS OF GRAND CENTRAL TERMINAL

ERIC K. WASHINGTON

LIVERIGHT PUBLISHING CORPORATION
A Division of W. W. Norton & Company
Independent Publishers Since 1923

Frontispiece: A sporty James H. Williams, seated with bowler hat. No date, possibly 1910s. *Schomburg/NYPL.*

Printed in the United States of America
First Edition

For information about permission to reproduce selections from this book, write to Permissions, Liveright Publishing Corporation, a division of W. W. Norton & Company, Inc., 500 Fifth Avenue, New York, NY 10110

For information about special discounts for bulk purchases, please contact W. W. Norton Special Sales at specialsales@wwnorton.com or 800-233-4830

Manufacturing by LSC Communications, Harrisonburg
Book design by Chris Welch
Production manager: Beth Steidle

ISBN 978-1-63149-322-5

Liveright Publishing Corporation, 500 Fifth Avenue, New York, N.Y. 10110
www.wwnorton.com

W. W. Norton & Company Ltd., 15 Carlisle Street, London W1D 3BS

1 2 3 4 5 6 7 8 9 0

FOR MY GRANDFATHER, JOHN MOSS, BORN IN 1843,
AND FOR MY PARENTS—ALL OF THEM

At the Grand Central . . . is a colored man who probably knows more people than any other Negro in New York. He is Chief James H. Williams, head of the Red Caps of the . . . station.

—*NEW YORK AGE*, 1923

CONTENTS

PART V: ECLIPSE

INTRODUCTION

New York City's Grand Central Terminal is a rightly celebrated tour de force that has captivated the traveling public for more than a century. Opened on February 2, 1913, the world's largest railroad station was built by the American firms Reed & Stem and Warren & Wetmore. It showcases a host of such artistic talents as Jules-Félix Coutan, whose monumental sculpture of Hercules, Mercury, and Minerva above a Tiffany clock crowns the building's entry; and Paul César Helleu and Charles Basing, whose cerulean painted ceiling transports a mind-wandering traveler to the blue heavens. Many regarded it as the "finest example of Beaux-Arts civic planning in New York,"[1] at once an architectural confection and a masterwork of innovative design and engineering. Yet the sublimeness of Grand Central Terminal's Tennessee pink marble concourses, its cascading ramps and stairs and opulent shadows, belies its once-essential operating model: the servitude of African-American workers.

The servitude in this case was rooted in the American tradition of racial exploitation. Northerners might have comfortably regarded their territory as a historically enlightened refuge from the harsh segregation practices of the South, or of a bygone era. However, twentieth-century New York City had ample evidence of its own Jim Crow policies—notably at Grand Central. The station's tightly run system deployed a singular corps of black men in red caps as baggage porters—"Red Caps," as they were popularly known—who at times numbered in the several hundreds. Travelers routinely hailed one of the ubiquitous wearers of red caps and put the porter through his paces. Or a porter, seeing no gain in being invisible, readily volunteered himself to unburden a traveler's grip. "The nature of a porter's work," the noted writer E. B. White observed in *The New Yorker*, "tends to put him in a class with beasts of burden."[2] Indeed, throughout the bustling concourses, a porter's often backbreaking and demeaning labor was integral both to the station's functional efficiency and to its glamorous ambience. It was perhaps inevitable that Grand Central's Red Cap porter system became the model for numerous railroad stations across the nation.

Made categorically identifiable both by their apparel and by their complexion, the black workforce at Grand Central embodied America's color line—the laws, bylaws, amendments, and social attitudes that closed doors to blacks. His travels through Europe had convinced Frederick Douglass by the 1880s that racial prejudice was "purely an American feeling" and did not innately belong to the broader white race. In the United States, the color line was a deep-seated cultural contrivance that had festered for generations. It was a panoply of contradictions. At times one felt its prohibitions only intuitively, yet they were as palpable as a taut rope. It could be woven into the collective subconscious by social mores or by deliberate legislative acts. But blacks also found ways to circumvent and mitigate impasses created when whites erected the color line: they bent and reconfigured it into opportunities and positions of leverage. Such was the case at Grand Central, where the color line afforded black workers the means, proverbially speaking, to make a way out of no way.

Indeed, "redcapping" flourished as one of the most iconic service occupations of the last century. It originated at Grand Central Depot in 1895 with a dozen white staff but had become exclusively black by 1905. A source of pride, the job was coveted by, and almost invariably associated with, African-American men. Whereas educated whites shunned the work as too low in status, educated blacks recognized it as a rare and propitious employment option in an era of rigid racial barriers. At Grand Central, African-American college students undertook redcapping as a means to pay their way through school. The man who created this opportunity for securing a foothold toward professional and social advancement was James H. Williams, a singular individual whose history at Grand Central Terminal is steeped in urban legend and the mythology of the landmark we know today.

Born to formerly enslaved African-American parents in 1878, Williams broke the color line of Grand Central's white Red Cap attendants in 1903. Upon Williams's hire, the former public reminder that attendants "are not porters," to carry baggage—but rather were on hand to assist station passengers—began taking on a new definition. Starting in 1909, Williams served as the chief attendant (or chief porter, or chief red cap) of Grand Central Terminal—its first and most notable African-American officer—and remained in that position until his death in 1948. In this capacity, he embodied a unique juncture between black and white America. His influential forty-five-year tenure made the monumental railroad station not only a gateway to America's greatest city but, just as much, a gateway to the nation's greatest African-American neighborhood: Harlem. For nearly half a century, Chief Williams supervised a staff of men who were relegated by dint of race to the lowest stratum of the station's workforce, though their role was integral to the railroad system. Like their rail-roaming kin, the sleeping car (or Pullman) porters—who were also African-American—the station-bound Red Caps were crucial to the Swiss-watch precision of the terminal and woven into the beguiling experience of early twentieth-century railroad travel.

Williams's life coincided with key periods in the evolving social and cultural world of African Americans living in the ever-changing metropolis of New York City. His experiences offer a window on post–Civil War America and the heady optimism of the Reconstruction era, a period that obliged the Williams family and their kind to discover strategies to sidestep financial dependency and social stigmatization in order to achieve some form of self-reliance. We follow Williams as a "race" man: he was an active, if unassuming, agent of the early twentieth-century ideological cause of "racial uplift"—which strove to quell white prejudice through black self-improvement in education, business, labor, civic interest, and the arts—that in the 1920s would fuel the New Negro movement and the Harlem Renaissance. And we follow him through two world wars, whose veterans from his earlier Red Cap workforce at Grand Central acquire greater resolve to surmount the racial bigotry on their home front.

It was Williams who redirected this historic labor force of railroad station porters, ingeniously transforming an outwardly self-abasing job into a coveted employment opportunity, be it interim, permanent, or moonlight. As the *New York Herald Tribune* would observe, Williams's chiefdom ushered scores of promising but fiscally strapped young black college men on "their way to a mortarboard by working under a red cap"[3] as luggage porters. Many of them were Greek-lettered men, a prime example of the countless social networks that blacks formed for themselves when they were categorically barred as personae non gratae from white fraternities and other private white institutions. Their academic credentials notwithstanding, these black "Greeks" as well as their unschooled "brothers of the race" worked as unsalaried laborers. They were ubiquitous throughout the terminal's opulent Beaux-Arts concourses, heaving trunks and valises, tucked with satchels and pets, and toting the golf clubs and hatboxes of bustling travelers whom they depended upon for tips.

James H. Williams's story reveals the qualities that ultimately positioned him and his legion of Red Caps as iconic cultural touchstones both of the Grand Central Terminal and of the Harlem community. While his story is obviously about race and labor, it is also overwhelmingly about personal industry, resourcefulness, and philanthropy. Over the course of his life, America roiled under some of the most seismic shifts in its history; the country's ever-changing social and political landscape shaped Williams into a remarkably complex man, at once a management functionary and a community hero.

As a New York Central Railroad employee, he ushered statesmen, movie stars, society elite, sports heroes, high clergy, and other notables to and from trains with marginal visibility. But he stood out conspicuously among African Americans as "the Chief," who created a platform to employ black men, to sustain black students, and to showcase the race in the most admirable light. In this capacity as the "boss of the grips" (*grips* being a term applied to both baggage and handlers), he was part of the central nervous system of the Harlem Renaissance, the storied era—from about the end of World War I through the mid-1930s—of Harlem's cultural, literary, and artistic expression. There was also a renaissance of vibrant business and industry as ancillary "race" enterprises, as well as inspirited African-American labor and civic movements in which Chief Williams was noted.

Some clarification may be needed as to how a porter may count as a professional—James Williams was, after all, not a banker, doctor, or priest. His responsibilities at Grand Central were more those of a general factotum: his executive duties, variously operational and diplomatic, included hiring, training, assigning, and supervising some five hundred men. "We make the first and last impression upon the patrons of the railroad we serve," he emphasized to his workforce. The sports author John R. Tunis concurred, observing that "the railroad red cap comes into contact with nearly all the famous people of his time, from Queens and Princes down."[4] Numerous profiles of Williams (from about 1909 to 1948) attest to his legendary sagacity and tact, which earned him acknowledgment from blacks and whites alike as "the Chief." The title was as affectionate as it was deferential, and it frequently opened doors that were traditionally closed to African Americans.

But while Harlemites admired him as a forthright advocate and power broker for their community, Williams genuinely touched others, too. The day after he died, the journalist Earl Brown had to go to Chicago, so headed down to Grand Central for a ticket on the *20th Century Limited*. For many, boarding that crack New York-to-Chicago train—which the New York Central advertised as "The Most Famous Train in the World"—anticipated the sight of Chief Williams at the gate. On the main concourse, Brown ran into some old-time friends, seasoned grips he knew from when he'd redcapped for a summer away from school. The vast majority of passengers weren't going to Chicago, didn't know about Williams's death, and did not miss a step. But Brown, and maybe some of the 'Caps, saw a couple of strangers: "Two old white passengers, friends of the Chief, said they had read about his death in the morning paper. They were crying."[5]

Who was this black man whose passing elicited grief among both friends and strangers? Indeed, tracing the life of James H. Williams is a dogged but fascinating task. The unobtrusive nature of his job rendered him nearly ephemeral—but not invisible. Though he was not a man of letters, in the letters and observations of others, and in the chronicles of his times, he takes shape, fleshes out, and breathes.

PART I

COMING OF AGE ON THE BRINK OF THE TWENTIETH CENTURY

CHAPTER 1

"To Hustle While You're Waiting"

"All things come to him who waits."
But that is merely stating
One feature of the case—you've got
To hustle while you're waiting.

—DR. WILLIAM HENRY JOHNSON (1833–1918)[1]

In the late morning of August 29, 1939, James H. Williams stood at the center of the upper concourse at Grand Central Terminal, waiting for a writer he'd agreed to talk to. Williams was a tawny-hued man of average height and medium build. The grayed temples below his cap betrayed his sixty-one years—thirty of which he'd spent surveying this station with keen-eyed assurance. As he waited, he occasionally blew into the pea whistle in his gloved right hand to signal his uniformed men to move to various parts of the terminal. The men were Negro baggage porters—a sizable army, several hundred strong, of rail station attendants—called Red Caps. The words CHIEF ATTENDANT in gold-embroidered letters above the visor of Williams's own red cap announced his rank, as did the rose or carnation that he daily wore in the lapel of his double-breasted coat. What was not part of his uniform, but common among men of his age, was a black mourning band hiked up over the right sleeve of his dark coat—it's not known who he was mourning.

He glanced at the clock atop the circular information booth. The great captivating orb, inset with four milk-glass faces, gave the kiosk the look of an ornate jewel box made of stone, glass, and gold. Its beauty was perhaps what made this clock the most popular meeting spot in the station, though Williams's appreciation of it was less romantic than practical. He prided himself on being punctual, and could easily read the clock from most anywhere in the great hall—always ticking toward the arrival of someone he was due to meet.

This morning it was the writer. Since his appointment as chief attendant in 1909, Williams had become used to interviews. America's number-one Red Cap, as a prominent railroad labor columnist acknowledged him to be, rarely had a day when he wasn't "besieged by some newspaper reporter, magazine writer, or other journalistic wag."[2] Although they often spoke to him about his daily duties as Grand Central's Chief Red Cap, he just as often suspected they were trying to coax him to tell how he came to be the first Negro Red Cap porter in the country. A seductive urban legend held that on Labor Day 1890, a colored teenage porter named James Williams attached a strip of red flannel to his hat to stand out in the crowded old Grand Central Depot. This conspicuous headwear eventually became uniform for the men hustling bags from railway waiting rooms to the trains and vice versa.[3] But that story was muddled in myth: the Red Cap system was started in 1895. Though Williams had been the first colored man whom Grand Central ever employed as a Red Cap, his hiring occurred in April 1903, and he wasn't made chief attendant until 1909. Still, he was more apt to shrug off credit for being the country's original Red Cap than either to own it or disclaim it. Williams knew this origin story was a considerable source of pride for many, even if it was only an amusing novelty to some. "That's what they say, and they've been saying it for some time," he told one reporter, kindling the mystery.[4]

Williams now eyed a tall dark young man pressing toward him through the heavily trafficked concourse, and removed his glove to extend a handshake. The two had never met, but Williams likely knew something of Abram Hill by reputation. At twenty-nine years old, Hill was a rising playwright in community theater. He had caught the attention of Rose McClendon, one of Broadway's most esteemed black actresses, whose troupe was poised to begin rehearsing Hill's latest play, *On Strivers Row*. Hailed as "the first high comedy of Negro manners," the play was set in an exclusive Harlem enclave in the West 130s.[5] It depicted, in Hill's own words, a black bourgeoisie self-absorbed with its own upward mobility and ostentatious status: "Neighbor competed with the neighbor to outdo one another. Musicals, teas, and soirees set the social vogue in their homes, whereas yacht parties, theater, concerts, opera-attending, weekend retreats at resorts and summer homes—added luster to the doings of the tribe."[6]

The comedy's setting was sure to provoke Williams's curiosity—and maybe a little discomfort, too. The Chief was one of the first Negroes to move into Strivers' Row in 1919—when restrictions against black tenants had lifted—and had called the neighborhood home for a dozen years, having sold his house there only four years earlier. Newspaper reports that Hill was the subject of rumors and threatened lawsuits—despite his insistence that his play was based only on his vivid imagination—may have fueled Williams's wariness. Of course, he understood that such controversies were often cooked up to enhance ticket sales. Still, the prospect of discussing old friends on Strivers' Row might have made him feel disloyal.

Despite his satirical aim, Hill himself lived at 795 St. Nicholas Avenue, at the southwest corner of West 150th Street, in Sugar Hill, Harlem's other prestigious enclave that had opened to blacks (as white residents fled) a few years after Strivers' Row. The two affluent areas perhaps represented a generational divide between Harlem's old and new guards—the former a bit more staid, the latter more freewheeling. During the early 1930s, the worst years of the Great Depression, Hill, his mother, and his sister entertained as many as seventy-five people at their annual summer bridge parties. Hill was relatively prosperous during those lean years, having worked as an administrative assistant to the national director of the Federal Theater, a product of the Federal Writers' Project (a program of the New Deal's Works Progress Administration, or WPA).

In 1938 much of Harlem had eagerly anticipated the Federal Writers' Project's "Portrait of Harlem," a chapter of *New York Panorama*, a book of the WPA's state-by-state American Guide Series. It discussed the city's African-American history from earliest colonial days under Dutch and British rule to its transformation into the world's largest urban Negro population. The WPA hired some of the country's best-known black writers, including Zora Neale Hurston, Claude McKay, and Richard Wright, to produce its guidebooks.[7] But some found the "Portrait of Harlem" irksome. Historian Dr. Willis N. Huggins, an early proponent of African and African-American studies in American schools, criticized its troubling oversights: "Neither Chief [Wesley] Williams of the Fire Department nor Lieutenant Battle of the Police Department [is] mentioned." Chief Williams's perplexity was predictable: fire battalion chief Wesley Williams was his son, and police lieutenant Samuel J. Battle—"Jesse," to all who knew him—as dear to him as a son, had been one of his Red Caps. Both of those men had broken the color barrier on the city's civil service forces.

Williams might have murmured a few conspiratorial amens to Huggins's litany of questionable omissions in "Portrait of Harlem." Where were the scenes of Harlem? Where were the educators? Where the "meritorious women" like the first self-made millionaire entrepreneur Madame C. J. Walker—"whereas [Josephine] Baker, who never was a part of Harlem life is lauded." Huggins bemoaned the absence of praise for the black press—such as the *New York Age*, *Amsterdam News*, *Chicago Defender*, *Pittsburgh Courier*, *Baltimore Afro-American*, *New Journal and Guide*, and the old *Messenger*—that reported on life in Harlem. He took a dim view of holding up "cultists and fanatics" to represent Harlem while the chapter made "no mention of sounder religious leaders" such as Adam Clayton Powell, Sr., Charles T. Walker, William H. Brooks, Lorenzo H. King, William Lloyd Imes, or Rev. David Elliott "D. E." Tobias—several of whom Williams and his family had personally interacted with through the years. Like Huggins, Williams could easily regard such curious omissions and questionable inclusions as profoundly disappointing for a government-sponsored publication focusing on Negro life in Harlem.[8]

Hill's mandate, in coming to the station, was to write profiles of Harlem's many notable Negro achievers, colorful characters, and vibrant institutions. His assigned subjects included the nightclub owner Ed Smalls; the fashion plate Blanche Dunn; the outré Hamilton Lodge transvestite ball; and Williams. According to Hill, Williams agreed to give an interview only "after I promised him that the write up would not be on the personal side." Williams politely but firmly shifted any question remotely about his private life "into something concerning his work and his many workers." He protested self-effacingly that there were "far greater men of his race to write about" than himself, but Hill sensed a certain pride during their meeting: "Of one thing he is sure. He has proved that the old superstition that Negroes would not work under a Negro is false."

Before long Chief Williams checked the big clock. In his characteristically gracious yet decisive manner, he excused himself from Hill, as an important traveler was soon due. He directed the young man to the New York Central Publicity Department over on Lexington Avenue. Hill conveyed the awkwardness of their meeting in a note he attached to his typed interview file: "Chief Williams was not in a very talkative mood."

"Well, everybody has to make a living," Williams said to Hill, then turned and disappeared through the crowd into the station.[9]

◆

Around noon on Thursday, May 15, 1873, a throng of the city's black citizens assembled at the corner of Fifth Avenue and Eighth Street. They had come to celebrate the passage of a New York Assembly bill that strengthened their rights more than did a recent federal civil rights bill. The citizens included some two hundred men of the Grant and Colfax Cavalry; about one hundred fifty from the Skidmore Guard; a Pioneer Corps from Jersey City; and several colored lodges of Odd Fellows, Freemasons, and Sons of Malta. There were also representatives from a coachmen's association, the Sabbath School of the AME Bethel Church, and benevolent societies of various monikers. As they settled into place, a long line of carriages pulled up behind them conveying leading black citizens and

Harried black food countermen kept up with the exigent demands of hungry railroad passengers, 1868. *Library of Congress.*

prominent friends of the civil rights movement. Most notable was Dr. William Henry Johnson, an Albany figure who, as chairman of the State Central Committee of Colored Citizens, a grassroots organization, had spearheaded the New York bill. The state bill was a swatch of legislation stitched to various acts passed in congressional sessions between 1870 and 1871, intended to enforce the rights and protections that had been promised to blacks in the Thirteenth, Fourteenth, and Fifteenth federal amendments.

On February 1, 1865, President Abraham Lincoln had approved the joint resolution of Congress submitting the proposed Thirteenth Amendment to the Constitution to the states. The document declared, "Neither slavery nor involuntary servitude, except as a punishment for crime whereof the party shall have been duly convicted, shall exist within the United States, or any place subject to their jurisdiction." Though the new law formally abolished slavery, the potent phrase "except as a punishment for crime" was an explicit deal-breaker. The provision allowed states to mete out servitude as punishment, and it also disabused emancipated Negroes of their notions of out-and-out freedom.

The Fourteenth Amendment, ratified on July 9, 1868, granted citizenship to "all persons born or naturalized in the United States," which included former slaves recently freed. In addition, it forbade states to deny any person "life, liberty or property, without due process of law" or to "deny to any person within its jurisdiction the equal protection of the laws." Abolitionists were constantly at odds with the fact that the amendment lacked explicit wording to prevent states from denying the right to vote based on race.

The Fifteenth Amendment, ratified on February 3, 1870, granted African-American men the right to vote by declaring that the "right of citizens of the United States to vote shall not be denied or abridged by the United States or by any state on account of race, color, or previous condition of servitude." But this promise would not be fully realized for almost a century. Through the use of poll taxes, literacy tests, and violent intimidation, Southern states were able to effectively disenfranchise eligible black voters. Only with the passage of the Voting Rights Act in 1965 would the majority of African Americans in the South be able to register to vote. Regardless of what the Thirteenth, Fourteenth and Fifteenth amendments guaranteed, their cumulative weight did not nullify common practices of racial exclusion, exploitation, and selective criminalization.

So on this celebratory day when all had assembled at the intersection, Chief Marshal George F. Mack, a prominent black leader strongly allied with President Ulysses S. Grant, led the parade of about three thousand people.[10] The picturesque line "was gay with uniforms, badges, and regalia, trim and orderly in arrangement," as it commenced southward to the musical accompaniment of a twenty-piece band (and the Skidmore Guards' own eight-piece drum corps). The procession moved down Fifth Avenue to Spring Street, where it turned east to Broadway and returned northward to Fourteenth Street—the demarcation in those days between "downtown" and "uptown"—snaking their way through the streets until they reached 24th Street, where they marched the two long blocks to Fifth Avenue.

The marchers commanded the grand Fifth Avenue for almost a mile until their parade came astride the great stone walls of the Croton Aqueduct's Receiving Basin at 42nd Street. From there, the former site of the Colored Orphan Asylum was a void, but was animated by an indelible memory: the asylum had been burned to the ground on the first day of the infamous Draft Riots. On July 13, 1863, some fifty thousand whites—mostly mobs of working-class Irish enraged by new federal laws to draft men into the Union Army—enacted a campaign of antiblack terror and lynchings. Though all the asylum's children and staff escaped the blaze, the building was the most famous collateral destruction of the riot. Even a full decade later, the marchers could not foresee that the site would still endure for generations to come as the country's greatest example of urban unrest.

From Fifth Avenue, the pilgrimage turned east again, to Madison Avenue, where once more it descended for almost a mile to 26th Street, where it suddenly paused. From a stand in front of the Union League Club, Maj.-Gen. James W. Husted (a chief champion of New York's new civil rights bill) reviewed the column of marchers. It was a small but poignant formality, for the Union League—established during the Civil War to promote loyalty to President Lincoln's policies—sponsored the corps of the Twentieth U.S. Colored Infantry soldiers among them, whom it had sent into battle with a ceremonious presentation of colors in March 1864. From the club, the march resumed southward along Fourth Avenue to Astor Place, where it disbanded at about three o'clock.

On that same May 15 evening, the celebration of the state's rigorous new civil rights bill carried over to the Cooper Union at Astor Place. The great hall was "uncomfortably full" with hundreds of black New Yorkers, some of whom were suing theater and tavern owners for thousands of dollars in damages in the Supreme Court. William H. Johnson recounted a grievance to the crowd about a stage driver who recently denied him and a woman companion from boarding because they were black. The new bill was meant to prevent such egregious behavior. "All we desire and all we demand is to be permitted to sail in the same boat, and no more," Johnson proclaimed from the stage. "You must not insult a colored lady or gentleman any sooner than you would those of a lighter complexion." The law stated at length that no citizen could be excluded by dint of "race, color, or previous condition of servitude." It mandated that all innkeepers, public transit operators, theater and entertainment house owners, public school administrators, and cemetery associations were bound to comply.

◈

James H. Williams would later receive passed-down memories of this controversial climate, having been only a generation removed from slavery. His parents, John Wesley Williams and Lucy Ellen Spady—both born in Northampton County, Virginia—had experienced the wretchedness of America's "peculiar institution" firsthand. According to family lore, John Wesley Williams, believed to be born in 1851, escaped via the Underground Railroad when he was only a teenager. Having grown into a wiry, olive-brown man of medium height, John Wesley could read and write, which would have given him an untold advantage when he rejoined family members in Virginia after the Civil War. By 1872, twenty-one-year-old John Wesley found work as a waiter at the Atlantic Hotel in Norfolk. His father, George W., was deceased, but his mother, Sarah Powell, lived in town as well as his four siblings: brothers Leonard F. and Henry B., and sisters Ada and Alice. Another sister, Malinda, lived in Brooklyn, New York.[11] The order of the siblings' births is unclear.

By 1873, John Wesley had moved to New York City, presumably for better work prospects. He lived in Greenwich Village at 218 Thompson Street, which was connected to the parallel Sullivan Street via a network of dark, ill-boding alleyways. The enclave was known as "Little Africa"—not an uncommon nickname for whites to bestow on just about any conspicuously Negro sector—but John Wesley did not find comfort in being among his own here. Steeped in abject poverty, the area was rife with sordid dives and rakish types

Though both former slaves from the same Virginia county, Williams's parents, John Wesley Williams and Lucy Ella Spady, met and married in New York about 1873. *Charles Ford Williams Family Collection.*

who preyed upon the unwitting. Not surprisingly, it was the subject of numerous case studies by such social reformers as Jacob Riis. But perhaps a redeeming aspect to the street's widespread infamy was that it induced John Wesley to move as soon as possible—which meant he must find work.

Despite the abolition of slavery in the South, even Northern states like New York would limit his employment options. Whether enforced by laws or by social customs, the strict color line effectively barred blacks from all but the most menial occupations. Just before the Civil War, New York's colored population amounted to some ten thousand men and women, the majority of whom worked in service-related positions.[12] As he had done in Norfolk, John Wesley found work in New York as a hotel waiter. Likewise, it was at one of the city's finest hotels, the Sturtevant House.[13]

During the Gilded Age, Brooklyn was known as the city of churches, and New York (just Manhattan then) as the city of hotels.

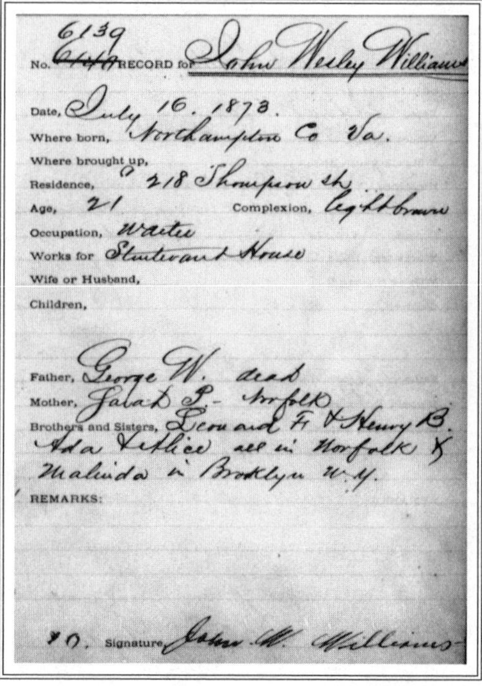

No. 6139 RECORD for John Wesley Williams

Date, July 16. 1873.

Where born, Northampton Co Va.

Where brought up,

Residence, 218 Thompson st

Age, 21 Complexion, light brown

Occupation, Waiter

Works for Sturtevant House

Wife or Husband,

Children,

Father, George W. dead

Mother, Sarah P. - Norfolk

Brothers and Sisters, Leonard F. & Henry B. Ada & Lettice all in Norfolk & Malinda in Brooklyn N.Y.

REMARKS:

Signature, John W. Williams

John Wesley Williams was a hotel waiter at Broadway's immense and sophisticated Sturtevant House. *Freedmen's Bank Records, 1873.*

In 1871 the noted hotel managing team Leland Brothers opened Sturtevant House on the southeast corner of Broadway at West 29th Street. It was one of several first-class public houses that were springing up on the city's main thoroughfare. Its prime location was an indicator of a hotel's stature, and another was its brigade of Negro waitstaff. And so in the spring of 1873, the Lelands hired the experienced colored hotel waiter John Wesley Williams to join the staff of Sturtevant House. That same spring a celebrity parricide at the hotel—a young man paid a murderous visit to the rooms of his father, the novelist Mansfield Tracy Walworth—might have shown John Wesley that in a fashionable district, in contrast to Little Africa, a gunshot exchange could oddly add cachet to a hotel.

John Wesley was fortunate, inasmuch as blacks could not be overly selective about their work opportunities. Needless to say,

Negro workers were often viewed as easily replaceable—a hotel manager could build up, and as quickly replenish, his service staffs of waiters, porters, maids, barbers, coachmen, elevator operators, and the like. Though these working conditions were tenuous, a number of black employees could muster some benefits from working under the roof of the same hotel. That is, black service employees frequently formed remarkable social organizations and networks. Sturtevant House, conveniently located near the theaters and the Grand Central Depot, was a case in point. In 1875 the *Clipper*, a theater trade magazine, praised "the waiters at the Sturtevant House" who had formed the Pastime Literary Club, "the first amateur dramatic society of colored men that was ever organized in this city." Their club's venue was a Negro social hall called the Lincoln Literary Musical Association, a three-story brick townhouse at 132 West 27th Street—a "black belt" address adjacent to the more exclusive white district of imposing Gothic churches and exclusive hotels. "The house was crowded," the journal claimed, with "a large number of the Sturtevant guests." The players enacted scenes from *Hamlet*, *Richard III,* and *Macbeth*, apparently eliciting generous praise from the audience. Their performances recalled the talents of Ira Aldrich and Morgan Smith, two "colored [American] delineators of Shakespearian characters who created quite an interest in Europe"—Aldridge from the 1820s until his death in 1867, and Smith since 1867. But for the Sturtevant House actor-waiters, surely a "laughable sketch" in the program was a knowing sendup of their proverbial "day jobs." Its title alone, "Wanted—500 Hands for the Centennial"—referring to the celebration fever spreading coast to coast over the nation's upcoming one-hundredth birthday—betrayed a wry, introspective humor about their livelihoods.[14]

One society writer in the early 1870s observed that male Negro servants, waiters, coachmen, and the like were quite the fashion, rendering many hotel establishments favorably exclusive and recherché. The fashion for black servants spread fast and far—and often unwholesomely. By the end of the decade, chic matrons at Paris receptions and in London lace shops employed "imitation

John Wesley Williams's new waiting job at Sturtevant House coincided with the sensational parricide of novelist Mansfield Tracy Walworth, a hotel resident. *David Rumsey Map Collection.*

niggers"—white men in blackface—to cater to the discriminating tastes of their guests, in the form of "gigantic ebony figures with enamel eyes, red lips, and glittering teeth, holding silver trays with refreshments."[15] And the Spanish painter Ignacio de León y Escosura had been so taken by a picture auction for the American centennial in 1876 that he attempted to emulate its "spectacle" at the Paris World's Fair of 1878 by having his own painting carried out by "negro waiters and white gloves complete."[16]

Not unlike other colored waiters, preparing for unforeseeable misfortunes as best they could, John Wesley Williams recognized the hospitality trade both as an occupational plight and as a lifeline. When he started at the Sturtevant in 1873, he and countless other black workers had accounts at the Freedmen's Savings and Trust

Company, best known as the Freedmen's Bank. The institution had been federally chartered at the end of the Civil War to encourage the economic development of newly freed slaves. But the bank was ill fated: lasting only nine years, from 1865 to 1874, it succumbed to mismanagement and fraud. Its failure left tens of thousands of its black depositors in financial ruin—how John Wesley fared is not known—but it introduced many inexperienced blacks to the potential benefits of savings.

Many black men and women also belonged to mutual aid societies in the form of fraternal and masonic orders, like the Terry Lodge no. 900, which celebrated its twenty-fifth year when John Wesley arrived in New York.[17] This local chapter of the Grand United Order of Odd Fellows (GUOOF)—unsanctioned by American whites, it was chartered in 1843 by the original eighteenth-century body in England—was one of several burgeoning black fraternal and Masonic orders in the nineteenth century. Others included GUOOF's Hamilton Lodge no. 710, whose masquerade parties were already setting the stage for the cross-dressing spectacles of 1920s Harlem, and the Prince Hall Lodge, a member of the oldest black order of Freemasonry in America, founded in 1784.

These and numerous other black fraternal organizations offered their members rare and invaluable opportunities for cultural fellowship, a means to unite an otherwise dispersed community: John Wesley Williams was for decades a drillmaster with the Odd Fellows. But such fraternal organizations also offered access to benefits germane to sickness, death, and certain economic reversals—the closest thing their members had to insurance. The model of the Terry Lodge was fairly typical: a member paid three dollars to join, and thirty-seven cents monthly dues. Each man paid a twenty-five-dollar burial fee; and a sick aid fee of three dollars and one-fifty for the first and next twelve weeks, respectively. Also typical was that fraternal societies counted numerous doctors, lawyers, teachers, and other professionals who—availing their expertise to the general membership—were the linchpins of the societies' social welfare mission. Their influence permeated enclaves where black residential life was evident.

Many social centers of black life were only a few blocks west of the Sturtevant House and the hotel district. Chief among these was a brownstone, at 252 West 26th Street, that veteran waiters would have pointed out reverentially as Porter's Mansion. Its owner was Peter S. Porter, freeborn in 1812 in Milton, Delaware, who since 1833 had made New York his home. Scattered citations of his various enterprises as whitewasher, butler, and caterer surely underplayed his business acumen, for Porter was decidedly one of the city's most illustrious colored magnates and bankers, said to be worth $10,000 (over a quarter-million today). The fact that Porter was the first vice-president of Brooklyn's branch of the Freedmen's Bank probably impressed John Wesley Williams, who was a depositor.[18] But aside from Porter's business success, it was especially his antislavery activism in the 1850s—"whether it was defying the fugitive slave law, by harboring, feeding, and otherwise succoring those who had escaped from bondage"[19]—that launched his celebrity among fellow high-profile abolitionists Frederick Douglass, educator and orator Rev. Henry Highland Garnet, physician Dr. James McCune Smith, and Dr. William H. Johnson. With Smith and others, Porter co-organized a State Suffrage Association in 1855, part of whose immediate mission was "to record the names and registers of the colored voters of the City and County of New York."[20]

By 1855 the arbitrary practice of refusing black passengers on the city's public conveyances was a matter of tremendous contention. Fed up, a young black schoolteacher named Elizabeth Jennings sued the Third Avenue Railway Company, after being forcibly removed from one of its horsecars. Judge William Rockwell of the New York Supreme Court ruled in favor of Jennings, effectively upholding the same rights for blacks to ride the city's public transportation as whites. A century later this benchmark case understandably cast New York's Elizabeth Jennings and Alabama's Rosa Parks as fellow travelers, two determined women who played similarly defiant roles in galvanizing the civil rights movements of their respective eras and places.

And much as the Rev. Martin Luther King, Jr., would do a century later, another activist had taken up and led the crusade. Catalyzed by Jennings's legal victory—which did not desegregate public transit either tidily or swiftly—black citizens of Manhattan and Brooklyn banded together to form the Legal Rights Association (LRA), which ardently bade blacks to resist the "Jim Crow cars." The organization's members included formidable church and business leaders: the oyster seller Thomas Downing, whom the city paid $2,200 in 1842 to cater its official reception for Charles Dickens,[21] and the Brooklyn abolitionist orator J.W.C. Pennington, who wrote the first book-length history of African Americans in 1841.[22]

But it was Peter S. Porter who became the most conspicuous advocate for black citizens' civil rights, often taking similar legal recourse as Jennings had. On December 16, 1856, Porter, his wife, and four other black passengers were ejected from an Eighth Avenue car, to make room for three city railroad functionaries. The incident took a violent turn, with the white passengers pummeling Porter as they kicked him out of the car, leaving his clothing torn and watch broken.[23] "Before we had access to the public conveyances, it cost us a dollar and a half to ride down or up town in a [hired] carriage," Porter reminded a crowd soon after the incident. "And at the same time all white persons could ride for the small sum of five cents—no matter whether rich or poor, clean or dirty, sober, or otherwise, they generally could get in."[24]

Porter's lawsuit against the railway company never reached a hearing. The rail company, whether it felt less confident due to the standing court precedent or was discouraged by Porter's reputation as a well-known citizen, settled the matter out of court and made an arrangement with Porter "permitting persons of color to ride in the cars on the same terms as white passengers."[25] But knowing rail companies to be recalcitrant, Porter schooled countless black passengers to carry LRA identification and know by heart their "rights that conductors and policemen were bound to respect."

In 1863 the Draft Riots furnished a new pretext to exclude black passengers, but a year later, when Ellen Anderson, a recent Union

The benchmark case of Elizabeth Jennings in 1855 positioned abolitionist Peter S. Porter to emerge as the foremost opponent of racial segregation on New York's public streetcars. New York Globe, *August 2, 1884.*

Army officer's widow was manhandled off a streetcar, her self-assurance made known she had been "for many years under the training . . . of Mr. Porter."[26] In 1867, Porter would accept a public tribute for his dogged commitment to black citizens' civil rights during the 1850s "horsecar wars," when a contingent of colored citizens of New York presented him with an ebony, gold-headed walking stick, on which the inscription expressed "a token of their appreciation of his services in obtaining Equal Rights in Public Conveyances."[27]

In the fall of 1871, a few months after Sturtevant House opened, Porter paid $15,000 for a brownstone townhouse and lot only a short distance away, at 252 West 26th Street near Eighth Avenue.[28] The *Evening Post* noted that the newly fitted residence would open on Thanksgiving Day as Porter's Mansion, a "club-house for respectable and intelligent colored men,"[29] although it welcomed a fair share of women of the same caliber.[30] Little wonder that Porter's Mansion resonated far and wide as a social magnet for the black community: Peter Porter exemplified Gotham's Negro citizens of intellect, respectability, and wealth. Guests moved freely through the house's elegantly furnished and well-ventilated rooms, where the walls featured a portrait gallery of honored men—"Abraham Lincoln, John Brown, Charles Sumner, Gerritt Smith and others"—who had been prominent agents in the abolitionist movement and the fight to enfranchise black voters.

Within months of its opening, Porter's Mansion became a nexus of black American social and political activity. On April 1, 1872, it became the seat of New York City's newly formed Thaddeus Stevens Club, named for the radical antislavery senator from Pennsylvania who was a key architect of the Thirteenth, Fourteenth, and Fifteenth amendments. Porter hosted the club's first annual dinner, called to coincide with its namesake's birthday on April 4. But the dinner was really held to celebrate the third anniversary of the passage of the Fifteenth Amendment, which gave black men the right to vote and which was still constantly being tested. About forty men sat down to table in Porter's dining room. The Rev. E.V.C. Eato, who five years before had been the first black American delegate to attend the YMCA convention in Montreal, arose to say grace over a sumptuous bill of fare.

Porter's legendary hospitality was indispensable to many visiting black travelers to New York City as well. On August 25, 1873, the house hosted a reception for former Louisiana governor P.B.S. Pinchback, the first colored governor of any U.S. state (albeit briefly).[31] But it was a particularly essential waypoint for students, like the young men and women who comprised the Hampton Singers, who toured the Northeast performing "Negro music" to improve and enlarge the campus of their school, the Hampton Normal and Agricultural Institute in Virginia. During a three-month itinerary that brought them to New York in the spring of 1873, one of the teacher chaperones noted the musical troupe "boarded—as they have always done in that city—at the comfortable and well-kept house of Mr. Peter S. Porter."

Their five-week stay at Porter's was particularly auspicious; they gave a private concert to a number of New York's white clergymen of various denominations who immediately afterward, and in a body, issued a unanimous endorsement for the singers and their musical mission. Apart from various churches and private invitational receptions, the Hampton Singers performed at several of the city's most notable public venues such as Steinway Hall, Union League Hall and Brooklyn's Academy of Music. The Hampton Singers sang a benefit for the Colored Orphan Asylum—which relocated to Washington Heights after the Draft Riots and was ever dependent upon charitable gifts—and were treated to a tour around Central Park. Reverend Garnet, himself a product of colored schools, invited the singers to his home, as did the white *Evening Post* music critic W. F. Williams; and they left the city for Boston with excellent reviews from the *Times, World, Tribune, Herald,* and other papers, plus a handsome collection of $485.[32]

The success of the Hampton Singers, whose strategy followed the Fisk Jubilee Singers, inspired other black colleges to bolster their respective schools by deploying student choirs for years to come. "When one of the companies of jubilee singers arrived at a building where we professionals were entertaining," a popular black vaudevillian later recalled, "the manager of the place would ask us to come in late in order to give the singers a chance to put on their concert." Whether black or white, the spellbound audiences were not stingy.[33]

The following year, in the spring of 1874, a call went out to anyone interested in meeting William Craft while he was lodging at Porter's Mansion. The Ku Klux Klan had destroyed Craft's cooperative farm school buildings and harvest in Woodville, Georgia, which he hoped to restore, but most everyone recalled his name from a storied incident a quarter-century before: the flight of William and Ellen Craft from Southern slavery had garnered them international fame. In December 1848, the husband and wife boarded a northbound train from Macon, Georgia: the fair-skinned Ellen, dressed as a man, passed for a white invalid "master" named Mr. Johnson; the browner William posed as his vital manservant.[34] Their breathless subterfuge got them to Boston, where they evaded arrest under the Fugitive Slave Act of 1850 with the aid of such abolitionists as William Lloyd Garrison and William Wells Brown, who were white and black, respectively. The Crafts then successfully expatriated to London, where they lived until their return to Boston in the summer of 1869. Since their return to the States, Porter's Mansion had invariably emerged in the often-tenuous network of reliable safe havens, even after emancipation. As a guest, Craft no doubt felt assured of Porter's partisanship and discretion that spring, and he likely roomed there again that December when he returned to New York to speak at the Union League Club.[35]

In the summer of 1875 artist Edmonia Lewis—the first black woman recognized internationally as a sculptor—returned to the United States after a long sojourn in Italy. Lewis had been part of a renowned group of expat American bohemians living in Rome, which included the stage tragedian Charlotte Cushman; the actress's partner, the sculptor Emma Stebbins (whose androgynous *Angel of the Waters* statue still stands at Bethesda Fountain, in the heart of Central Park); and the novelist Henry James. Lewis's monumental *Death of Cleopatra* sculpture would be acclaimed at the Centennial Exhibition in Philadelphia the next summer, but now, on July 29, she was in her room at Porter's Mansion, penning a letter to a venerable old abolitionist in Albany, William H. Johnson, whose interest she hoped to direct toward accepting a two-hundred-dollar work of art:

> *Dear Sir.—I have just returned from Rome, Italy, with a large number of works of sculpture and among them is a life-size bust of our noble [Charles] Sumner.*

Johnson replied enthusiastically, and at length, on August 3:

> *My Very Dear and Much Esteemed Miss Edmonia Lewis:*
>
> *—I am profoundly sensible of the great honor done me by your distinguished recollections of my unworthy services. . . .*
>
> *To simply say that I would be delighted to be the possessor of a life-size bust of the dead Senator, and to assure you that I would be proud to know that that work of art was the creation of your*

talent and labor, would but faintly express my true feeling; still, language at my command is inadequate to express more. With distinguished consideration, I have the honor to remain

Yours truly,
W. H. Johnson, 27 Maiden Lane.
Albany, August 3, 1875.

The bust in question was of the late Republican senator from Massachusetts Charles Sumner, who had died the previous year. A hero to most American blacks, Sumner was caned unmercifully in 1856 on the Senate floor by Democratic congressman Preston Brooks of South Carolina, who objected to Sumner's antislavery speech. Edmonia Lewis's transaction was successful. She raised the necessary subscriptions and ceremoniously presented her Sumner bust to Johnson in Albany on August 25.[36]

As they pertained to John Wesley Williams, such were some of the notable black figures who populated the overlapping districts where he worked and started a family—amid events that foreshadowed James's view of New York City, such as the passing of local heroes like Porter.

James Williams was just shy of six years old when Peter S. Porter died on July 24, 1884. It mattered little whether his father, John Wesley Williams, had ever set foot in Porter's Mansion. However incidentally John Wesley and Lucy Ellen Williams might ever have spoken of it, little James would surely have detected the esteem with which black New Yorkers by and large regarded the place: a touchstone for race enterprise, altruism, and high repute. Porter's funeral took place at the Union African Methodist Episcopal (AME) Church, where he had been a longtime member and Sunday school superintendent; it had been located since at least the 1830s on West Fifteenth Street, a block east from where James was born. Little James's parents had moved the family up to 151 West 33rd Street about a year before, but it's easy to imagine them shepherding all five of their children back down to the church, all gaining an incremental appreciation of their rapidly shifting neighborhood.

CHAPTER 2

"A Gilded, but Gritty Age"

For in gay New York where the gay Bohemians dwell, there's a Colony called the Tenderloin, though why I cannot tell. A certain man controls the place with no regard for coin—the Czar, the Czar, the Czar of the Tenderloin.

—BOB COLE AND BILLY JOHNSON, "THE CZAR OF THE TENDERLOIN," 1897

James Henry Williams was born on August 4, 1878, a Sunday, at 227 West Fifteenth Street. His mother Lucy gave birth in perhaps the very same bed in which she had birthed two sons before him and would birth another son and a daughter after him. It was a building filled with working poor tenants in varied occupations: waiters (his father), laundresses (his mother), carpet cleaners, a music teacher, servants, and housekeepers. The presence of a calciminer evokes a city still amply built of wood for some to whitewash for a living. About nine families lived in the building, which included a separate apartment in the rear. Although the building was black throughout, the adjacent house on the right was mixed with black and white tenants, as was its block between Seventh and Eighth avenues.[1]

Though the specifics of young James's childhood are uncharted, a prominent church, a school, and various businesses nearby attest to his being born into a considerably established black community. At barely two years old, he was too young to recall a controversial incident (but surely grew up amid its retelling) that shook the antebellum Union AME Church, a block east on Fifteenth Street: one of the most sensational murder trials of the Gilded Age. The widely covered case involved a black porter, Chastine Cox, who was sentenced to hang for killing a white socialite, Jane De Forest Hull, during a burglary. "If there was ever a cold blooded murder or a man who richly deserved to be hung, Cox is that man," Frederick Douglass, by then a U.S. marshal, said, urging that the fullest legal penalty be meted out promptly.[2] But while the course of Cox's murder trial patently engaged race and class, it also interwove fraught issues of medical jurisprudence (involving suspended animation and phrenology), cultural solidarity, and even celebrity sympathy (some called him "the handsome criminal"). Ashton's waxworks exhibit, near City Hall, added to its life-size figures of Napoleon, Queen Victoria, Pope Pius IX, and Washington Crossing the Delaware, a figure of "Chastine Cox, murderer of Mrs. Hull."[3] On July 16, 1880, Cox was hanged in the Tombs. Until the night before, reports had held that his body would be taken to the Union AME, where the Rev. James Cook had promised Cox a church funeral. But congregants and neighbors descended on the church—perhaps little James among them, clutched in his mother's arms—and "condemned the project in unmeasured language."[4]

James, and likely his two older brothers, John and Charles, attended the venerable Grammar School no. 81, at 128 West Seventeenth Street—called until recently Colored School no. 4. The three-story brick building had numbered in a series of racially segregated schools that, despite the unkind cause of its inception, had become a source of pride for generations of black New Yorkers. The schools were begot from the first African Free School that had been established on Mulberry Street in 1787 by the New York Manumission Society (whose prominent members included Alexander Hamilton and John Jay) to educate Negro children in preparation for the abolition of racial slavery in the state—which ostensibly came about on July 4, 1827. The society's longtime president Cadwallader D. Colden—a former abolitionist mayor of New York, though namesake to a prominent slaveholding grandfather[5]—founded seven African schools before he died in 1834. A number of their thousands of alumni were prominent members of young James's community and integral to shaping his world. The iconic representation of African Free School no. 2 was a student drawing by master engraver Patrick H. Reason, whose brother Charles L. Reason was principal of Colored School no. 3, on West 41st Street—where Elizabeth Jennings (now Graham) was a longtime teacher—which became Grammar

Established decades earlier in Harlem before moving around 1871 to 128 West 17th Street, Colored School no. 4 was born of the city's late-eighteenth century African Free School movement. *New York Municipal Archives.*

School no. 80, on West 42nd Street. The Williams's next-door neighbor was Richard Robinson—who had succeeded William Appo, one of the country's most renowned black musicians—music teacher for both Colored Schools no. 3 and 4 and a former pupil at the latter. In the mid-1880s, James entered a singular African-turned-Colored-turned-Grammar-School system with long, intimate connections and proprietary sentiments.

Another esteemed teacher, Joan Imogen Howard, from Massachusetts, had also brought her considerable musical experience to New York's Colored School no. 4. Howard had been noticed by James Monroe Trotter, the country's first black music historian (and father of civil rights activist and newspaper founder William Monroe Trotter). "When in Boston this lady exhibited commendable zeal in the study of music, and at an early age was quite noticeable for good piano-forte performance," the senior Trotter wrote.

Trotter also noted the unfolding career of one of Howard's critically promising young graduates, Walter F. Craig, who "will ere long

JOAN IMOGEN HOWARD, A. M.

Teacher Joan Imogen Howard, of Colored School no. 4, became the only black manager at the Chicago's World Columbian Exposition of 1893.
Women of Distinction: Remarkable in Works and Invincible in Character, *L.A. Scruggs. Raleigh, 1893. Internet Archive.*

be ranked with the first violinists of the day. He has lately composed a march."[6] The debut of Craig's march, "Rays of Hope," coincided with Williams's infancy. Over his career, the composer would produce such notable works as "Selika's Galop," which he dedicated to his one-time partner, the coloratura soprano Marie "Madame Selika" Williams—hailed as "the queen of the staccato"—who on November 18, 1878, was the first black artist to sing at the White House, at the invitation of President and Mrs. Rutherford B. Hayes. James Williams likely knew Craig his entire life, for the maestro and the Williamses' neighbor Robinson had been classmates at the Seventeenth Street school. As James grew up, any program featuring Craig—who was said to be the first black allowed to join the all-white Musical Mutual Protective Union—signaled that entertainment's high social magnitude,[7] for black and white audiences alike. Unquestionably, "W. F. Craig's Famous Orchestra," as it was often billed, was a central musical backdrop to James's boyhood. And he came of age under the same watch as the maestro's: Sarah

In 1863 noted educator and suffragist Sarah J. Tompkins Garnet, of Colored School no. 4, became the first black principal in the New York City (then just Manhattan) public school system. *NYPL Digital Collections.*

J. Tompkins Garnet, who was the first black principal in the city's public school system.[8]

But the continued existence of the colored schools was in question, a consequence of the state's 1873 civil rights bill ensuring that black children could attend any public school. Despite its century-long lineage, no. 4 had already suffered evident attrition by the year James was born, when the board of education began agitating to disestablish all the separate caste schools. During Grover Cleveland's two years as governor of New York, 1883–85, a movement arose in the state legislature to absorb the city's colored schools into the general ward school system. The initiative fueled concerns that the new organizational schemes would disenfranchise black teachers.

So on February 12, 1883—Lincoln's birthday—throngs of black New Yorkers descended on Chickering Hall, at Fifth Avenue and Eighteenth Street, a popular social hall where the colored schools frequently held commencement exercises. A letter of support from Frederick Douglass galvanized an action committee (which included Peter Porter) to confront the board of education: either give black teachers parity with their white counterparts, or leave the colored schools as they were.[9] Their argument proved effectual and appeared to turn the tide in their favor: the following year at Chickering Hall, about 150 boys and girls, all dressed in white, for Grammar School no. 81's commencement ceremony, cheered as a former graduate praised the governor for refusing to close the colored schools.[10] A few months earlier, Cleveland had signed a legislative bill that allowed Colored Schools no. 3 and 4 to continue independently (as Grammar Schools no. 80 and 81) of the predominantly white schools. "I know that whatever I did was in favor of maintaining separate colored schools instead of having them mixed," Cleveland later recalled.[11]

Even after Cleveland's action, the colored schools had to struggle to retain some of their racial singularity for a few more years. At Grammar School no. 81, principal Sarah J. Tompkins Garnet was the widow of the former U.S. minister to Liberia, Rev. Henry Highland Garnet, who was himself an African Free School graduate. In March 1887, Principal Garnet chaperoned a number of her pupils to a celebration of the Fifteenth Amendment at Bethel AME Church in Greenwich Village. The children, who perhaps included eight-year-old James, "illustrated the four epochs in the history of the American negro—slavery, freedom, citizenship, and suffrage."[12] But by the next year, Principal Garnet saw attendance drop as the community shifted. Black children were increasingly going to predominantly white schools, like the Williamses, who five years earlier had moved from West Fifteenth Street to West 33rd Street. "This was formerly known as an exclusively colored school and our pupils came from all parts of the city," Garnet said, "but now they have left in order to attend schools nearer their homes."[13]

More than just new school access, many pupils were also finding new job opportunities. At a time when child labor was more liberally practiced, it was conceivable that James's schooling began to instill in him a work ethic at the threshold of adolescence. And perhaps James got a little push from his father. It's easy to imagine John Wesley Williams dashing out of Sturtevant House in his waiter's apron and making a beeline to the fancy flower shop at Coleman House, just across Broadway, and unrolling the newspaper for the proprietor to confirm the advertisement's message. One can imagine him boasting that he had two good boys, three if needed: John Jr. and Charles were twelve and eleven; and James was nine. For in the hard era that they lived in, the boys had come of age to at least be trade apprentices, if not breadwinners. Thorley's Roses would be as good a place as any to start.

On December 4, 1887, Charles Thorley, renowned as the florist of New York's aristocracy, had advertised in the *Herald* for "two boys as messengers; must live with parents."[14] Whether he was looking to hire two colored boys specifically is not known—nor whether James started working for him that year—but it is known that Thorley's shops became familiar for decades for their almost exclusively colored staff, which at some point included James as a florist messenger.

◈

At six feet tall, Charles F. Thorley looked imposing within his element: handling delicate, vividly colored flowers. A soft helmet of auburn hair topped his round face, which balanced a faint mole on the right side of his upper lip. Born in New York City in 1858, Thorley had followed his English-born father in the flower trade, in which he proved himself a prodigy: an 1872 city directory listed the teenager as a florist on West Street. By 1883, the twenty-four-year-old had been running two successful greenhouse businesses around Fifth Avenue's posh Ladies' Mile shopping district, where he regularly provided free bouquets for women patrons of Tony Pastor's (called the "Father of Vaudeville") Fourteenth Street Theatre.[15] But on February 2, ruined by a financial recession, he auctioned all his stock-in-trade of plants, wire frames, baskets, counters, piping, and the boiler to pay off creditors.[16] Soon afterward, as a story had it, Thorley was walking dejectedly up Broadway until he reached Coleman House, between 27th and 28th streets: he stopped to ponder a sign advertising the little vacant storefront for rent, but not feeling even a dollar's worth of coins in his pocket, he continued on.

However, Thorley returned the next morning. The sign in the store still directed him to inquire at the hotel a block away, the famous Gilsey House. Looming like a picturesque white château above the northeast corner of Broadway and 29th Street (across from Sturtevant House, where James's father worked), the Gilsey's five-story cast-iron pile was topped by an additional three-story mansard roof. The elegant hotel was the irresistible focal point of the hotel and theater district. It was where the English writer Oscar Wilde had stayed the year before, when beginning his American lecture tour at Chickering Hall.

On this day, Thorley found himself face to face with old Peter Gilsey, Jr. (whose late father had also built Coleman House), who asked for $2,500 a year, three months in advance, for the storefront's rental. Though Thorley feigned indifference as he heard out the terms, his fingers worried a gem in his pocket, which he hastened to pawn as soon as he left. He returned and managed to talk

Charles F. Thorley, one of the most influential florists of Gilded Age Gotham, notably employed black staff. American Florist, *Internet Archive.*

By the mid-1890s, Thorley's Broadway flower shop under Coleman House thrust young Williams at the intersection of Broadway shoppers, Tin Pan Alley music makers, and idling tourists. *MCNY.*

Gilsey into accepting fifty dollars for one month's rent. Upon his success, Thorley went back to the store and noticed a secondhand lumberyard nearby, as well as a place to buy two chairs, a counter, a mirror, and a chandelier. He repapered the walls. When the place looked once again like a shop, he stocked it with flowers. He stepped outside his new store, and spying old Gilsey approaching—no doubt to look in on his new tenant—he turned out the last few coins from his pocket and toyed with them for Gilsey's benefit. Then he suddenly tossed them clear across the street to the roof of an old boardinghouse. "That's the last sixty cents I have," Thorley confessed to his baffled new landlord. "If I haven't got more than that by to-morrow night you are going to have a bad tenant."[17]

Gilsey had no reason to worry. In the early 1890s, working poor families of the Tenderloin like the Williamses saw businesses like Gilsey House and Thorley's Roses defining the posh fringe of their district. Charles Thorley was largely credited with promoting the orchid to its viability as a market flower. The bloom usually appeared only occasionally at some opulent event, but suddenly it thrived exponentially among his fashionable clients. Due to Thorley's penchant, "at least five hundred Orchid-flowers are sold to-day," it was claimed, "where one was sold half a dozen years ago."[18] Gilded Age versifiers frequently dedicated couplets to his blooms or services: a "liv'ried messenger / With cocky, flippant air—gamin depraved—/ Brings Thorley's roses at two 'plunks' the head."[19] But the florist's high reputation suggests some poetic license was taken in the unflattering allusion to the delivery boy, who by this time might well have been a fourteen-year-old teenager like James Williams.

In a fictional family portrayal a century later, a Williams descendant would invoke Thorley's flower shop as the setting of James and his sweetheart Lucy's first meeting. The apt conjecture is not surprising. More than most retail stores, Thorley's had the theatrical magic to stir romantic sentiments, and it was indeed the likeliest place for the youngsters to court. Even before entering, customers often paused in stupefied admiration at the florist's delivery wagon at the curb, "resplendent in gold trimmings and uniformed driver."

Thorley's shop quickly became a dazzling feature among Broadway florist and dry goods merchants: the "oriental magnificence" of colorful delivery wagons belonging to various firms.[20] It is easy to imagine Lucy Metrash stepping inside Thorley's—sometime in 1895, when she was about twelve or thirteen—chaperoned by her grown-up sisters Caroline and Mamie (who were nineteen and eleven years older, respectively), and losing herself instantly in the ecstatic decor. The ceiling was barely visible, covered by a canopy of orchids and other flowers and greenery. Thorley's undulating maidenhair ferns were "finer than all the feathers on all the fine birds unshot," Mary Bacon Ford wrote, offering a weirdly telling allusion to the millinery fashion of the time.[21] Thorley's was the likeliest place for Jimmy and Lucy to court. Lucy would have shopped as James worked (or each at least pretended to), he asking if they (but caring only if *she*) had ever smelled this or that blossom, and Lucy coming up with more questions for the genial attendant.

Though Williams and Lucy's affections were mutual and deepening, the two were hardly from the same social worlds. Racial mores and prejudices were levelers. Both of Williams's parents were former slaves from Virginia and had to work hard—his father as a hotel waiter, his mother as a laundress—to keep the family in good financial condition.

But Lucy's parents were northerners, descended from generations of free blacks. Though her father's side was from Connecticut, she had old New York connections. Indeed, a traffic accident had put her grandfather's name in the papers some fifty years before, a time when reckless coachmen were "almost universally in the habit of racing furiously through their routes."[22] It was on one of the spectacular Broadway coaches owned by Francis A. Palmer, president of Broadway Bank. In spring of 1844, Eaton, Guilbert & Company, a renowned coach manufacturer in Troy, New York, made fifteen new coaches for Palmer's fleet of public omnibuses. One paper described the horse-drawn carriages—uniformly painted with scenic panoramas of City Hall Park and its environing mayoral manse, sparkling fountain, St. Paul's Episcopal Chapel, and adjacent buildings—as "far more elegant than any omnibuses now running in the streets of New York."[23]

But on July 3, a driver crashed one of Palmer's new conveyances into a lamppost. The impact threw Adam Metrash, "a respectable colored man"—and the grandfather of James Williams's budding sweetheart Lucy—from his Jim Crow seat beside the coachman. Few New Yorkers were surprised: just two months before, another of Palmer's stages had crushed a three-year-old Irish girl.[24] The constantly ignored demands to protect the public against heedless coachmen now fueled anger over the Metrash case. One outraged citizen wrote to the *Commercial Advertiser* of this "flagrant case of inhuman misconduct." Not only had the crash thrown Metrash from the carriage, the driver had abandoned his injured passenger on the pavement. Metrash had to make his own way home, an arm "broken just above the wrist and one of his legs much bruised." The irate writer insisted that a mayoral inquiry start with the omnibus owner Palmer himself.[25]

This episode happened before Williams's time, but he was raptly interested in any utterance from this young lady, Lucy Metrash, from Connecticut. Her father, Adam Metrash, Jr., was a boatman and oysterer, whose family "had made their home in the coastal town of Norwalk since the 1790s." Her mother was from New Jersey. Their paths had crossed by way of a singular social circle within and without the Negro community: both her parents were deaf. According to record, a cannon discharge had deafened her father Adam Jr., born in 1837, when he was only one and a half years old. Her mother, Elizabeth Pepinger, born in 1838, was four when a bout of scarlet fever left her deaf. If accident and illness had caused both of her parents' losses of hearing, it appeared to be an ill-fated coincidence that her eldest sibling Robert was also born deaf.[26] The sight of Lucy's family signing fluently introduced a world perhaps unfamiliar to Williams.[27]

In 1852 fourteen-year-old Elizabeth Pepinger attended school in

Descended from generations of free blacks, the late parents of Williams's wife, Adam H. Metrash and Elizabeth Pepinger (circa 1860s) of Norwalk, Connecticut, were prominent in black deaf society. *Charles Ford Williams Family Collection.*

New York. In 1858 she was in the first graduating class at Fanwood, the New York Institution for the Deaf's new building facility in Washington Heights. The principal awarded her a premium for her obvious artistic talent: a drawing book, two lead pencils, and a rubber eraser.[28] Pupils in the deaf community—who often knew disparagement both at home and in society—had a certain advantage over hearing pupils: unlike students at the city's segregated public schools, black and white classmates of antebellum schools for the deaf commingled in scholastic learning as well as recreational and ceremonial activities and general deaf community events. Still, some black applicants surely erred on the side of caution. Elizabeth's inconsistent racial descriptions suggested to one historian that "she may have been passing for white at school."[29]

Whatever the school's progressive stance on integrating, inevitable events highlighted the prevailing prejudice. During Elizabeth's tenure at Fanwood, twelve-year-old Charles Wia Hoffman came to the school from Cape Palmas, Liberia. Three decades earlier, in 1822, the American Colonization Society had established Liberia to "repatriate" formerly enslaved African Americans. Cape Palmas—annexed to Liberia in 1849—became a prominent outpost presided over by the Rev. C. Colden Hoffman, a New York Protestant Episcopal missionary. Charles was eventually brought to the New York Institution for the Deaf, probably by Hoffman himself. Unfortunately, in 1858, only a few months after he arrived, the boy died of tuberculosis. His body was interred a few blocks away in Trinity Church Cemetery, where Fanwood maintained the institution's communal plot. But irrespective of the racial integration within the asylum's walls, the cemetery's rules sadly obliged that the boy be buried in its segregated "colored ground."

Where and how Lucy's father met her mother is unknown. Adam Metrash, Jr., was an 1857 graduate of the preeminent American School for the Deaf at Hartford, founded by Thomas Hopkins Gallaudet. He and Elizabeth were wed in 1861, but their marriage record did not specify a date or place. Though they belonged to St. Paul's Episcopal Church in Norwalk, whose churchyard still retains many of their family members, the couple very likely wed at St. Ann's Episcopal Church for Deaf-Mutes in New York. Founded in 1852 by Gallaudet Jr., the church on Eighteenth Street and Fifth Avenue was the best known in the deaf community. Of Lucy's three older siblings—Robert, born in 1864; Mary (called Mamie), born in 1869; and Caroline, born in 1872—at least two, plus their adult father, had been baptized at St. Ann's.

The church document listed only three of the Metrash children: Robert, deaf, born in 1864; Mary, hearing, born in 1869; and Caroline, hearing, born in 1872. Lucy was born a year after the census, on October 8, 1881. Already entering middle age, their father Adam got himself baptized at St. Ann's in 1874, and ten years later, on July 21, 1884, he died at forty-seven. In 1887 Robert married—

Mary ("Mamie") Metrash, one of Lucy's two older sisters, probably in the 1890s. *Charles Ford Williams Family Collection.*

he and his wife, Anna, had a baby girl named Grace the following year—and worked as a boot and shoe maker in Bridgeport. But in the late summer of 1893, six years after his marriage, he was reportedly living alone in Stamford when he died at twenty-nine. Just months after her brother's death, twelve-year-old Lucy's widowed mother Elizabeth died, too, on February 5, 1894. Probably not long afterward her big sisters Caroline and Mamie put things in order and fetched her to move down to New York City.

With Connecticut behind them, the Metrash sisters had good reason to frequent Thorley's, apart from the enchanting floral displays:

his stores were conspicuously staffed by Negroes. The owner was well known among blacks as a friend. At Thorley's Roses on Broadway and at the subsequent House of Flowers on Fifth Avenue, the florist's able staff of liveried messengers, a chauffeur, a valet, shop clerks, and a purchasing agent were by and large race men. This fact no doubt made Thorley's retail shops a nexus for refined colored society folk to communicate matters both urgent and trivial that contributed to racial uplift. What conversations caught fire in Thorley's that mid-week day of February 20, 1895, when the sorrowful news spread across the nation that Frederick Douglass had died? Lucy, at thirteen, might have asked sixteen-year-old James what he thought about it. The two teenagers would have discussed family matters, like James's newborn baby brother, Richard Alexander, as well as more political issues like the Malby Bill, yet another new civil rights law that meant they had the right to stay in the same hotels, eat in the same restaurants, and buy the same theater seats as whites.

Did Williams tell Lucy and her sisters the pie-girl story? Though the shop clerks were not invited guests, they were privy to details of a sensational party that spring that culminated in a gossamer-clad artist's model leaping from the crust of a giant pie. About a dozen Negroes had been essential to the festive ambiance: "To insure ample entertainment, four banjo players were employed and the same number of colored jubilee singers were engaged. . . . Thorley provided the flowers."[30]

It could very well have been over such news or gossip that, if her guardian sisters were not paying attention, James and Lucy first touched hands.

◈

In 1895 railroad passengers arriving in New York learned that a new amenity awaited them at the Grand Central Depot, unlike anything they recalled in the station's quarter-century history. By the War of 1812, the teenage Cornelius Vanderbilt had already shown enough promise in the harbor trade to be nicknamed "Commodore," as the shipping magnate was still known during the Civil War, when he sold his last vessels to focus on railroads. He bought and consolidated several of New York's steam locomotive lines and laid plans for a new terminal on East 42nd Street—sinking Fourth Avenue northward into the track bed that became first a tunnel, then Park Avenue. It opened in 1871 as Grand Central Depot. Later in 1898 the depot was rebuilt as Grand Central Station, and again in 1913 as Grand Central Terminal. Observers remarked that certain traveling disadvantages in the station's earlier years had not much improved for women or strangers who arrived in New York City by train. Women risked "falling into the hands of bunco men or worse,"[31] and foreigners unable to speak English were at the mercy of those who did. The situation was endemic to transit terminuses.

But on March 1, 1895, passengers arriving at Grand Central Depot on the New York Central and Hudson River Railroad found leaflets in the cars informing them that station attendants would be waiting to assist them in various ways. These new attendants would be easy to recognize by their blue uniforms trimmed with bright red, and by their red caps. Their distinctive uniforms were meant to make them unmistakable from others worn in the station or from casual street garments, and therefore easy for a passenger to recognize. "One of these men will be found at the end of every car on the arrival of all trains,"[32] the railroad's general passenger agent George H. Daniels explained. He'd hired a trial staff of twelve men, preferring men over boys to instill a greater sense of professionalism. Daniels was widely known for his constant efforts to perfect passenger comfort on the New York Central's "Great Four-Track Line," and it was a rare periodical that didn't describe or advertise the railroad's new feature of "twelve uniformed men to be known as attendants"[33] put on duty at the Grand Central Station.

The new free service was a wonderfully practical idea from the point of view of the general traveler, especially those in the rear cars of long trains who had to walk some five hundred feet to the street exit. The attendants' explicit duties were "to help women with their hand-baggage, to lead a child if necessary, or to assist a feeble person."[34] And mindful of New York's nonnative visitors—often

An 1883 depiction of a black public porter in a vivid red-sashed hat suggests a precursor to Daniels's red-cap system, and to its origin with Williams. *Library of Congress.*

bewildered strangers—Daniels noted that "the foreigner will be as readily served as the American,"[35] as he installed a polyglot force that included speakers of French, German, Spanish, Italian, Danish, and other languages in addition to English.

Despite general public enthusiasm, some of Daniels's railroad industry colleagues were perplexed as to why his new uniformed attendants should be classified separately "from the ordinary porters at the station, who attend both outward and inward passengers."[36] But Daniels intended them to be out of the ordinary. More chaperones than lugs, the men would direct passengers to the right streetcars, or flag them cabs. Though they would carry hand-baggage, they would not handle heavy baggage—as Daniels emphasized, "They are not porters."[37]

Daniels's directive was probably naive. One couldn't please

everyone. A woman having "alighted from incoming trains fully six times this summer, laden with flowers, packages, valise, &c.," was incensed that "the red headed men" at Grand Central just "stood idly by."[38] Her injured vanity aside, one might appreciate the woman's mortification as she realized her alternatives. There were the city's licensed "public porters," who, black and white, were impudent and boorish. Or there were the half-dozen or so street urchins who likely clustered around her, worrying at the handles of her handbags. These "baggage smashers," as everyone knew them, were a familiar sight at railway stations—Grand Central, the Cortland Street Station of the Pennsylvania Railroad, and the Barclay and Christopher Street stations of the Lackawanna Railroad—and at riverfront ferryboat landings.[39] Such hustling opportunities were where many boys first honed their entrepreneurial skills and tested their powers of charm. They were mostly adolescent boys, around the age of Williams, who was about seventeen, though a fair number of man-sized fellows sometimes stood out as well. A stranded lady commuter could not avoid hearing their full motley chorus: "Smash your baggage, miss?" The age-old greeting was as familiar as a folk ballad.

Despite a few misfires, Daniels's experiment proved a clear success within a year. He had simply piped the company's standard blue garments with red trim and topped the ensemble with a red cap. By fashioning the free-attendant service as a distinct unit of the railroad's workforce, he had also codified the ancient practice of livery—special uniforms worn by servants or officials. This dress code redefined and promoted the impression of the entire corps of uniformed help as an essential component of a great railway station. Daniels quickly built up the attendant system at Grand Central, where travelers soon encountered neat and tidy redcapped men throughout the station. Red Caps greeted them at entrances to waiting rooms, ready to assist them from carriages and escort them to trains, and they stood on all the arriving train platforms. Articles and advertisements reiterated that the service was "absolutely free," that "no tips are necessary," and that the attendants were "active and intelligent, polite and well posted; they speak several languages and are walking encyclopedias."[40]

New York Central Railroad's general passenger agent, George H. Daniels, generated the most company publicity, such as an 1896 ad for its new "Red Cap" service. *Author's collection.*

Beyond New York City, the traveling public was soon enjoying Daniels's "free-attendant service" at Buffalo and Albany and in other large stations of the sprawling network. The system subsequently spread even farther away, to the Northwestern Line's Chicago station, to the Pennsylvania's Jersey City station, and to numerous other railroad stations nationwide. Within a few years, a traveler would have been able to identify the free amenity anywhere by the presence of a red cap.

To be sure, the railroad companies' uniformed employee system reflected an increasingly discrete, military-like regimentation of dress standards for laborers. Just two months after Daniels installed his Red Caps, the city's street cleaning superintendent, Col. George E. Waring, inducted his iconic army of White Wings, clad in white duck-cloth uniforms and helmets. Not all workforces liked the idea; while City Hospital physicians agreed to wear white duck coats on duty, nursery maids objected to wearing "a livery" ensemble of caps and aprons. But by and large, the art of discipline appeared to induce other managers of labor to court public trust with work teams whose attire exemplified tidiness: clean clothes, polished shoes, bright buttons, and shaven faces combined to imply trustworthy authority. The trend in heightening, or tightening, dress standards was visible among doormen, hallboys, elevator operators, and messengers in first-class hotels and apartment houses.[41]

It was in this decade that young James Williams moved in the ranks of varied uniformed service, although he may also have picked up some plain-clothed baggage smashing on the streets for extra money. The nimble teenager's various hats included the pillbox and elastic chin strap of a hotel bellhop, which he also wore while on duty as a florist messenger at Thorley's.

In January 1897, two years after he met Lucy, Williams was still living with his parents at 454 Seventh Avenue, just above 34th Street, across from where Macy's department store would eventually dominate for generations. The area was infamously known as the Tenderloin, an epically sordid entertainment and red-light district. The sector stretched amorphously up Manhattan's West Side from about 24th Street to 62nd Street, between Fifth and Ninth avenues—including a foreboding swatch of blocks around 39th Street known as Hell's Kitchen. The zone abounded with so-called "disorderly houses," gambling dens, saloons, and pool halls that were the constant target of antivice crusades, police shakedowns, and exchanges of graft. Indeed, its colorful nickname was attributed to "Clubber" Williams, a fearsome police captain transferred there in 1876, who savored the prospective bribes that would advance him from his usual chuck steak to "tenderloin."[42]

Yet a newspaper's map illustrating the "proximity of evil to schools and churches" revealed pulses of respectability dispersed throughout the area as well.[43] The joyful noises around the intersection where the Williamses lived—if raucous even by the Tenderloin's peculiar standard—were often more sacred than profane: some local residents had recently complained to the board of health that "two rival negro congregations" kept them up nights, worshipping too vociferously in an avenue meeting hall.[44] James and Lucy were restless for other reasons: they were about to get married.

Lucy was living about ten minutes away from James, at 321 West 41st Street, possibly with one or both of her elder sisters. On January 31 the teenagers met each other at the northwest corner of Seventh Avenue and 39th Street, the path to Hell's Kitchen, where they entered St. Chrysostom's Episcopal Chapel. In 1883 the church's black members had formed the Guild of St. Cyprian (an African saint and a usual indicator of black congregants), a mutual benefit society that, like a fraternal order, collected a membership initiation and monthly dues "for colored men and women, providing for its sick, and burying its dead."[45] Yet the formality of their wedding at this particular church, to which neither belonged, had the ring of elopement to it.

Despite its sacred authority, this church had a dubious history with marriages. A few years earlier, St. Chrysostom's Chapel was "apparently much sought after by runaway couples and others desirous of entering the matrimonial state as expeditiously as possible."[46] The church's marriage certificate did not request birth dates, and watching the Rev. Thomas Sill fill in their answers to his questions in his own hand, James and Lucy gave only their ages. "Twenty years," the bridegroom replied confidently. "Eighteen," his bride diffidently murmured. The vicar recorded their ages, but truth be told, James and Lucy were eighteen and sixteen, respectively, two years younger than they claimed. No matter the age of consent, the teenagers had good reason to want to appear older on record, or at least more mature: Lucy was pregnant. Less than eight months later, James moved to Lucy's address where, on August 26, 1897, she gave birth to their first child: Wesley Augustus Williams. The baby's birth certificate incidentally listed James as nineteen, which he had turned earlier that month, and Lucy as seventeen, which she would become in October—making them younger than on their marriage certificate.[47] Within a year, they moved directly across the street to 318 West 41st Street, where on August 22, 1898, their second child, Gertrude Elizabeth Williams, was born. Their father's occupation as a hotel bellhop, as the birth certificates of both children indicated, attests to Williams's vigorous work ethic if he determined to eke out a living beyond the flower shop.

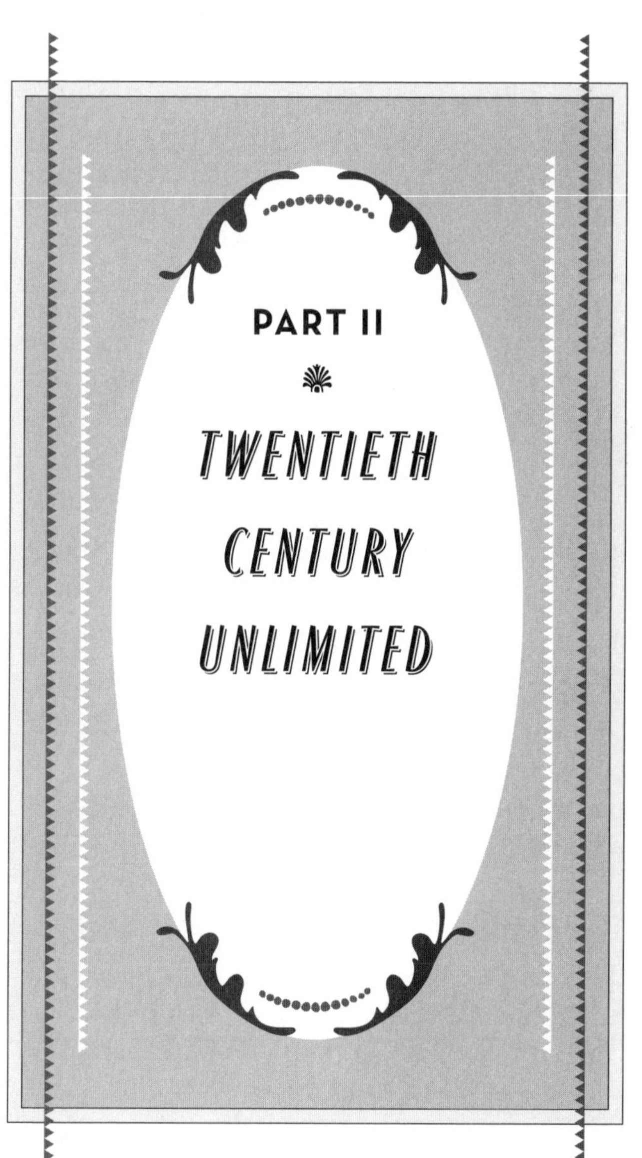

PART II

TWENTIETH CENTURY UNLIMITED

CHAPTER 3

"If We Cannot Go Forward, Let Us Mark Time"

We ask for no money consideration—the rights of citizenship we value above money.

—W. H. BROOKS, 1900

By the summer of 1900, Williams had moved Lucy, Wesley, and Gertrude out of 318 West 41st Street down to 228 West 28th Street, which at the time was still considered "uptown." The surrounding neighborhood, still part of the Tenderloin, had supplanted the old black belt around Sullivan and Thompson streets, where his father first landed from Virginia a quarter of a century earlier. Greenwich Village's black population had now thinned out, with residents moving even well beyond the closer tenement blocks to the suburbs of Brooklyn, and to the Bronx sections of Williamsbridge and Kingsbridge. Zion AME Church was still on Bleecker Street, and the Abyssinian Baptist Church was still on Waverly Place and Grove Street, but other black churches were already dotting the map uptown from 25th Street to 163rd Street.[1]

Migratory and professional progress appeared to go hand in hand. Whereas for years the public had patly assumed black men, by dint of race alone, to be barbers, hostlers, coachmen, and waiters, they were now entering "many of the most respectable callings" of doctor, dentist, and entrepreneur. One white writer observed that blacks were at the helm of at least two full all-Negro theatrical companies—Williams & Walker and Cole & Johnson were leading black performance teams—but black New Yorkers knew there were others. A Negro owned a prosperous Seventh Avenue cigar store, and on Sixth Avenue a colored man was the instructor of a school of podiatry and manicure that was "attended only by white pupils."[2]

Even if Williams did not own his own business, such observations no doubt fueled his enterprising nature. Though he had not yet moved his young family out of the Tenderloin, his walks to work barely three blocks east were now infinitely more convenient. That year's census gave his occupation as a florist messenger, but his actual duties at fashionable Thorley's Roses at 1173 Broadway belied that lackluster title. Williams's "messenger" duties often required diplomatic finesse and intuition, sometimes even a hint of corporate sleuthing. His boss was the flower merchant of choice for the "Four Hundred" of New York's exclusive Gilded Age society. His association with Thorley's modish shop was auspicious inasmuch as it seasoned him, like an apprenticeship, in the art of service with discriminating taste and tact.

Charles Thorley's creative genius stimulated the practice of giving particular cut flowers for particular occasions—roses, orchids, violets—and presenting them in ceremoniously wrapped paper and boxes. Citywide, nationwide, and even thousands of miles away in Europe, the trends of romantic aspiration, consummation, breakup, and patch-up were traceable through flower orders in Thorley's business ledgers. His enterprise eventually became the three-story mansard-roofed House of Flowers—its exterior walls cascaded florid tendrils from every window—at the corner of Fifth Avenue and 46th Street. It was reputedly the largest cut-flower business ever built in the country. Williams likely also witnessed the event for which his boss acquired his most recent fame. Thorley owned a lot at the corner of Broadway and 42nd Street, and he now leased it for $8,000 to *The New York Times*, whose later skyscraper would mark that intersection—then known as Longacre Square—as Times Square, the crossroads of the world. Years later, when Thorley died, many black New Yorkers would mourn the loss of a sincere friend, whose

Negro employees in executive positions "practically managed his business for a number of years."[3] His carriage driver was Henry Crum, an unassuming former South Carolinian whose brother, Dr. William D. Crum, was one of the most prominent Negroes of that state. In 1902 President Theodore Roosevelt would appoint Dr. Crum collector of the Port of Charleston. (Not incidentally, Dr. Crum's wife Ellen was the daughter of the legendary fugitive slave couple William and Ellen Craft, who stayed a spell at Porter's Mansion after the Civil War.)

Another place of considerable advantage to Williams was en route to and from work: Jack Nail's, the most upright colored saloon in the Tenderloin, was at 461 Sixth Avenue, near the southwest corner of his street. Between the predominantly black staff at Thorley's and the black clientele of Jack's, Williams was attuned to the constant flow of news pertaining to the race, wherever the geography. That July, for instance, news of American Negroes heading to London for a Pan-African Congress—which summoned worldwide representatives from Great Britain, Africa, both Americas, and the West Indies—surely provoked countless discussions over a few rose thorns here and a few beers there, especially given the current reports of a genocidal campaign in South Africa. D. E. Tobias, an American student organizer and speaker (whom New Yorkers would know better in a few years as the "colored whirlwind"), impressed attendees as he wryly suggested that "the only solution of all the problems lay in according to black men the same justice that white men claimed for themselves."[4] In a few weeks' time, the claim for justice was deafening in the Tenderloin, as the district became the epicenter of the West Side Riot, the city's bloodiest campaign of wanton violence since the Civil War.

On August 12, 1900, a white man approached a young black woman standing on a corner at Eighth Avenue and West 41st Street. Robert J. Thorpe was actually a patrolman in plain clothes, and he summarily arrested the woman, May Enoch, for "soliciting." Enoch protested that she had been waiting for her man in a nearby store, as Thorpe proceeded to usher her to the station. At that point a young black man, Arthur J. Harris, came out of the store and, seeing a white stranger manhandling his girlfriend, rushed to her rescue. In an ensuing scuffle, Thorpe pulled out a billy club to beat Harris. Harris retaliated with a penknife. Thorpe collapsed into a lifeless heap. Then Harris went on the lam.

Williams might have tried to place May Enoch's face, for the papers said she fled home and gave her address as 241 West 41st Street, just one block east from where he and his family had last lived. In fact, a witness called to Harris's trial—who testified he saw Harris and Thorpe "holding each other with one hand and striking at each other"[5]—was a man named Wesley Commodore, who lived at Williams's old address at 318 West 41st Street.

Thorpe had been a popular officer at the Twentieth Precinct. On August 15, three days after his killing, his body was laid out at his home, where the notorious police chief William S. "Big Bill" Devery, Inspector Walter L. Thompson, and various other officials paid their respects. With Harris still at large, the collective grief devolved into a spirit of vengeance against blacks in general. That day rumors of trouble surged, enough to prompt many blacks to close shops or stay indoors. The rumors proved well founded. That night numerous white gangs known to be "hostile to Negroes and friendly with the unofficial powers that are now potent in police affairs"—that is, Tammany Hall political bosses—ran through the city streets for hours uninhibited, hunting down blacks.[6]

Under the pretext of restoring order, the police ordered every saloon closed from Twentieth to 42nd Street, between Sixth and Ninth avenues. "Noisy hoodlums" hurled stones at fleeing blacks and drove fists into those they could corner. Cries of "Kill the nigger" filled the night air. Aboard an Eighth Avenue streetcar near 40th Street—around the corner from where the Williamses had recently moved—police rushed to break up several white men punching a black passenger as "two women tried to stab him in the face with hatpins."[7] A mob of fifty men and boys waylaid a 34th Street streetcar and were about to lynch two black passengers from a lamppost with a clothesline when a squad of policemen thwarted them. But apart from a few noted instances of officers keeping the peace, a greater number of them, in compliance with Chief Devery's orders, clubbed rioters freely to foment the lawlessness.

For weeks following the unrest, newspapers across the country raptly reported accounts of police colluding, by and large, with the vicious gangs. "If the accounts are true, some white men acted last night like beasts," Magistrate Robert C. Cornell said, censuring the police in the Tenderloin whose own hatred aided and incited abuse of innocent blacks.[8] An Ohio newspaper later commended the judge for stopping the police from "dragging Afro-Americans indiscriminately into this court room," warning that they "ought to arrest more whites to do justice to the riot."[9]

One of the victims was Alfred Akins, a thirty-year-old parlor car porter heading home from Grand Central Station, unaware that the white gangs were raging through town. Although a policeman rescued him from being beaten almost to death, a newspaper reported, he "barely escaped rougher treatment at the hands of the police." The Jamaican-born Akins and fifteen other West Indians filed similar complaints with the British consulate.[10] Wherever Williams was during the unrest, the enormous anxiety surely engulfed him as his family's safety grew questionable: his wife and babies were on West 28th Street, and his parents, along with eight of his brothers and sisters, still lived at 474 Seventh Avenue near West 34th.

It's uncertain if Williams yet knew either Bert Williams or George Walker of the comedy duo Williams & Walker personally, but news that Walker was attacked no doubt personalized the horror unfolding on the streets. Walker's affable persona among audiences and in the theater community was already famous enough that several newspapers reported the shocking account: at about one o'clock at night, a horde of whites surrounded Walker and the comedy team's secretary Clarence Logan on a streetcar at 33rd Street and dragged them out. Walker escaped the flail of their fists via Trainor's Hotel, but Logan was overtaken and beaten terribly before he could escape into a drugstore, "which the proprietor locked and kept the mob out of."[11] For two days, similar attacks flashed throughout Manhattan's

West Side, from the West Twenties up to the black San Juan Hill enclave in the West Sixties. Not surprisingly, the wanton assaults prompted a rush to acquire weapons in kind: all over the Tenderloin, pawnshop clerks quickly sold out of their stocks of small arms as terrified blacks bought "everything from blackjacks to Colt's 44s."[12]

Springing into action, the Negro pastor Rev. William H. Brooks insisted that the real story of the riot was being silenced. In the following several weeks, he railed from his pulpit at the injustice being "whitewashed" by political authorities. "Colored people who break the laws must not expect sympathy from us," Brooks told the crowd that filled St. Mark's Methodist Episcopal Church—one of the city's most notable black churches—but nor should they countenance lawlessness from Tammany's police, who "are guilty of incapacity, brutality, and rascality." He had spearheaded an initiative to collect signed affidavits attesting to police misconduct, and he readily ticked off a litany of damning charges from his list. Innocent men had been assaulted, nearly every case by officers on duty. Not a single "tough character" was among the victims, "but decent, honest, hardworking people." Officers, instead of providing respectable helpless women their protection, had instead cursed and threatened them. Officers had kicked in the doors of upstanding colored businessmen who "were mercilessly clubbed upon their own premises." Terrified men and women who threw themselves on the mercy of the law and sought refuge from the mobs in police stations were beaten by officers while getting out of patrol wagons. Officers recklessly shot at women and children looking on from windows. They drove men out of saloons to feed them to the mob. They shielded white offenders and abused innocent blacks. They broke into homes, rousted men and women from bed, and paraded them naked to the station. And "officers turned thieves and stole," Reverend Brooks recounted.[13]

And then, when the mayhem seemed to subside, violence struck Williams and his family. On the evening of August 20, just days after the random attacks, twenty-five-year-old John W. Williams, Jr., Williams's eldest brother, was found stabbed around the corner

A strong influence for Williams, Rev. W. H. Brooks of St. Mark's Methodist Episcopal Church condemned police lawlessness that fueled the West Side Riot in 1900, and conducted special sermons for Colored Elks and Red Caps. *NYPL Digital Collections.*

from their parents' home. It was down the block from the famous Koster & Bial's 34th Street music hall, whose management the Hashim Brothers—a noted Washington-based sibling trio of vaudeville house managers—had just taken over. The theater's luck must have suddenly looked ominous as someone from Koster & Bial's—maybe N. H. Hashim himself, who was in the house—put in an urgent call to Bellevue Hospital for an ambulance. A surgeon arrived to find the wounded man was already removed to a nearby doctor's office. Struggling to stay conscious, Williams's bloodied brother tried to explain what had happened: he'd been helping a drunken friend get home, but then the latter suddenly turned on him and stabbed him. His account satisfied the surgeon, who found a four-inch knife puncture in the young man's abdomen; it raised eyebrows for the police, who could find no correlating cuts on his trousers or vest. But the gravity of Williams Jr.'s condition made the veracity of his story irrelevant, and the coroner was dutifully summoned to take an antemortem statement.[14] As fate would have it, John W. Williams, Jr., recovered and lived eight more years, but his near-death experience was but another reason James Williams and other black residents viewed the Tenderloin with trepidation.

On the morning of Monday, September 3, 1900, Reverend Brooks and others organized the Citizens' Protective League, to afford mutual protection and to prosecute the guilty in the aftermath of the West Side Riot. Its membership would reach five thousand. Brooks even found numerous allies among the white public. He challenged the police to answer the serious charges he had canvassed and conveyed. Dr. Hamilton Williams, the city coroner's physician, publicly denounced Devery as the "procreator" of the riots "which convulsed a large quarter of our great city."[15] On the evening of September 12, the league held a public protest against the "whitewashed" inquiry into the sworn charges of police brutality, and to raise funds to prosecute the offending officers. The mass meeting was held at Carnegie Hall: the crowd filled the plush rows of orchestra seats, ascended the stairs to the tiers and boxes. The meeting opened with the singing of the national anthem and a prayer by one of the several clergymen speakers.[16]

On September 12, Reverend Brooks submitted an open letter on behalf of the league to Mayor Robert Van Wyck, beseeching a fair and impartial investigation. While condemning Harris's act, and all lawlessness of the race, he was quick to add that "this crime, as black as it may be, does not justify the policemen in their savage and indiscriminate attack upon innocent and helpless people." No monetary reparation was sought, Brooks emphasized, but rather that those officers, whom he assured the league could prove guilty, be convicted and ousted from the force. Failure to do so would otherwise encourage both the mob and the police to commit the same misdeeds, and would sow bloodshed as blacks inevitably took measures to defend themselves. The reverend deferred to the mayor's influence to forestall all of this. "The color of a man's skin must not be made the index of his character or ability," W. H. Brooks wrote to Mayor Van Wyck, voicing the league's appeal for common justice. On December 8 the inquiries concluded. The police were neither disciplined nor faulted.

Perhaps searching for some conciliation, Reverend Brooks found at least one unforeseen effect of the riots that the police and mobs never counted on: their disgraceful actions increased the demand for colored help. He told his congregation a white couple had just called on him intending to engage some colored servants. The woman said it was her first time, but that "she and some of her friends had been talking over the riots and they had concluded to give a chance to some of our people." She knew a number of other wealthy white families now determined to do the same, from whom Reverend Brooks could relay an offer of "two good places now for two good girls."[17]

Even if he hadn't yet narrowed down his own goals, Williams was aiming, without cant or condescension, at some calling higher than domestic service. He understood that even increasing turn-of-the-century appreciation of Negro progress was predicated on an age-old assumption of service jobs as the prerogative of blacks. Despite the former prevalence of black men in such occupations during the 1870s and '80s, their diminishing presence in hotels, restaurants, and homes by the turn of the twentieth century was obvious to some. White social reformer Mary White Ovington, who would later co-found the NAACP, recollected, "Frederick Douglass said that his color was an unfashionable one, and it is even more so now than it was in his time."

It's possible that Douglass's wry sentiment, felt widely among fellow blacks, was unwittingly fostered by the man who would appoint him minister to Haiti: President Benjamin Harrison. In March 1889 the relocation of the newly inaugurated president to Washington, D.C., resulted in murmurings over his family's imminent housekeeping arrangements: "Mrs. Harrison is replacing the servants in the White House, substituting white help for the negro servants who have had control of the domestic machinery there for many years." Reports that the new first lady had drawn the color line at 1600 Pennsylvania Avenue began to concern blacks well beyond the nation's capital. Many blacks dependent on service occupations dreaded that, if white households north and south emulated White House etiquette, Mrs. Harrison's example might result in loss of jobs and destitution.[18]

The Harrisons themselves did little to stem the rumor. Gossipy, uneven accounts cropped up in newspapers for days and weeks before other papers refuted the story. Some noted that at least three of the black domestic staff from the first family's Indianapolis home had accompanied them to the capital. Other reports claimed the Harrisons employed more colored staff than any previous administration. The most impressive refutation came on November 28, 1890, when the Harrisons hosted a reception for a squadron of visiting Brazilian military officers at the White House. An awestruck account noted their "colored servants . . . not in livery, neither are they in the evening dress in which servants are often clothed in private residences. They stand about in plain business garments, and apparently have the success of the reception as much at heart as if they were the hosts."[19] It might hardly have mattered if rumors of the wholesale removal of "colored attachés" about the White House had been true. In the fateful interim between the first reports and recognition of their apparent baselessness, the fecund gossip had rekindled a latent prejudice that was thriving by the turn of the century.

Since 1900, Williams had seen old loyalties lose their adhesion. "Very few of the New York restaurants employ colored waiters," a keen city observer reported, "the favorite waiters being white men."[20] Williams could attest to this through his father's world; for quite some time, the advent of white foreign waiters from England and the Continent had edged out colored hotel waiters in first-class establishments.

In the spring of 1901, a resolution at the venerable Union League Club "to dismiss the colored help employed on the second floor and in the dining room" threw the organization into upheaval. Many saw the decision as betraying the original mission of the gentlemen's club and its branches: the Union Leagues, or "Loyal

Leagues," had been founded during the Civil War to promote Union solidarity, the Republican Party, and the policies of President Lincoln. This New York chapter, which was especially proactive in its civic-minded missions, had initiated, organized, and outfitted the state's first colored regiments. Nevertheless, the old racial prejudice they had shed blood to dispel still prevailed, even at the dawn of the twentieth century. Fortunately, some voting members at the Union League Club intervened and "overwhelmingly overruled" the votes previously cast to oust the black waiters—but not without stirring resentment. Outraged by the results, over a dozen governing committee members promptly resigned. Observing this controversy from the equally exclusive Lotos Club, the black waiters there penned a formal letter of thanks to the club's manager, John S. Wise, who championed the cause of the Negro waiters in the midst of the Union League debate.[21]

It's not known how long Williams's father stayed on as a waiter at the Sturtevant House; some three decades since his first shift in 1873, the hiring prospects for the old colored waiters of his father's generation were less promising than for at least a few young men in the flower shop nearby. In their place now, a few white girls waited tables in lunch rooms here and there, then made way, at an appointed hour, for white men to take over the dinner shift. And likewise a growing number of private homeowners were casually replacing their black American domestic servants, like a new floral centerpiece, with some white European variety.

Ironically, it was a particular European import about this time that would cast black New Yorkers of James Williams's immediate circle in a fleeting, but glowing, light. Williams and Herbert Cummings, the chief shipping clerk at Thorley's Roses, were but two of the numerous young colored men who staffed the chic floral operation. Williams and Cummings were of a type: both were born in Manhattan the same year and were of similar light complexion, medium height, and build—but Cummings was singled out on an eventful occasion.

On February 23, 1902, the popular Prince Henry of Prussia

arrived in New York on the *SS Kronprinz* for a goodwill tour of several American cities and towns. Although Henry was not a ruling monarch—he was the younger brother of Kaiser Wilhelm II and the grandson of Queen Victoria of England—the prince was the first European royal to visit the United States. The occasion thrust New York into one of its most extravagant welcomes on record, most notably a gala performance in the prince's honor at the Metropolitan Opera House—the "Yellow Brick Brewery," as some mocked the industrial-looking pile—which was then located on Broadway and 39th Street. The prominent architect Stanford White completed a decorative overhaul of the theater's interior, dividing the parterre with a vestibule, to reorient the royal box as the central focus. The Elblight Company installed nearly nine thousand incandescent bulbs of four candlepower (a third of them on a moveable sixty-foot-square drop curtain), an impressive feat of electrical technology for the time, achieved "without driving a single nail or screw, without breaking a single lamp or blowing a single fuse."[22]

Not surprisingly, Charles Thorley was commissioned to execute the gala's floral features, which rivaled the live entertainment on stage. The curtain rose on time at eight o'clock, and Prince Henry was expected to arrive at nine, fashionably late. The musical program unfolded under the notable batons of German-born Walter Damrosch, musical director of the New York Symphony Society; the Italian conductor Armando Seppilli; and Belgian composer Philippe Flon, who had conducted that country's premiere of Puccini's opera, *La Bohème*, two years earlier. The program comprised select acts from six operas—*Lohengrin*, *Carmen*, *Aida*, *Tannhäuser*, *Le Cid*, and *La Traviata*—for which over a dozen "luminaries of the operatic firmament" had agreed to perform.

The motley cast and crew in the wings were doubtless abuzz when word spread around 9:40 that Prince Henry's entourage had at last arrived. Probably none of the artists were aware of the cause of the guest of honor's distraction: he could not ignore the dazzling floral display that surrounded him. Arcing in both directions from his central seat were tier upon tier of flowers, the rows undulating over all the box and balcony fronts. Lush vines of southern smilax were "relieved with frequent bunches of azaleas and marguerites, and with stars of white lights shining through the green leaves." Leafy streamers draped the sides of the proscenium, from the top of its opening to the boards of the stage, and were strewn throughout the great hall in festoons that gleamed with tiny white and green lights. The prince was overwhelmed. By the time *La Traviata* came up on the program, the act had to be omitted: the prima donna Marcella Sembrich declined to sing, having learned "the Prince had already left his box and part of the audience was following his example."[23] But Prince Henry would not quit the opera house before he knew just who was responsible for the floral decorations, which he thought were superb.

Probably James Williams was present at the opera house to help mount and break down the daunting floral installation—it must have required an army of hands—but it is not on record. Still, word that Thorley, an astute businessman, was not on the scene for his royal highness to pay a compliment was weirdly impressive. According to *The World*, "Mr. Thorley had left Cummings in charge," so that was whom Prince Henry sent for. If the florist's unceremonious absence was a show of faith in his employee's consummate proficiency, it was aptly rewarded: Prince Henry offered the talented Cummings a position as his own florist when his tour through some of the other states brought him back to New York.

As towns across the country sprouted reception committees to welcome his royal highness, the black press noticed the conspicuous absence of black citizens. One Illinois paper asserted that committee officials "must have concluded that the 'niggers' must keep out of sight when Prince Henry arrives in town."[24] Another, in Kansas, urged that Prince Henry "be given a chance to see the Negro in some other capacity than a servant."[25] But it came as a surprise to blacks and whites alike to learn that Prince Henry was a bit of a Negrophile who had given some advance thought to aspects of black American life he wanted to explore. Black readers who followed the princely itinerary in the dailies would have noticed occasional ad hoc adjustments that revealed his royal highness as at least an inadvertent champion of the race.

All along the itinerary, members of local German societies quite naturally turned up for the rare opportunity to celebrate their Teutonic heritage. Indeed, when Prince Henry's special train arrived for a fifteen-minute visit to Nashville, Tennessee, some of the seven hundred ticketed townsfolk who greeted him at the depot were all done up in their Tyrolean Sunday best. Eager to indulge any matter of royal caprice, they were no doubt surprised to learn that an explicit request had been wired: "Prince Henry will be pleased to hear Jubilee Singers during his stop at the Nashville station."[26]

Back in 1871 the Fisk Jubilee Singers, of the town's historically black Fisk University, had introduced the wider world to slavery-era "plantation songs," which had been preserved in the American musical lexicon as Negro spirituals. Their renown as a musical group lent plausibility to the German royal's pressing request, but few would have guessed at the prince's more sentimental motive: when he was about fourteen, the Jubilee Singers had performed those very melodies in the theater of his family's royal palace at Potsdam.

Though over a quarter of a century ago, he longed to hear them again. In fact, his first request upon arriving in the United States was to hear "some of the old Southern melodies, if possible, sung by the negroes." According to Rear Adm. Robley D. Evans—the official American chaperone to his royal highness, who received him in New York—Prince Henry confided "he was passionately fond of them, and had been all his life—not the rag-time songs, but the old negro melodies."[27] The prince was once again deeply moved by some of the old spirituals, of which "Swing Low, Sweet Chariot" had been given as a preference. However, the combined arrangements of Nashville's mayor and Fisk's president exceeded the Prince's wish: the soprano leading the singers was Mrs. Ella Sheppard Moore, "who led them at the time the Prince heard them in Germany" and was the only member remaining from the original company at its inception in 1871. Enraptured, Prince Henry rose and grasped Mrs. Moore's hand (said to be the only hand he shook at Nashville) as he recalled the joy the group's visit had brought to the entire royal family at Berlin.[28]

Back in New York, Prince Henry made a point of attending two concerts of the visiting Hampton Singers, in a reception hall at the Waldorf-Astoria Hotel and at Carnegie Hall, respectively. At the former, he turned excitedly to Admiral Evans to ask, "Isn't that Booker T. Washington over there?" Evans, somewhat surprised, confirmed that it was indeed the famous Negro educator from Tuskegee Institute. The prince urged Evans to introduce him. "I know how some of your people feel about Washington, but I have always had great sympathy with the African race," he said. "I want to meet the man I regard as the leader of that race."

The two men talked for fully ten minutes. "Booker Washington's manner was easier than that of almost any other man I saw meet the Prince in this country," Evans recalled. Prince Henry left overjoyed by Washington's promise to send him published copies of the old Negro songs he had cherished since his German boyhood,[29] but in the meantime he happily discovered the new Negro music at a saloon on West 53rd Street. The colored musicians, singers, and dancers at the Hotel Marshall's cabaret were blithe to share their new repertoire of vaudeville "rags" and show tunes to the attentive royal fan.[30]

Certain loyal followers of Prince Henry's itinerary read the papers with personal interest. On March 11, 1902, Cummings was to accompany his highness back to Germany aboard the *SS Deutschland* as Thorley's official representative. Preparing for their friend's departure at the flower shop, Williams and his co-workers understood it was no trivial matter for their boss to give Cummings a $700 (about $19,000 today) stipend for expenses and place him in charge of an estimated $6,000 worth of flowers (about $161,000 today). Approximately fifteen thousand fresh blooms—American Beauty roses, winter roses, sprays of lilies of the valley, orchids—were painstakingly picked, swathed in moss, and laid out in the ship's hold in iceboxes at the last moment.[31]

Once the *Deutschland* set sail, Thorley's staff pored over the reports from Cummings, who was now essentially the personal floral steward to the Kaiser's brother. "Every morning I supplied the Prince's stateroom with fresh flowers and at each of the three meals the decorations of the royal table were changed," Cummings said, adding, "The Prince talked to me a lot about the greatness of the United States."[32] Cummings's overseas adventure was extraordinary: he returned with the prince's gift to him of a royal letter and a $500 gold watch with diamonds encrusting its face. Thorley would eventually make him shipping clerk for his famous House of Flowers shop at Fifth Avenue and 46th Street. But even after he returned, Cummings was somewhat independent of the bustling district of the shop: he was living up at 4 West 134th Street in Harlem. For Williams, that remove may well have added to the place's allure.

Whether Williams heard it directly or not, he seemed to take something to heart that Reverend Brooks later recommended. The pastor spoke fervently of building up the race through self-reflection, political consciousness, financial stability, and even real estate: "Buy property, and buy more property, and use your means in the ways of righteousness."[33] He railed impatiently on a later occasion against the disheartened of the race who preached expatriation: "The ship is not to be deserted because of stormy weather. If we cannot go forward, let us mark time. Here we have toiled, here our dead lie sleeping, and we have no other home. But we claim here more than food and clothing—we claim the right to be honest and industrious."[34] Perhaps Brooks or Cummings or even Thorley inspired Williams's own diligence.

Around 1903 Williams moved his family out of the Tenderloin, and some five miles farther uptown. Though he hadn't the means to buy property yet, he was a part of the first great wave of black renters to venture to Harlem. How Harlem's white landlords begrudgingly came to open up their restricted properties to "respectable colored tenants" is a story of legend. The advent of the city's first subway, in 1904, triggered an explosion of speculative development in Harlem. Block after block, a building boom of new apartment houses, anticipated an influx of white tenants. But those white tenants did not come as envisioned, so many an overzealous builder found him-

James and Lucy Williams, circa 1903, about when they moved from the Tenderloin to Harlem, with children Gertrude, Wesley, and James Leroy ("Roy"), about a year old, on his father's lap. *Charles Ford Williams Family Collection.*

self in an unscripted financial dilemma. The predicament offered a decided advantage to such pioneering and savvy African-American realtors as Philip A. Payton—often extolled as "the father of Harlem"—who now persuaded crestfallen white property owners and managers to accept black tenants if they wanted to avoid financial ruin. He also swayed a number of blacks to consider investing—if not through stock purchases, then through foresight—in his newly incorporated Afro-American Realty Company:

> Beyond a reasonable doubt, the completion of the new Pennsylvania Depot will bring about a great change in the character of the [Tenderloin] neighborhood now surrounding it. . . . This section is largely inhabited by our people. Where are they going when this and other changes take place and they are driven out?[35]

By 1905 James H. Williams was among those pioneering arrivals to Harlem, having moved his family to 18 West 134th Street, a five-story brownstone tenement between Fifth and Lenox avenues.[36] Though it was not one of Payton's buildings, the black property manager, Clarence Hutchinson, worked and lived in the building, which boosted the place's sense of security and respectability. However, the neighbor who lent this new uptown address the most prestige was Jesse A. Shipp—who would be called the "Dean of Colored Showmen"—a Broadway star who'd come to live in Harlem, "the choicest location of all the big [Afro-American] actors in New York."[37] Shipp co-wrote and appeared in the recent hit *In Dahomey*, the first African-American musical to be performed on an indoor Broadway stage. It affiliated him with "the highest rank of actors of his race" who were then influencing American theater, including Bert Williams, George Walker, Aida Overton Walker, Will Marion Cook, and Paul Lawrence Dunbar.

Whatever their disparate vocations, Williams and his new neighbors personified essentially similar quests for self-betterment, familial security, and prosperity and, as Reverend Brooks had invoked, to "uplift the race." Their example induced thousands of other black families to pull up stakes from Manhattan's scattered "black belt" enclaves in Greenwich Village; in Chelsea; the vibrant West 53rd Street spine of the Tenderloin (today's Penn Station and Hell's Kitchen areas); and in San Juan Hill (today's Lincoln Center area), a black neighborhood in the West Sixties, whose nickname was purportedly inspired by the "colored" 24th U.S. Infantry that distinguished itself during the Spanish-American War in 1898. The uptown relocation of Williams and other black families, in turn, encouraged the Great Migration of rural southerners to the urban centers of the North, prior to World War I. The linchpins of this extraordinary demographic shift to Harlem—a once-sleepy white suburb, suddenly revitalized as the capital of America's "New Negro" race—were a wide array of African-American business folk, artists, entrepreneurs, and others whose professional circles now regarded Williams, in his new capacity at Grand Central Station, as a man of position.

CHAPTER 4

Fraternity and Ascendancy

Mr. Williams holds one of the most responsible positions—as little as it is known—at this great railway station, that of chief of the Red Cap attendants.

—JOHN E. ROBINSON, 1909

Even before it selected an architect or determined a design, the New York Central Company started building its new $200 million terminal complex around the old Grand Central Station. On July 18, 1903, workers broke ground on East 42nd Street and, to maintain regular service during construction, adapted the Grand Central Palace exhibition hall on East 43rd Street into a temporary terminal. For the next ten years, as crews executed their strategic demolitions and elevations, Grand Central Station carried on as the seminal railroad gateway to the metropolis.

For his part, as general passenger agent, George H. Daniels continued to welcome travelers with ever-freshened promotional enticements: "Nineteen red-cap attendants in handsome uniforms meet all incoming trains." Numerous publications reminded travelers that these attendants were at their disposal for free, being employed by the railroad company. Without giving salary figures, the New York Central's *Four-Track News*—an onboard magazine that Daniels launched two years earlier, and that would become *Travel* magazine—suggested that Grand Central Station's Red Cap attendants earned twice as much as counterparts elsewhere in the company's network, even on par with "the average railroad conductor." Whether it was true "that passengers can here get good service without feeling obliged to tip the porter,"[1] a railroad attendant might forget to reiterate it. Despite Daniels's brochure parlance, one might wonder if a white attendant's salary was truly lucrative enough to dull his aspirations to a higher position.

Of course, for Williams and other members of the race in general, the challenge of securing a regular salary through gainful employment was all too familiar. The sociologist Mary White Ovington (who actually knew Williams's sister Ella through their mutual connection to the Quaker-run Colored Mission) was among numerous white "progressives" who were elucidating the troubling social conundrum to the broader public. A prolific informant on the subject of Negro family life in New York, Ovington helped further the subject's topical interest. Numerous black civic leaders, ministers, and teachers would soon endorse her important mission to investigate employment opportunities, housing conditions, and the efficacy of relief agencies pertinent to the race.

Ovington cited countless cases of trained and qualified black women whose color alone routinely denied them access to trades above laundry work or domestic service: "They cannot be saleswomen, stenographers, telegraphers, accountants or factory workers, because in the great majority of these positions they would be obliged to work side by side with whites." She also pointed out black professional men who were acutely aware that, whatever their status amid their own people, no credentials ensured them positions in trades obliging their constant interaction with white peers or clients. "For this reason we seldom find a colored architect or engineer or electrician," she observed, "while there are plenty of doctors, lawyers and clergymen." But brushing aside her own many citable caseloads, Ovington judged there were "really few people who entertain this strong race prejudice."[2] She hazarded that if employers simply refused to listen to biased complaints, racial tension would soon disappear from the workplace. Her optimism remained to be tested.

In anticipation of the new station being built, the New York Central hired a Negro to the Red Cap attendant service team. "I was the first colored man ever employed at Grand Central as a red cap," Williams averred many years later. The all-white workforce that Daniels created eight years earlier would soon become almost all black. Williams recalled he was hired to replace a white man named Walsh, who had been promoted to a clerical position in Grand Central's Information Services.

If in most occupations breaking the color line was inherently controversial, Williams's hire did not noticeably touch off any polemical objections. And though white workers often adamantly refused to work alongside black ones, instances of whites and blacks working together tolerably were not unknown. Some employers sympathized with social reformers like Ovington and, defying the prejudiced indignation of their white workers, chose to "stand by their colored employees and refuse to dismiss them."[3] But the virtual absence of reports soon after he replaced Walsh suggests that Williams's hire was but the first step of Grand Central's orchestrated stride toward a complete racial overhaul of its Red Cap station attendants. If the white attendants made any concerted protest over a colored man's admission to their ranks, or objected on grounds of a perceived threat to their incomes, it did not reverberate in the press. A better guess is that the ensuing rapid attrition of other white attendants was due to their rise, as with Walsh, into other, more highly regarded departments of the terminal.

Although Daniels had mustered a dozen white men into the station's Red Cap attendant service in 1895, most educated white men shunned the job as too menial. A white attendant's mandate to relieve encumbered ladies—and increasingly gentlemen, too—no doubt heightened his popularity with those he assisted. But every valise, hatbox, and baby thrust at him emphasized the humbleness of his position and effectively nullified Daniels's earlier claim that "they are not porters"—a term the word *attendant* did not really displace. Perhaps the constant hauling of others' property reminded him that this job was a low echelon of the railroad station's workforce hierarchy. Yet if a white attendant was apt to bemoan self-comparisons to the colored Pullman porters on the train, or to the baggage smashers on the street, he could reasonably hope to ascend to another position, even if unschooled, simply because he was white. It was unthinkable, considering the many rigidly obeyed racial barriers, that Daniels would nonchalantly replace a white attendant with a black one. Even without knowing who vouched for Williams—though Thorley seems the most plausible candidate—Daniels would certainly not have risked the company's censure by hiring a Negro with less than the highest recommendation.

Though Walsh's vacancy might have given him an in, Williams understood the palpable boundaries of the terminal's color line that debarred him from opportunities that were available to his white predecessors: as Negroes, he and others who might follow him could not count on promotions. How apt now was Reverend Brooks's challenge of a few years before. "Work may be difficult to secure," he'd said, "but if we cannot get what we want, let us take what we can get."[4] Williams could surely imagine it to be auspicious for the race to corner this disdained job category, as a sort of bird in the hand until something superior was in the offing. Later claims that he convinced the eminent New York Central railroad company to give Negro workers the Red Cap attendant franchise are less than persuasive. Indeed, irrespective of Williams's sentiment, the company was hiring blacks rapidly enough to suggest that it was already contemplating a full revision of its Red Cap attendant system into one that racial caste defined as a porter system. Indeed, the byword of "porter" or "Red Cap" quickly supplanted that of "attendant," which all but vanished.

For some thirty-five years, colored sleeping car porters had been serving Pullman cars of the New York Central and other railroad lines across the country. Negro station porters, a logical extension of Negro sleeping car porters, would have obviated company concerns about white attendants who, disgruntled by their lowly position (perhaps aggravated by being nevertheless referred to as porters), were less inclined to hustle than black attendants striving for job stability. Whether by happenstance or by design, Grand Central Terminal's new all-black Red Cap porter system rapidly swayed a similar racial shift in railroad stations across the country. Though employing blacks may have been less altruistic than intuitive, for it assigned blacks the same genre of jobs to which they had been traditionally relegated: service.

The Grand Central Station workforce transformed precipitously. By the spring of 1904, the Red Cap staff, which Williams had integrated the previous year, was almost exclusively black. (The notable holdout was Milt Newman, apparently as novel for being Jewish as for being white, who had started in 1900 and continued into the 1940s.) Grand Central's hierarchy was not unlike that of other U.S. railroad stations at the time. It employed multiple thousands of people. Williams and the other Red Caps were supervised by the stationmaster, who in turn fell under the jurisdiction of the terminal manager—a position that was described as a "neutral terminal official" who served the New York Central and the New Haven companies equally. Under his control were four principal departments of the station: seven stationmasters, the gatemen, the information service, and the Red Caps. By dint of their race, the last were ineligible for promotion into the other departments.

If advancements were impossible, some Red Caps discovered other ways to improve their lot at one of Grand Central's most coveted posts: the Vanderbilt Avenue entrance, a principal point of arrival, on the west side of the station. Since the company paid them only sixteen dollars per month (less than it had paid the white porters), they soon figured out how to make up the difference—and at a profit. By turning up the charm as they hustled, they earned tips from travelers, often trebling their small salary. But upon learning they were doing so, the stationmaster docked the men from the payroll altogether and insisted—over the porters' strongest objections—they would have to get by only on tips from now on.

In defense of his retrenchment, the stationmaster informed the men that the company considered their services to be inessential and actually "only consented to have them stay out of pure goodness of heart." But was that true? No record places Williams at the Vanderbilt entrance, although he was the likeliest to have been if the seniority system that entitled men to that post in later years was already in effect. At any rate, Williams knew the stationmaster's baseless barb contradicted everything he'd ever heard the company say to promote the free Red Cap attendant service, and which it would repeat for years. The comment more likely revealed a bitter recognition that white Red Caps were from a bygone era. Williams and the other Red Cap attendants could easily see through the stationmaster's indignation. His subsequent action was too familiar to them, merely another instance of exploitative supremacy over black workers—who could not advance or transfer from redcapping like their white predecessors.

While the New York Central patently discouraged passengers from tipping, the stationmaster hadn't pointedly objected to Red Caps taking tips per se. It rather seemed he resented these Negro porters being so successful.[5] And some were astronomically successful, according to one former porter. "The salary as a Red Cap was $32.10 a month, and I was saving $300 a month," Jesse Battle recalled of his last days as Williams's assistant chief in 1911, before he became the first black police officer in Greater New York. "I was making three or four hundred a month as a Red Cap."[6]

By 1905 Williams's hire may have sparked predictable resentment from the stationmaster. It perhaps resonated elsewhere, too: a Brooklyn pharmacist mockingly "rigged up a little darky with a red cap and yellow coat" that summer to promote his shop.[7] But it surely inspired others: William Ernest Braxton's painting, *The Red Cap*, in the Brooklyn Colored YMCA's first annual exposition of American Negro artists that fall, visually codified the Red Cap railroad porter as an iconically Negro occupation.[8] And a story serial in the *Ladies' Home Journal* that same year began: "When we got to the Grand Central Station to start for Newport we had a number of the delightful café-au-lait-colored porters in gray livery and red caps to help us with our bags and things getting into the train."[9] Maybe one was Williams, who toted baggage during the station's expansion over the next few years. If chivalry was dead, as some wistfully conceded, then Jim Crow servitude would have to make do.

◈

Probably sometime in 1905, Williams went to sit for his portrait at the prestigious photography studio of Otto Sarony, at 1177 Broadway near 28th Street. Sarony's shop was directly next door to Thorley's, and Williams had likely known him through his duties for the latter.[10] What occasion prompted this sitting is not known, but the full-length portrait seems telling: smartly attired in evening wear, Williams dressed not to reflect his job as railroad attendant but more likely to convey his readiness to claim some promising prospect in the offing. Though not dressed for work per se, this broad-shouldered young man in his twenties was apparently suited for something of considerable importance, something that very likely had to do with his recent affiliation with a particular fraternal order.

For this photo, Williams had slid tight the knot of his white silk cravat to the white batwing collar that splayed beneath his fair brown throat. He fastened the six vest buttons of his well-tailored dark three-piece tweed suit, and he tucked a patterned silk pocket square into the coat's left flank pocket. Williams could not have been unaware, as he poked a tiny brass pin into his lapel, that many took exception to the ornament. The shiny antlered head was the emblem of the Improved Benevolent and Protective Order of Elks of the World—IBPOEW, or Colored Elks. They were part of the phalanx of black American fraternal organizations that had been forming since 1787, when Prince Hall of Massachusetts chartered, and became namesake of, the first Masonic lodge for members of African descent. As Williams was aware, bands of white Elks often set upon any unwary black man who dared to sport their beloved mascot on his own lapel—and it was a litigious offense in New York. In the photograph, the modest but potent little symbol suited Williams, both as an adornment and as a badge. A comb had marshaled the unruly curls of his raven hair. His calm, doe-eyed face already exuded the confidence and goodwill of an ambassador—a sort of minister without portfolio, gamely awaiting an assignment.

James H. Williams, in an Otto Sarony Studio photograph, circa 1905. Williams's "antlers" lapel pin defied a law—which his lodge overturned in court—barring blacks from wearing Elks insignia. *Charles Ford Williams Family Collection.*

About this time, in 1905, some local acquaintances had begun raising Williams's interest in the Elks. That year realtor Sandy P. Jones, one of Harlem's increasingly patrician Negro colony along West 134th Street, took notice of Williams, a fairly recent person of note on the block. Jones surely knew it was Williams who broke the color line at the august Grand Central Station, and was intent upon making the fellow's acquaintance. Jones was not just a real estate man—he was connected to black real estate royalty. He was a stockholder and member of the board of directors of the Afro-American Realty Company, the firm established by the putative "Father of Colored Harlem" Philip A. Payton, Jr. With the discerning eye of a cobbler-turned-broker, Jones now sized up his neighbor for a purpose. He happened to be the Exalted Ruler of Manhattan Lodge no. 45, a fraternal order of the IBPOEW, with a tireless mission to institute new lodges in towns throughout the Northeast. To Jones, this James H. Williams appeared a worthy race man to recruit.

Jones's invitation was flattering and perhaps acknowledged the rarity of a colored man flourishing from Thorley's flower shop to Vanderbilt's railroad terminal. But Williams could not have savored that invitation without tasting its potential danger. The very existence of the Colored Elks, as the order was best known, was the bane of the older white fraternity, which was on the whole unbrotherly—indeed, it was litigious and vindictive. Yet knowing the Colored Elks sought only the best characters for membership would surely have stoked Williams's enthusiasm about them. Williams was already known in fraternal orders. He and his father both counted among the "gentlemen of standing and integrity" of Ivanhoe Commandery no. 5, under the Knights Templar, a Freemasonry-affiliated order with a specifically Christian-based membership requirement. The Ivanhoe's drill corps was widely praised for its demonstrations, at black social functions, of intricate and precise military maneuvers.[11] James was also a member of the Manhattan Lodge of Odd Fellows, the Royal Arch and Blue House Masons, and Medina Temple, so the Manhattan Lodge of Elks was probably not a hard sell for him.[12]

Given Williams's vocation, he had very likely heard Colored Elkdom's creation story—which, coincidentally, unfolded from the railroad. One Billy King—an impresario who worked a backup job as Pullman buffet man between theatrical bookings—picked up a certain book that some white passenger had left behind on a New Orleans–to-Cincinnati train. Unimpressed, he tossed it into a linen locker. A. J. Riggs, the porter of the same Pullman car, found the book but, unlike his colleague, lost himself in page after page of its strange accounts of secret rituals. The white passenger who had so carelessly left this mysterious volume on the train turned out to be the Grand Exalted Ruler of the Elks, who soon reported his precious lost item to the Pullman Company. Upon investigation, the book was discovered, and King, who had originally found the book but failed to properly turn it in as lost, was suspended. Riggs was fired, but the book's magic had already turned him in a fatefully creative direction. He and his friend B. T. Howard organized the country's first chapter of Colored Elks. As a result, White Elks embarked on a campaign of costly lawsuits that endured for years.

Founded in 1898, the still nascent order of Colored Elks had fashioned itself upon the bylaws and principles of its white predecessor. As tensions mounted between the two organizations, the Colored Elks quickly pointed out that "the seven original members, who constituted the first lodge in New York City, February 16, 1868, did not have any 'Jim Crow' annex clause in their By-Laws and Constitution"; rather, it argued, "good Southerners" had added the clause later.[13] For their part, on June 9, 1868, the jolly good Northerners organized a Minstrel Festival at New York's Academy of Music to benefit their new Benevolent and Protective Order of Elks. Revealing their own racial prejudices, the publicity promised to feature "Ethiopic arias"—using a commonly exotic nickname for Negro—and a popular headlining act named Emerson, Allen and Manning's Ethiopian Minstrels.[14]

By the early twentieth century, Colored Elkdom had grown rapidly into a powerful movement for financial and spiritual self-empowerment in black communities across the country. Manhattan Lodge no. 45, organized in the fall of 1904, was the first on the island borough.[15] The lodge enlisted Williams during its distinctive emergence in the struggle for black civic equality, when the Colored Elks constituted the institutional forerunners of the modern civil rights movement. Whether purposeful or intuitive, the lodge probably valued Williams's practical experience from working at Thorley's and Grand Central Station: both jobs called upon his convivial forbearance under pressure from an often demanding public.

At the time, white Elks societies across the country were strong-arming black Elks, whether physically or by systematically forcing them into litigation. In New York, Assemblyman William J. Grattan, a chief ally of the white Elks, introduced legislation that made it a misdemeanor statewide to wear an order's copyrighted emblem. Grattan feigned ignorance that black Elks existed at all, but members were certain the newly enacted law was targeted at them. On April 12, 1906, police arrested one of Williams's Manhattan Lodge brothers, Oldridge R. Johnson, for wearing his Elk lapel pin. Johnson was arraigned for violating three counts of Section 674-A of the Penal Code, or the "Grattan bill."

After a few adjournments, on June 19 Johnson's case went before the court of general sessions, where about three hundred white Elks filled the chamber. Three justices examined the evidence put before them. They compared the names of the two societies—the "Benevolent Protective Order of Elks of the United States" versus the "Improved Benevolent and Protective Order of Elks of the World." They examined the white Elks's copyrighted button, which bore an elk's head with the letters BPOE above the antlers. Then they examined the colored society's button, with its abbreviation, IBPOEW, on the same plane as the antlers. The justices conceded the similarity but nevertheless threw out the case on the grounds that the word *white* in the white society's constitution was an impropriety: they held that, being black, the Negro society could not practice a deception. They also determined there to be no evidence that the colored society had willfully violated any provisions of the white Elks' constitution or bylaws. Accordingly, they upheld the Colored Elks' right to adopt and wear the emblem of any secret society that exluded their membership. The justices acquitted Johnson unanimously.[16]

By now Williams was a conspicuous member of the Manhattan Lodge of Elks, with essential organizational importance. He was elected Esteemed Leading Knight, making him second in command in the hierarchy of Manhattan Lodge officers, after Exalted Ruler Sandy Jones. He was keeping enviable company: "Mr. Sandy P. Jones, the present Exalted Ruler, is a man of good executive capacity and a skillful parliamentarian. It is mainly through his efforts and ability that the lodge holds the enviable position it does in the order of Elkdom."[17]

Another officer of the tribe (as lodge members called themselves), holding the rank of Esquire, was Jesse Battle.[18] Although Williams was only a few years older, he regarded his friend as something of a protégé: Jesse had followed him as a Red Cap at Grand Central in May 1905. Not only did Williams and Jesse share both employment and Elks membership, their families grew as extended relations to each other in Harlem as neighbors, mutual house guests, and even occasional traveling companions.

As fellow officers and friends in the Manhattan Lodge of Elks, Williams and Jesse helped to coordinate a pivotal event in the lodge's maturation: On June 8, 1906, the First Annual Picnic and Summernight's Festival took place at Sulzer's Harlem River Park. Williams, on the event's floor committee, mingled and made introductions among the vast, interchanging crowd as it enjoyed the music furnished by Hallie Anderson, one of the preeminent dance music leaders of the black society circuit whose full orchestras, not uncommonly at the time, were often mixed with white musicians.[19] The event was a formality, albeit a judicious one: it set the stage for the Manhattan Lodge to impress and garner support from Negro Harlem society. It also gave the two-hundred-member Manhattan Lodge visibility in the eyes of the national body, Grand Lodge of the IBPOEW: it showcased the fledgling lodge as having the political gumption to host the seventh annual session of the IBPOEW Grand

Lodge that would take place in Brooklyn two months later. That late-summer national conference would constitute a signal turn in the Colored Elks history.

Indeed, Williams's lodge was facing a newly dispiriting battle against the Elks' national leadership. "Trouble is hotly brewing in Elkdom for Grand Exalted Ruler B. T. Howard," the *New York Age* wrote of the Grand Lodge's first titular head, who, it opined, "got cold feet about meeting in Brooklyn." Before Johnson's trial, Howard had effectively capitulated to the threat of the Grattan bill. Citing New York's statewide prohibition of Colored Elks wearing pins and badges, he declared it "wise and beneficial to move said Grand Lodge to the city of Columbus, Ohio."

Howard's overcautiousness struck many members as an impolitic show of weakness, not to mention a lack of solidarity. Many were also irate that he presumed to usurp the governing authority of the Elks body: he had not consulted any of the numerous member lodges whose votes at the Grand Lodge session in Washington the previous year had determined the location of this year's session. The Manhattan Lodge, duly galvanized by the triumphant outcome of its costly legal defense, lost patience with the Grand Exalted Ruler's unilateral decision. Joined by Brooklyn Lodge no. 32 (the mother lodge of the Elk order in New York State) and Jersey City's Progressive Lodge no. 35, the three lodges together challenged Howard's one-man rule. The Grand Exalted Ruler retaliated by suspending all three for insubordination, which prompted dozens of other lodges to defiantly close ranks against him.

On August 28, 29, and 30, 1906, the seventh annual Grand Lodge session took place in Brooklyn as planned. But the estimated "one hundred lodges, with an aggregate membership of 12,000 American citizens" at the borough's Sumner Hall, formed the dissenting faction of a schism in Negro Elkdom: the matter of deposing the autocratic Howard topped their agenda.[20] The two factions split, and Dr. W. E. Atkins was installed as Grand Exalted Ruler of the new faction.

After the session adjourned, the Manhattan Lodge to which Williams belonged gave "the delegates an opportunity of seeing Coney Island and other points of interest." At Coney's Luna Park, many would have been eager to see, among its myriad diversions, the artist E. J. Perry, "the negro silhouette cutter" who limned portraits on the spot with a pair of scissors in lieu of pen and ink. The Manhattan Lodge also treated conventioneers to "trolley cars and a band of music." Even lacking a song list, the high quality of the entertainment—no doubt dance music of symphonic proportion and style—may be deduced from the names of a few of the Manhattan Lodge members in attendance. James Reese Europe was a bandleader nonpareil who a few years later would found the Clef Club Orchestra and during World War I would become lieutenant leader of the 369th U.S. Infantry "Harlem Hellfighters" Band. Arthur "Happy" Rhone was an orchestra leader who would become the principal Harlem nightclub owner in the 1920s. And both Wilkins brothers would gain renown for promoting and giving succor to black performers: Barron as a hotelier and cabaret owner of Harlem's Exclusive (né Astoria, later named the Executive) Club, and Leroy as owner of the Cafe Leroy.[21]

By the fall, Williams was clearly ensconced in the inner circle of the country's largest black fraternal lodge. On the evening of November 22, Manhattan Lodge no. 45 gave its first Grand Annual Ball and Reception, again with Hallie Anderson's orchestra. Williams served on the arrangements committee and was able to secure the Grand Central Palace as the venue.

By January 26, 1907, Manhattan Lodge no. 45—having emerged from the split with the Grand Lodge's Howard faction a few months before—was newly rechartered and incorporated. Among the eleven names appearing on the new charter were the indefatigable Sandy P. Jones, James H. Anderson (who would found the *New York Amsterdam News* two years later), and James H. Williams as trustee.[22] That spring the lodge elected Williams its treasurer, and he also officiated as grand treasurer for the West Chester Lodge no. 116 in

Tarrytown. "Forty good men," the IBPOEW's recruitment philosophy proclaimed, "are far better than a hundred bad or unreliable men." Williams thrived in this good company.[23]

Late on Sunday, December 1, 1907, Williams and several dozen other finely dressed men gathered on West 53rd Street as St. Mark's Methodist Episcopal Church let out its regular evening service. The gentlemen exchanged brief greetings with the exiting parishioners and, at the behest of Reverend Brooks, helped themselves to the just-vacated seats. These members of Manhattan Lodge no. 45 of the IBPOEW had come in force to formally issue a proclamation: by authority of the factional Grand Exalted Ruler, Dr. W. E. Atkins, the first Sunday in December of each year was designated "Elks' memorial day," to be commemorated thereafter "by every lodge of Elks to the memory of our departed brothers." James H. Anderson, who replaced Sandy Jones as Manhattan Lodge's Exalted Ruler, delivered the opening address; the Elks' Quartette rendered "Nearer My God, to Thee"; a roll was called, revealing 187 of the full membership of 292 in attendance; and Reverend Brooks delivered his second sermon of that evening, which he closed with a benediction: "I am glad that you came here tonight. I wish you success, for I know that you have difficulties."[24]

The difficulties that Reverend Brooks referred to were the battles that the Elks would persistently face on behalf of the race. From the collective fraternities of Elks, Odd Fellows, Masons, Knights, and other orders, including their women's branches and counterparts, Williams surely drew ample experience and confidence to shape his "uplift" mission of community building at Grand Central Station. It was a mission that other family members were striving to carry out in their own way.

Around the time Williams was joining the Elks, his wife Lucy delivered their fourth child, Dorothy; while his sister Ella bore her and her husband's first child, Lloyd Meegee Cofer III. Ella and her husband were still fairly newlywed when their boy came. On January 6, 1904, she had been twenty-two and Lloyd Cofer, Jr., nineteen when they stood before Reverend Sill at St. Chrysostom's Chapel (where James and Lucy had wed seven years before). Despite the joy of Lloyd III's birth the following year, the young couple's marriage was tragically cut short a year after that by Lloyd Jr.'s death.

The passing of Williams's brother-in-law drew an affecting response from Mary White Ovington, who was gaining wider notice as a keen social reformer. Before she would co-found the NAACP in 1909, Ovington gave deference to the deep, invaluable friendships she made among black New Yorkers—like the Williamses and Cofers—in the course of her research and prolific discourses on Negro family life in the city. That she so generously eulogized Lloyd Cofer in *Colored American* magazine perhaps softened Ella and her family's personal sorrow—if that were even possible at the time—but Ovington was their good friend, who had known the two young sweethearts, and their ambitions, for years.[25]

Williams's widowed sister had a life just as busy as his, albeit in religious circles. Though Ella and Lloyd Jr. were active in pious church work, they also were ardent race workers. The couple had met as teenagers at the Colored Mission on West 30th Street, a Quaker philanthropy established just after the Civil War, that was a meetinghouse, a school, and an employment center. While a fair share of associations existed for Negro men, there were too few for women, particularly the "many green southern Negroes" newly arriving on New York's docks. The Colored Mission was known particularly for its work, in conjunction with other community-based charities, on problems unique to industrious Negro women, who, in their naïveté, were vulnerable to all manner of exploitation. The Colored Mission strove to get them proper lodgings and work.[26]

Lloyd Jr.'s mother was the cleaning woman at the Mission, so he had practically grown up there and became an unusually young member of its staff. Ella was one of the Mission's social workers. She was three years Lloyd's senior, but his gentle nature, his studiousness, and his ambition inflated him with maturity. The affable young Lloyd Jr., "whom every one was attracted to," was bookish but athletic. He was musically gifted as well, with a beautiful voice that he likely inherited from his mother, who in earlier days had had a dalliance in the theater. His father, Lloyd Sr., was the head hall man at the Lotos Club, one of the city's most venerable Gilded Age gentlemen's clubs, founded in 1870, on Fifth Avenue at 21st Street; member Mark Twain had wittily dubbed it the "Ace of Clubs."

When the Mission formed a boys' club, Lloyd Jr. joined and was soon its director, meeting with the boys six nights a week, when he was just nineteen. "It was a great task for so young a lad," Ovington wrote. "Some of the club members were older than he, they all knew him, and there was the danger that they might not submit to his authority as readily as to that of a stranger. But this, instead of proving a hindrance, was a help. The boys knew him, and therefore they trusted him." In charge of thirty boys, he taught them music and organized five of them into a skillful singing quintet; he also coached them in basketball in the Mission's yard. At seventeen, carrying over his passion for organizing from the Mission, Lloyd had joined the Bethel AME Church, where he and Ella together became diligent members of the community.

In 1905 the Cofers were living in the Tenderloin—in the household of Williams and Ella's parents—at 117 West 30th Street. Lloyd Jr.'s ambitious labors were exacting a toll on his health that no one had begun to fathom. Employed as a stenographer for a neighborhood tobacco firm, he was reportedly "so anxious to advance himself that he overworked." In mid-August 1906, he fell ill with typhoid. Now, stressed even more about "the little round bundle of a third Lloyd Cofer at home," he surrendered to others' urgings to go to Bellevue Hospital for the best care. But shortly after midnight on August 29, following a two-week bedrest, Cofer awakened in a delirium. The ward's nurse was absent when he dove out the window to his death in the yard thirty feet below. "That such a thing should have happened in the hospital is a terrible indictment upon its management," Ovington wrote mournfully. And perhaps upon a society where a man's wholesome striving to excel should usher him to the breaking point.

Williams's parents had at some point bought a family plot at the Evergreens Cemetery in Brooklyn, where their son-in-law appears to have been the first laid to rest. Unfortunately, another family member would be buried there less than two years later. In the spring of 1908, James's eldest brother, John Wesley Jr., who had miraculously rebounded before a coroner's mortal pronouncement in 1900, died at the same West 30th Street apartment, from tuberculosis.[27]

◈

By the end of December 1906, James Williams and his co-workers had adjusted, along with Grand Central's constant bustle of travelers, to the temporary terminal on Lexington Avenue. The following summer he witnessed the New York Central line switch all its trains to electric operation, then likewise the New Haven line a year later. In January 1909, as the last steam engine was removed from Grand Central, a golden (if troubled) age of America's national rail system slowly receded like a fog.[28] But nostalgia evaporated quickly for Williams in the face of new prospects. Sometime between 1908 and 1909, C. L. Bardo, superintendent of Grand Central Terminal, was mulling over the necessary interplay between train passengers and station crew. He zeroed in on the station porters, the kinetic flow of their crimson hats—bobbing, idling, gathering, dispersing, appearing, vanishing—among the constant throng of travelers in the station. Bardo determined that, as more would now need to be hired, their duties ought to be regulated and supervised.

In April or early May 1909, Superintendent Bardo promoted Williams chief attendant of the Red Caps.[29] Despite the official word ATTENDANT on their uniform caps, "Red Cap" was their bona-fide appellation. The term would classify their station assignments, pay, wages, locker room designations, and recognition by the traveling public.

That black New Yorkers felt a collective investment in Williams's achievement was little surprise, for it counted as a significant stride toward racial uplift. Even John E. Robinson—an up-and-coming journalist who wrote the first full profile of Williams for the August 1909 issue of *Colored American* magazine—might have had some personal motive in promoting his subject: Robinson and Williams were brother officers in the Manhattan Lodge of Elks. Robinson had a faster connection still: the fledgling newsman worked under Chief Williams, his profile subject, at Grand Central Terminal. Robinson, who would soon become an editor at the *New York Amsterdam News*, was one of the city's many black men who worked as Red Caps while aiming for other professions.

Inevitably, Robinson's profile of Grand Central's auspicious race man thrust Chief Williams into public view. The article, which featured Williams's handsome Sarony portrait, cropped in oval cameo, surely stoked a proprietary fondness among black subscribers, and the interest of its fewer, but mindful, white readers. "Mr. Williams holds one of the most responsible positions—as little as it is known—at this great railway station, that of chief of the Red Cap attendants," Robinson wrote. "When C. L. Bardo, superintendent of the Grand Central Terminal, promoted Mr. Williams to the position it is said the he did so largely because the young man had for seven years shown himself to be an honest, faithful and trustworthy employee, one who had the ability to succeed where rare skill, devotion and diplomacy are prime requisites."

Having had ample occasion to hone his interpersonal and managerial skills at Thorley's, it came as no surprise that Williams had fine-tuned the Red Caps' working performance: "The men are considered by the traveling public to be the best attired and disciplined body of men to be found at any railway terminal." And Red Caps demonstrated their esteem for their new boss. If Williams ever worried that any of the Red Caps might begrudge him his promotion, attendants from the night division disabused him of such concern, as they "presented him with a fine traveling bag made by one of the best manufacturers of leather goods in the city." The day men celebrated his titled promotion likewise.[30]

On Saturday, August 7, 1909, brimming with his newfound celebrity, the Chief and Lucy left Grand Central with their friends Jesse and Florence Battle for Michigan. The friends then lived across from each other on West 136th Street, the Williamses at number

44, the Battles at number 27. Williams and Battle were both Manhattan Lodge delegates to the Elks' annual Grand Lodge session taking place from August 9 to 12 in Detroit. While the trip was only about a week long, it was no doubt an anxious one for Lucy, thinking constantly about the kids at home. There were plenty of family members to supervise them, but four-year-old Dorothy, the youngest, needed the most attention. James and Lucy got back from the Detroit convention by mid-month, nevertheless their return coincided with a tragedy inside Grand Central Station.

Early on the morning of August 17, a thirty-year-old Red Cap, Louis H. Blackwell, had a fatal accident. The porter was towing a heavily stacked baggage truck along a train platform, when an incoming suburban train clipped some of the trunks. The baggage truck overturned, sending Blackwell to his death on the tracks. Reverend Brooks presided over the funeral the following Saturday at St. Mark's Methodist Episcopal Church. Chief Williams selected the pall bearers, who included his friend Lloyd Jones and other Red Cap section officers. Although some years later, after litigation, the New York Central and Hudson River Railroad Company would pay a $500 judgment to Blackwell's family, Williams understood how unprepared his men were for sudden misfortunes.[31]

That harsh lesson became even more painfully clear a month later, when personal tragedy consumed the Williams home: On September 24, James and Lucy's four-year-old daughter Dorothy died. Sick for over a year, she had finally been confined for a couple of weeks in the Hospital for Ruptured and Crippled Children—which was next door to Grand Central Station—where she succumbed to "tuberculous meningitis and hip disease."[32] Dorothy's funeral took place in the family's apartment two days after she died. Her baby photo, which James and Lucy had had taken four years earlier, downtown at the Sol. Young Studio (next door to Gilsey House on 29th Street), now haunted the parlor. The intimate service was presided over by the Rev. E. G. Clifton of St. David's Protestant Episcopal Church, where Lucy used to take little Dorothy to Sabbath School, in the Morrisania section of the Bronx. The church's location, near the New York and

Harlem Railroad lines, accounted for its congregation's considerable number of Pullman porters and Grand Central Red Caps, who now formed the mournful gathering. Williams's old boss Thorley likely provided many of the overflowing floral tributes that followed the little girl's funeral cortege to the Evergreens Cemetery in Brooklyn.

Injury, illness, and death that found Williams both in and out of the workplace: his eldest brother's death the previous year (John Wesley Jr. had survived being stabbed in 1900), his baby girl's death, and his man Blackwell's fatal tragedy in the station fueled his call to action toward improving the Red Caps' working conditions. On the evening of September 14, a week before Dorothy died, Williams had summoned his men to the True Reformers' Hall—another church, a block east of St. Mark's, at 153 West 53rd Street—where the gathering organized "a beneficial and benevolent society, to be composed exclusively of Grand Central employees."

The twofold mission of the Attendants' Beneficial Association of Grand Central Terminal was to promote fellowship among Red Caps and to provide aid in case of sickness, injury, or death to their uninsured, and unsalaried, members who depended on tips. The men elected Williams president, and Battle (then studying for the police exam) as sergeant-at-arms. Williams no doubt modeled it after similar mutual aid, or so-called "sick societies," that black citizens were familiar with.[33] Even without the advantage of organizational records, the present writer can see its importance: fifteen years later, on November 18, 1924, the song team of Noble Sissle and Eubie Blake would dedicate a performance of *Chocolate Dandies*—their Broadway musical hit, which launched the comedic dancer Josephine Baker—as a benefit for the Red Caps Sick Fund of both Grand Central and Penn stations.[34]

The attendants' resolved solidarity coincided with a new sense of permanence around their common workplace: the New York Central announced that its executive offices, traffic operations departments for both freight and passengers, legal and financial bureaus, "have removed to the new Grand Central Terminal," even as construction was still under way.[35] Just as Grand Central Station was setting new standards for rail travel, Williams was instilling in his Red Caps a new sense of purpose and self-confidence—not to mention an essential sense of community empowerment and self-reliance in the face of occupational disfranchisement. In addition, he was effectively shaping a Negro workforce that would become an exemplar of grassroots enterprise, lobbying, and philanthropy.

CHAPTER 5

Harlem Exodus to the Bronx and to the Sea

There has been quite an exodus from that neighborhood to the Bronx and Williamsbridge.

—*NEW YORK AGE*, 1908

By summer of 1910, the Williamses' grief over little Dorothy's death had somewhat waned with the needs of their four other children—Wesley, Gertrude, Leroy, and Pierre. Wesley, the eldest, played a particular role in lifting the household's spirits. A few weeks shy of his thirteenth birthday, he distinguished himself on behalf of his school by bringing home "one of the medals in the *Evening World* athletic games." Public School no. 89 at West 134th Street and Lenox Avenue was one of the venerable old schools from Harlem's sleepy decades past, and Wesley's achievement would have imbued the burgeoning black community with pride. Like any other striving community, Negro Harlem measured its prospects by the achievement and potential of its progeny. Wesley, like colored boys all across America that summer, likely imagined that prizefighter Jack Johnson's superhuman sweat anointed his own victory as one for the Race.

During the late spring of 1910, keen anticipation over the imminent "fight of the century" had steadily swelled to a national cause célèbre. Though Johnson reigned as the World Colored Heavyweight Boxing Champion, the color line that ran through other organized sports barred him from matches sponsored by the white World Heavyweight Boxing Championship organization. As potential white opponents routinely refused the black boxer's challenges, Johnson took a creative tack by doggedly following his worthiest white contender around the globe. On December 26, 1908, he entered a ring in Sydney, Australia, squared off against Canadian boxer Tommy Burns, and duly relieved him of the World Heavyweight Champion title. Back in the United States, Johnson's victory over Burns unleashed the nation's deep-seated racial tensions. Sportsmanship gave way to explicit avowals of defending white supremacy. Somewhat despairingly, white promoters coaxed a former pugilist champion out of his five-year retirement: Jim Jeffries would be America's "great white hope" to defend the heavyweight title against the audacious black contender. Jeffries aimed to put Johnson in his place on the Fourth of July.

The historic Johnson-Jeffries fight took place in Reno, Nevada, on July 4, 1910. Obsession over its outcome was countrywide. The florist Charles Thorley—Williams's former boss, who was also a well-known sportsman—witnessed the fight and bet $5,000 with odds on Jeffries to win. Years later the florist recalled the fight as the greatest, but most disappointing, match he ever saw. "Johnson outclassed Jeff, or rather the shadow of the once great Jeff, from the start."[1] In New York's Times Square, a mostly white crowd of thirty thousand watched play-by-play bulletins on the Times Building as Johnson decisively won the bout. Depending on who one rooted for, the disappointment and the satisfaction were equally palpable. Up in Harlem, the Williams household was surely apprehensive of sudden mayhem—only ten years earlier whites had spontaneously attacked blacks in the city.

Johnson's victory immediately ignited plans for feting his return to the city, and Chief Williams was thrust directly into the maelstrom of celebratory preparations. The process had been in the making since Johnson won the World Heavyweight Champion title from Burns in Sydney. Black fans in New York had been effusive in their recognition of Johnson as world boxing champion. In the spring of 1909, Colored Elks and black businessmen had offered consecutive evening events to kick off a weeklong series of receptions for the boxer. On March 30, Williams's Manhattan Lodge had entertained Johnson at Palace Hall. Then on March 31, the reception committee chairman Barron D. Wilkins, said to be Johnson's closest friend, spearheaded a three-dollar-per-plate dinner and reception (about $75 in 2018 currency), sponsored by many other black business leaders, at American Theater Hall. (The affair likely enabled Barron Wilkins to wire Johnson $20,000 in Reno some weeks later to bet on himself.)[2] Though he held no official office, Wilkins owned Café Wilkins in the Tenderloin district, which served as Johnson's de facto headquarters. The place's innocuous name was perhaps a purposeful distraction from its former name, the Little Savoy, an infamous "black and tan" hotel-saloon that catered to a Tenderloin clientele of sporting men, ragtime cabaret acts, and white revelers.

Barron Wilkins and the boxer's personal lawyer, J. Frank Wheaton, were two of the most prominent brother "antlers" in the Elks' Manhattan Lodge. Now as Wilkins was charged with arranging the celebrations for Jack Johnson's victorious return, his effort to engage "every sight-seeing car in the city" surely drew support from the ranks of his own lodge—support particularly from Williams, one assumes, who frequently teamed with Battle in organizing important lodge functions. Wilkins also headed up the Jack Johnson Diamond Belt Subscription Fund, a corollary committee that formed with the mission to engird the new world champion in a $25,000 gem-studded gold trophy belt. That the Chief of course knew the principals surely impressed his raptly interested son Wesley. One of them was "the colored whirlwind," the eloquent public speaker D. E. Tobias, whose kaleidoscopic roles included publisher, economist, criminologist, psychologist, and political gadfly, who also did a fair amount of dabbling as a Tin Pan Alley music publisher (he cofounded the black-owned Gotham-Attucks Company), and theatrical press agent. Tobias also happened to live in the same building in the Tenderloin as young Wesley's grandparents, Aunt Ella and little cousin Lloyd, and a few uncles who had yet to move up to Harlem.

The city readied itself for Jack Johnson's arrival as the *20th*

J. Frank Wheaton, formidable attorney for Manhattan Lodge no. 45 and boxer Jack Johnson, was a force behind Samuel J. Battle's historic appointment to the New York City Police Department. *Photo: Circa 1899, by Charles Alfred Zimmerman, Minnesota Historical Society.*

Century Limited carried the champion from Chicago, like a long-burning fuse. The train was to deliver the hero to Grand Central, whose old station building had been abandoned just a few weeks before. On Monday morning, July 11, crowds descended on the station to greet Johnson's arrival at nine-thirty. A wreck upstate of the Northern and Western Express delayed the train, but the crowd—which by most accounts numbered several thousand blacks and several hundred whites—waited resolutely for their idol with his gold-filled smile. At about a quarter past two in the afternoon, nearly five hours late, the *Century* finally appeared. As the train backed slowly into the station, James "Gentleman Jim" Corbett, another former heavyweight champion, "stood, grip in hand," in the vestibule of the first car, which "slid past and nobody's eyes followed it." Rather, messengers from Johnson's reception committee dashed off to alert waiting autos. The committeemen trailed a motley crowd of black and white fans as they hustled down the platform toward the train. Williams tried to bring order to the frenzied scene on the platform, where passengers stepping from the cars were at pains to get a Red Cap's attention to take their bags—all of them bent on greeting Johnson.[4]

As much of white America begrudgingly acknowledged Johnson his world title, some recalcitrant forces in white Harlem were stalwartly resistant. Only a decade into the twentieth century, the black foothold in Harlem was unambiguous, with a steady influx of black tenants, thriving new businesses, and flourishing organizations. A number of white property owners found the change irksome enough to wage a battle to determine "whether the white man will rule Harlem or the negro."[5] Yet as white property owners closed ranks, black Harlem, having a burgeoning population in its favor, stood its ground.

A pivotal voice of opposition belonged to John Goldsburgh Taylor, a sixty-two-year-old realtor who emerged as white Harlem's self-appointed paladin. As founder and president of the Property Owners Protective Association, he raised $20,000 to bankroll the purchase of Harlem properties on the market before black buyers or agents "of 'Little Africa,' just east of Lenox Avenue," might obtain them. Built for intimidation and strong-arming, the southern-born Taylor stood six feet four inches tall and weighed more than 250 pounds. His dense mustache hung from his nose like the brooms he sometimes suspended from building windows to signify his "clean sweep of negroes from the white resident districts of Harlem." He spent the next four years confederating his like-minded white neighbors to drive back their "common enemy," the Negro invaders who appeared poised to move westward across Lenox Avenue into West 136th Street. As Taylor stirred up fellow whites to confront their existential crisis, his campaign particularly sought to oust an explosively successful new colored saloon on the intersection's southwest corner.[6]

On a Tuesday evening in November 1910, Williams's Elk brother Leroy Wilkins had opened Café Leroy at 513 Lenox Avenue (many years later to become the site of the Schomburg Center for Research in Black Culture). He had sold his other Harlem cabaret—the Café Astoria—to his older brother, Barron, who would give the address greater fame as the Exclusive Club. At his new place, Leroy obviously spared no expense transforming the three-story building into the city's most modern restaurant for a colored clientele. Café Leroy was extravagant: "One of the features is the $3500 organ which can be heard throughout the building," the *Age* reported, adding that in the "rathskeller"—as basement-level eating halls were still commonly called—the proprietor had installed a smaller organ.

First-night Harlem customers poured in. They pressed through the first floor to the bar, some of the men to the wine rooms. Some ascended the stairs to fill restaurant tables on the second floor; others continued yet higher to the third floor to join parties in the private dining rooms. While many exalted the swank Café Leroy as the "Colored Rector's," evoking one of the city's poshest white establishments near Times Square,[7] John Taylor disparaged the grand place as being frequented "exclusively by negroes or dissolute white persons." He succeeded in convincing the court to revoke the proprietor's saloon license, which he asserted Wilkins's partner had forged names to obtain.[8] Leroy Wilkins ultimately moved his café to Fifth Avenue and 135th Street, which was close enough to retain his devoted clientele—and also close enough to deprive Taylor of feeling comfortably smug.

Williams and other black Harlem residents might have remembered Taylor from the Tenderloin. The zealous realtor was a retired police officer, whose strapping figure was unmistakable among the rank and file of the 30th Street Station. Still burly and imposing, Taylor might have been itching to avenge Jim Jeffries's recent loss of glory to Jack Johnson, as he now poised himself for battle. He advised white homeowners to build twenty-four-foot fences to separate their properties from those of their black neighbors. Though such outlandish industry was never realized, his organization did succeed in closing the first sale of a property "restricted against use by colored tenants for fifteen years." The sale of the townhouse at 210 West 136th Street appeared to be the first recorded transaction on Manhattan "of property restricted against use by a particular class of tenants," reported the *Times*. Insurance for the property title was contingent upon it remaining in that condition.[9]

Taylor's schemes may have been more foolhardy than foolproof. One of his prolific newspaper ads boldly proclaimed, "200 WHITE FAMILIES MOVE BACK TO HARLEM," as its cartoon of a horse-drawn moving van assured of "MORE COMING EVERY DAY." It is true that for a time restrictive covenants effectively barred black tenants from several Harlem blocks. However, Taylor's strategy to attract new white tenants with the promise of low rates, by special arrangement with property owners, appeared hopelessly flawed—some cosigners broke the covenants themselves. After selling her house on West 136th Street to a black buyer, one white owner reportedly declared her right to sell it "to any person she saw fit," and dismissed the covenant as "a big joke." Another owner, on the north side of the exclusive Astor Row block of West 130th Street, found white renters were unwilling to pay a fair rent in his brownstone, so he put out signs for "respectable negro tenants" instead. "Yes, I think I can get more from negro than from white tenants," he said, "and I have two or three propositions under consideration." And why would he not? An owner wanting to sell or lease property, having no white buyer at the door, was unlikely to ignore the knock of a prospective black buyer.[10]

By 1914 more and more white property owners had defected, and Taylor's most recent strategy, to sue covenant breakers for damages, was made moot by his death. As Taylor lost influence in his neighborhood and his association, then lost his life, the black Harlem of Williams's generation thrived and expanded.

Jack Johnson's victory might have steeled the resolve of black Harlemites to resist Taylor's relentless attempts to oust them. And their resistance may have bolstered a cultural sense of place and entrepreneurial confidence, for a considerable number of Harlem's professional class now appeared poised to leave the neighborhood of their own volition. Without pulling up stakes entirely, a number of Williams's friends were moving from Harlem up to the Bronx, and they encouraged him to consider doing the same.

In 1910 the Bronx neighborhood of Williamsbridge had seen the establishment of a recreational center, probably catalyzed by the commotion surrounding the Johnson-Jeffries match. The nationally segregated Young Men's Christian Association (YMCA)—whose Jim Crow "colored" branches were central to black communities around the Tenderloin and elsewhere—contributed to the growth of black Williamsbridge. In 1910 the white Williamsbridge branch of the YMCA leased out a disused building to the Williamsbridge Colored Men's Association (WCMA), or Wicoma. The Wicoma reclaimed the castoff space at 706 East 215th Street near White Plains Avenue with gusto and carried out the similar physical, recreational and spiritual mission of the white facility. A local ladies' auxiliary furnished the club's well-equipped gymnasium, which opened daily at hours staggered for boys and girls. The basketball court was evidently popular, as its two basketball teams showcased promising athletes the first winter after opening.[11] There were also bowling alleys, a pool table, and showers. The white Williamsbridge branch Y's physical director and gym leader conducted classes at the Wicoma. A glee club and a debating club were organized. The black Wicoma in Williamsbridge—which operated out of the white YMCA's old rooms until 1918—predated Harlem's 135th Street Y by several years.[12]

The impressive board of managers elected to the Wicoma expressed their commitment to "uplifting the young men of the vicinity" with the new facility. Several, including Jacob Charles Canty and Sandy Jones, were noted "property owners of no small extent." Jones now worked with Nail and Parker, Harlem's best-known real estate firm; he had known Williams since both lived on West 134th Street, and both were fraternal officers of Manhattan Lodge no. 45, working on the arrangements committee for big Elks events. Jones, who knew James's family, most likely encouraged the Chief to seriously think about moving to the "Bridge."[13]

In March 1912, Chief Williams was already comfortably settled in Harlem. A move to Williamsbridge, about six miles north, seemed unnecessary. But some of Williams's friends had moved there, and he knew the realtors Nail and Parker personally, so he looked over the ad that his friends put before him. The house was in the north-central section of the Bronx: "1st floor of 6 rooms and bath, steam heat. Rent $23."[14] The monthly rent was comparable to rents in Harlem.

Prominent colored folk had been venturing to Williamsbridge for more than a decade—most notably Jacob Charles Canty, a southerner who had come north for a medical degree. In 1886 the limited prospects in Negro communities induced him to give up his professional ambitions and become a railroad porter. He was assigned to the original crew of the New York Central's *Empire State Express*. For forty years he rode back and forth between New York and Buffalo, totaling more than six million miles by his retirement in 1926. "Doc," as his Pullman co-workers referred to him, had bought several pieces of Bronx property in Williamsbridge. "Even before the first influx of colored people had started toward the Harlem River from the Tenderloin district," the *Age* reported, "he was advocating that section of the city to his friends as the coming residential section."[15] One Martha Jefferson, wife of a railroad porter who had run a colored lodging house on West 134th Street, was happy to quit Harlem for quiet Williamsbridge. "There has been quite an exodus from that neighborhood to the Bronx and Williamsbridge," the paper quipped. "Upon closer acquaintance that latter place don't seem to be as far removed from civilization as was formerly believed by some."[16]

Indeed, by 1912 Williamsbridge was a buoyant community, plugged into the circuitry of black Manhattan. St. Mark's Methodist Episcopal Church, which Williams knew from West 53rd Street, had just opened a mission church there. It was farther from Williams's workplace, but the direct rail line between Grand Central Terminal and the Williamsbridge station along the Bronx River would make the commute faster than by subway. And annual company passes

While assistant Chief Red Cap under Williams, Jesse Battle prepared for the exam that made him New York City's first black police officer in 1911. *New York Police Department Museum.*

permitted workers to ride the line for free. As improving transit had induced other friends to move from Harlem's tenements to greener suburbs, Williams soon succumbed and moved his family to 823 East 223rd Street in Williamsbridge. The Williamses were not long without their friends, as the Lloyd Joneses (no known relation to Sandy Jones), the Battles, and others joined the influx of middle-class Harlemites. Harlem's cultural annexation of Williamsbridge as a "race" suburb was apparent by the summer of 1913, when the *New York Tribune* reported that "a new colored settlement has sprung up in The Bronx in the last six months," with a population of five thousand.[17]

That summer a group of thirteen black teenagers from Williamsbridge clacked across the wooden floorboards of a photographer's studio. Wearing smart, colorful uniforms, with cleated shoes, banded leggings, knickers, piped and embroidered jerseys, and brimmed red baseball caps, they constituted the Grand Central Red Caps baseball team. In the photograph, two additional young men pose with the team in suits and straw boater hats, likely athletic managers from the Wicoma. These young men were sons of Grand Central porters (and maybe a few worked as porters themselves). Chief Williams's sixteen-year-old son Wesley sits on the floor beside a tripod of crossed bats. Wesley was developing into an all-around athlete in Williamsbridge, a fact that surely informed the gusto with which Chief Williams approached his leadership at Grand Central. Baseball and other athletics clearly had the potential to strengthen the fraternity of porters.

Lucy and James's teenage daughter Gertrude also thrived in Williamsbridge. In February 1914, it was probably she who placed an ad from the family's address: "Colored Girl wishes position at housework; good references."[18] She certainly had references. By the summer of 1918 Gertrude had graduated from high school and, recently appointed a postal clerk, was cited among "the young Race women of Williams Bridge . . . taking advantage of the opportunities now afforded by the present war" as the nation was fighting in Europe.[19]

For his own part, James Williams appears to have joined the Butler Memorial Methodist Episcopal Church, at 719 East 223rd Street, near White Plains Road. Established by St. Mark's in 1912, it was one of the community's three black churches. On one Friday evening in June 1916, Williams was floor manager for an event at the Masonic Hall at East 216th Street and White Plains Avenue to benefit the church's Lyceum (which, organized in 1883, identified itself as "the oldest literary society in the State of New York"). The amateur players had a full house for their presentation of two one-act plays (one being *Bargain Day*, a popular vaudeville farce by Mary H. Flanner), followed by an evening of dancing.[20]

But on November 6, 1915, Butler Memorial's doors opened for the most important event in the Williamses's lives: Wesley Augustus Williams married Margaret Russell Ford, his sweetheart from New Rochelle. Like his father, Wesley was a Red Cap, though at Penn Station; and similarly as well, he was eighteen as he stood at the altar. The Chief's eldest daughter Gertrude and his own older brother Charles stood as witnesses,[21] as other family members and close friends crowded the little frame church. The Chief and Lucy Williams, perhaps taking turns holding their baby daughter Kay, beamed as their firstborn, Wesley, entered married life.

◈

On a mid-August evening in 1913, Chief Williams hosted "a Red Caps stag" dinner in honor of Jesse Battle, who was celebrating his second anniversary as New York City's first Negro policeman. Williams's own sense of personal achievement might have equaled that of his guest of honor: he had drawn Jesse from the ranks of his luggage porters, promoted him to his assistant chief, and encouraged him to study at night for the civil service examination. For this high celebration, whose details are unknown, Williams had chosen the Hotel Lincoln in Arverne-by-the-Sea, a swank colored resort on the city's Rockaway shoreline.[22] The sea retreat's conspicuous black visitation had coincided with Harlem's wave of black settlement.

Almost a decade earlier, on the sunny Sunday afternoon of June 26, 1904, several white residents of Arverne-by-the-Sea strained to look over two six-foot-high board fences on the boardwalk. Employees of William Kemble's Halcyon Casino Company were holding a pleasant outing with about "a dozen or more negroes sitting in willow rocking chairs" and enjoying basket lunches and ice cream. The uncommon scene so perturbed the white residents at the fence that some hurled racial slurs at the guests. Others "took snapshots of the negroes as they were being served" to later incriminate their host.

Kemble had apparently been upsetting his neighbors for some time, as he intended to build an amusement park and casino on the site. The attraction was certain to mar the residents' sea vista and disturb their tranquility, so Arvernites had secured a court injunction to forestall construction. Kemble responded to this preemptive strike by setting up a number of small shanties on his casino property, where several local passersby heard—coming from behind the tall plank barricade—the distinct voices of black people "enjoying themselves with banjos, rag-time, and plantation melodies." Many thought Kemble's retaliation played upon his neighbors' dread—not of a proposed carousel but of Negroes.[23]

White property owners organized themselves into the Arverne-by-the-Sea Association, which resolved to "starve out" a black realtor's expensive new boardinghouse elsewhere for wealthy Negro patrons, by imposing a covenant warning "storekeepers who sell to the negroes are to be boycotted."[24] But fashionable colored folks were undeterred. In fact, the next summer, on July 10, 1906, a particular function might have made the seaside locale still more enticing: "Booker T. Washington, the famous educator, entertained a large audience . . . in the Ocean Casino with a discussion on the race problem." Perhaps celebrity itself, that all-American obsession, fueled Arverne's appeal to black social circles as a convenient getaway.[25]

In the summer of 1908, Williams likely heard about the opening of a new hotel at Arverne-by-the-Sea. The Hotel Lincoln was the latest seaside resort for colored patrons to dot Rockaway Peninsula's communities of Seaside, Rockaway Beach, and Hammels. The Lincoln's close proximity to the city made it a choice refuge for middle-class and affluent blacks looking for a reputable getaway. Indeed, at the end of July, the overflow of nearly a hundred guests from Manhattan, Brooklyn, and New Jersey necessitated turning many away. But those who found accommodations for the weekend enjoyed an afternoon auto outing, reveled at a "hop" in the pavilion, took advantage of the excellent bathing, and delighted in an impromptu concert arranged by the noted newspaper correspondent Cleveland "C. G." Allen, whose investigation of the U.S. Navy's discrimination against its enlisted Negro seamen would catapult him to national prominence four years later.

Whether Williams was there that weekend is unknown, but he knew from the papers and the talk that it was quite a celebration. If Wiley H. Collins and Vincent Taylor, the Hotel Lincoln's managers, had the regrettable task of turning away guests, their regret was mitigated by the guilty pleasure of success. They reserved a special table in the main dining room for Mme. May Belle Becks, a modiste. A few months earlier she had opened a special school in Manhattan: the Mme. J. H. Becks School of Dressmaking, Designing, Cutting, and Fitting, and it was gaining much attention. William Jay Schieffelin, a noted white philanthropist who chaired the New York Committee for Improving the Industrial Condition of Negroes, publicly asked "those who can [to] give work to colored dressmakers and milliners."[26] Madame Becks's dressmaking school was securing her a redoubtable stature as "the foremost colored designer in this country."[27]

In the spring of 1910, numerous black periodicals advertised the resort at 22–24 Lincoln Avenue. Williams saw the photo of a squarish three-story, wood-framed manse, the central door recessed in a porticoed porch. The Lincoln, only a block from the beach, offered such seasonal diversions as cruising, boating, bathing, and fishing. It was easily reached from the city by taking any Rockaway Beach train to Hammels Station. A succession of at least three proprietors—Emma I. Dorsey, F. M. Allison, and C. A. Breckenridge—were all women.

During the Fourth of July weekend of 1913, James Van Der Zee—who would earn eternal renown as a photographer—was an accomplished violinist and pianist when he checked in at the Lincoln with his wife Kate Brown, as leader of the Harlem Orchestra.[28] Bandleader James Reese Europe and his wife Willie Angrom Starke checked in exactly two years later; and businessman John W. Rose—owner of Harlem's first restaurant chain, Rose's Dairy Lunch System—relaxed there with his wife Theresa in July 1916.

In mid-July 1914, Chief Williams spent a weekend at the Hotel Lincoln. His name appeared first on the hotel's registry of notable patrons, which must have tickled him—it preceded that of an international star, Bert Williams. The two Williamses were unrelated, but they shared something: James Williams was Chief of Grand Central's Red Caps, while Bert Williams played a Grand Central Red Cap in *Ziegfeld Follies of 1911.* Bert Williams's legendary interpretation of the Red Cap character had convinced Florenz Ziegfeld himself to offer a three-year contract to the black comedian.

The convenience of Arverne's Hotel Lincoln did not deter the

Chief and other black New Yorkers from traveling farther afield for beach relaxation. Throughout the late nineteenth century, the railroads facilitated the flow of New Yorkers to summer in the seaside resorts of New Jersey. Asbury Park (named for Francis Asbury, the father of American Methodism) was founded in 1874 as a Protestant temperance resort but grew in a decade to become an intemperate pleasure ground of 15,000 permanent residents, some 2,000 of them black. The town flourished as a leisure campus of hotels, music pavilions, and a boardwalk punctuated with flowerbeds, piers, and fanciful bathhouses. As affluent whites flocked to Asbury Park's myriad posh establishments—about "200 hotels, the majority of them with colored waiters"—proprietors tried to dissuade, then to restrict, the use of beach facilities by blacks, be they local workers on leisure time or those arriving on seaside excursions. A number of black clergy, like the Rev. Andrew J. Chambers, an influential AME Church pastor, expressed outrage about the proposed color line: "A man with a black skin is not a menace to the prosperity of the place." Of course, the white resort economy of Asbury Park was dependent on hundreds of black service staff: the hotels employed two-thirds of the town's black population.[29]

In fact, Williams was a patron of a number of black entrepreneurs who ensured the prosperity of Atlantic City, the foremost "Mecca of pleasure" of America's leisure circuit, founded in 1854. For some thirty years, until white businesses pressured him off in 1925, entrepreneur George H. Walls, a former hotel waiter, ran the only black business on Atlantic City's famous seven-mile Boardwalk: Walls' Bath Houses. Numerous other bathhouses on and off the Boardwalk welcomed white hotel guests and beachgoers, but Walls's was the only one for blacks. Located on a four-lot strip at the foot of Texas Avenue that had once demarcated "the extreme end of the inhabited section of the old ramshackle promenade," it quickly became an attraction. In the mornings, the so-called "400" of influential black society—like violinist Joseph H. Douglass and poet Paul Laurence Dunbar, who toured together—arrived at Walls's, eager to take the waters. Then in the late afternoons, hotel workers

A 1913 advertisement for George H. Walls's four-lots-wide bath houses, the only black-run business on Atlantic City's seven-mile Boardwalk for three decades until 1925. *Author's collection.*

off their shifts came to bathe in turn. Passing the stretch of hotel beaches, black beachgoers concentrated in the few-block area from Walls's, at Texas Avenue, to Missouri Avenue beyond. Until 1906, when a racial segregation policy was set, there was no law to prevent blacks from bathing there. And the shore in front of Walls's—like any promenade where one went to see and be seen—offered blacks the most vibrant sense of community.[30]

By the 1910s, George Walls was a preeminent figure in Atlantic City's flourishing community of black businesses, social centers, and

In 1916, James and Lucy Williams and their son, Pierre, posed for a photo postcard in Atlantic City. *Charles Ford Williams Family Collection.*

fraternal organizations. He increased his posh facilities with novel "shower baths" to accommodate "up to 500 bathers at one time." Here black visitors came to rent bathing wear, lounge under a shady pavilion, and feel at home. In the summer of 1909, Walls had augmented his bathhouse's comforts by adding full-service dining and refreshment rooms featuring a $5,000 soda fountain.[31]

James Williams frequently brought his family to Atlantic City, when the briny sands that rolled down from Walls's to the surf were the center of colored attraction. An advertisement for Walls's read:

> Where you can see the moving thousands
> on the Boardwalk, on the Sand.
> While other delighted thousands "Jump the Breakers," hand in hand.
> Far beyond the happy bathers you can view the Ships at Sea;
> While refreshing billows whisper, "Come and take a dip with me."
>
> —COL. GEORGE H. WALLS, PROPRIETOR,
> WALLS' BATH HOUSES, ATLANTIC CITY[32]

At the end of August 1916, James, Lucy, and their son Pierre went down to Atlantic City with their Williamsbridge neighbors Sandy and Mary Jones, who had been friends since West 134th Street in Harlem. They all stayed at Lipscomb Cottage at 1632 Arctic Avenue, whose owners, Mr. and Mrs. C. D. Lipscomb, were familiar in Williamsbridge black society. The Lipscombs' modern amenities and year-round service made it the town's principal colored hotel. C. D. Lipscomb and his businessman colleague Walls were both officers of New Jersey's Grand Lodge of the Knights of Pythias fraternal order. The ad for the inn featured a cameo photo of the round-faced, mustached namesake, but the fine print read "Mrs. C. D. Lipscomb, Prop." The three Williamses stopped in a boardwalk shop to pose for a souvenir photo.

And Williams was also discovering welcome getaways even much farther beyond the city. George H. Daniels's *Four-Track Series* promoted the delights of nature awaiting travelers along the New York Central's lake routes through the Adirondack Mountains, promising, "if you visit this region once, you will go there again."[33] The Chief was privileged to do the tourists one better: for about twenty-five years, between 1910 and 1935, he took an annual fishing vacation: as the guest of Edward C. Smith, a former governor of Vermont. at Camp Madawaska, the governor's lakeside hunting lodge in the Canadian woods.[34]

CHAPTER 6

War at Home and Abroad

"It's quite wonderful, isn't it?" I continued. "A city in itself. What did it cost? And if all the red caps were laid end on end, how far would they reach?"

—PARKHURST WHITNEY, 1916[1]

As Grand Central Terminal took shape, New Yorkers grew rapturous. For ten years they had watched in awe as skyscrapers spiked in the city—the Singer Building (1908), the Metropolitan Life Building (1910), and the Woolworth Building (1913), and other iconic towers.[2] The railroad terminal would be lower and stouter, but maybe as an inherently public premises, it loomed more personally than others. By 1911, the feat of engineering that was creating a new station on the old one's site impressed one observer as "a project that requires more of God than of man to accomplish."[3]

Williams probably felt less inclined to marvel. The terminal's construction—the sheer, measured magnitude of it—certainly inspired contemplative wonder, but its grand incompletion made it the irresistible stuff of parody, which might not put him in the best light. Just a few blocks west, *Ziegfeld Follies of 1911* was cinching Bert Williams's reputation as a Broadway star by lampooning the terminal's epic building-in-progress state. The legendary Negro entertainer "appeared as a 'red cap' to pilot an English tourist" to his New Rochelle train—a rope tethering the pair, each to each, like alpinists—by traversing the bare steel rafters of the rising terminal. In typical low comedy fashion, the wary white traveler and his black porter guide ultimately plummeted, one after the other, into the void of the building's works—to convulsions of side-splitting audience laughter.[4] Chief Williams could ill afford such burlesque missteps. As the new terminal at last prepared to open, he and his men were in the crosshairs of ineluctable scrutiny and unflattering slapstick comparisons. They were now the personification of its completion, and they must be perfect.

As the four opaline clock faces struck midnight on February 2, 1913, Chief Williams, a red carnation in his lapel, inspected his army of Red Caps in formation one last time. They numbered about 150 men of varying brown complexions, all comprising a uniform body by their identical crimson hats. Their natty uniforms bade good riddance to the days of motley so-called "public porters" who haunted the outside curbs; they stood poised to represent the new station's exalted expectations. The doors to the new terminal were thrown open. Many local travelers ignored the railroad's promo-

In *Ziegfeld Follies of 1911*, black entertainer Bert Williams uproariously parodied a Red Cap at the new Grand Central Terminal under construction, informing Chief Williams's determination to keep his Red Caps ever on point in the traveling public's eye. *Schomburg/NYPL.*

tional assurances that the station was simplicity itself and instead "placed themselves in the hands of attendants who knew every angle."[5] Indeed, many appeared to seek out members of the Chief's amicable crew, as if they were playing an amusing connect-the-dots game with the dart and dash of the men's red caps.

A central information booth anchored the main concourse, but Chief Williams's men were the terminal's most recognizable agents in public view. By dint of their uniform clothing and their general dispersion, Red Caps had considerable authority in the eyes of visitors, at least enough to ask a question. Throngs of sightseers flocked to Grand Central not to go anywhere but to see the spectacular new station for themselves. These "railbirds" lingered endlessly up on the mezzanine gallery gazing at the main attraction, the cerulean blue "sky ceiling" that canopied the main concourse. The marble floor was visible only fleetingly through the sea of people. The Chief and his men navigated through the shoulder taps and called-out questions. "Every attendant was a walking *Baedeker*," someone observed. "He had to testify hundreds of times as to the number of stars in the sky above the main concourse, as he did to most of the other unusual features of the station."[6]

Not knowing Chief Williams's relationship to William C. Brown, president of the New York Central, it's hard to judge if seeing him on the congested concourse made him anxious. Few other railroad folks would have recognized Brown, weaving nonchalantly through the throngs. The conspicuous Red Caps were fielding a barrage of visitors' questions, comments, and suggestions, while Brown was circulating, pausing now and then to listen unobtrusively. Williams knew that the president's dissatisfaction with his men's performance could be baleful. And opening day was a performance to be sure, an unusually exhausting one. One attendant tallied all the questions people asked him; he figured 310. *What's the architect's name? What kind of marble is that? How does the electricity system work? Those figures painted on the ceiling—what do they mean?* When a question about tracks in the upper express level tripped up one unlucky Red Cap, Brown, who was within earshot, stepped in to provide the answer. Brown appeared to be pleased at the opening, a report the next day noted, so Williams no doubt exhaled.[7]

Although the uniformed porters constituted part of the new Grand Central Terminal's official "staff," they were barely salaried and subsisted basically on tips. Nevertheless, the Red Caps recognized they had a position of advantage, that it was a linchpin of opportunity in a time of racial work barriers. No sooner had the new station opened than Williams's men proactively organized business and leisure pursuits, sometimes in conjunction with other stations. His close Grand Central friend Lloyd Jones, a community activist who years earlier cofounded the Manhattanville Colored Republican Club, was an officer of the Amalgamated Railroad Employees Association, which the Pennsylvania Station Red Caps had founded two years before. While less a labor union than a traditional mutual aid society, the Penn's Amalgamated aimed—beyond just relieving members with financial troubles—toward acting as an organizational stakeholder for their business ventures. The association not only expanded its membership to include fellow Red Caps from Grand Central, it also diversified its ranks with Harlem businessmen like the saloonkeeping brothers Barron and Leroy Wilkins. Even more ambitiously, it envisioned a countrywide network of headquarters that would serve both as social centers and as training schools for its members, whose New York base drew from both Grand Central and Penn stations. To that end, the Amalgamated leased a brownstone townhouse at 447 Lenox Avenue near 132nd Street. The *New York Age* described the Red Caps social club as a "commodious and up-to-date headquarters" that provided members with a restaurant "conducted on a first-class basis, and sleeping apartments, with all conveniences." The premises were also fitted with "reading rooms, pool room, writing rooms and parlors."[8]

While many of the Red Caps had known each other before, or through mutual connections, neither Chief Williams, nor any of his men at Grand Central Terminal, had likely ever met an Abyssinian. The Abyssinian was their own Oualdo Gorghis, the given name of the Red Cap they knew as George Gabriel—though to the traveling public he was simply Red Cap no. 20. Born on April 26, 1888, in Addis Ababa, he immigrated to the United States on January 14, 1913, in time for Williams to hire him for the newly opening terminal on the recommendation of none other than former U.S. president Theodore Roosevelt. Side by side, Gabriel stood just slightly taller than Chief Williams, whose café au lait complexion seemed pallid compared to the African's chiseled dark face, which was made even more remarkable by a pair of light eyes that sometimes appeared brown or gray.

Williams had heard Gabriel's story as the public did, in the papers or at the station. Gabriel had been a boy during the first Italo-Ethiopian war that killed his father, a ranking officer in the Abyssinian army of Emperor Menelik II. The war separated him eternally from his mother and any knowledge of her fate. Around 1896 a senior British Army officer, Herbert Kitchener, adopted the boy, who then accompanied the military forces to the Sudan, India, and Egypt. Kitchener returned to England, where in the fall of 1898 he was made Lord Kitchener of Khartoum, but before he left, he placed the boy in a Muslim school in Cairo. Using funds that Kitchener sent him from London, Gabriel determined to perform the hajj—the pilgrimage to Mecca, forbidden to non-Muslims. Though he was born an Orthodox Christian, Gabriel had learned enough of Islam to present himself confidently as a convert named Abdullah Mohammed. Succeeding in Mecca, he continued by camel to the second holy Muslim city, Medina. Spiritually enriched but broke, he accompanied Syrian pilgrims on foot across the desert to Damascus, then went to Jerusalem for six months. His next location changed his fate dramatically.

In 1900 Lord Kitchener was back in Cairo, where Gabriel rejoined him. There the officer arranged for his appointment as interpreter to the British embassy at Constantinople. Gabriel thought Constantinople a fine, beautiful city, and its thousands of people kept him enthralled. "You can learn many languages in Constantinople," he said. And he studied every language he heard there—over a dozen—for some five years. Gabriel was later transferred to the

Although former president Theodore Roosevelt engaged Abyssinian-born George Gabriel as an interpreter in Africa in 1909, the linguist's American journey culminated at Grand Central as a Red Cap. *Baltimore Afro-American.*

British consular services, for which he traveled around the world. In Vienna he married an Austrian woman, Therese, with whom he had two children. Gabriel was at the Paris consulate when Colonel Roosevelt advertised in a French paper about his imminent hunting expedition in Africa: he needed an interpreter for his travels, and so Gabriel answered the call.

George Gabriel acquired two souvenirs from Roosevelt's 1909 African safari. One was a bullet wound to his leg; the other was the colonel's promise to provide him with employment should he ever visit New York. North America being the only continent Gabriel had yet to see, on December 8, 1912, he boarded the *SS Grant* in

Cuxhaven, Germany, bound for New York, with a letter in hand in which Roosevelt attested to his desirability as a citizen. In January 1913, Gabriel reportedly visited Roosevelt's home at Oyster Bay, and obtained his host's letter of recommendation to William Jennings Bryan, President Woodrow Wilson's secretary of state. Gabriel's résumé would have been impressive for any man, white or black. He was proficient in thirteen languages and five African dialects; he had served in military campaigns, diplomatic missions, and expeditions of adventure. He bore (and sometimes wore) honors from several sovereign nations. Yet despite his résumé, and despite testimonials to his competence and character from a former president of the United States, Gabriel was informed that he could not qualify as a government interpreter because he was not a citizen.[9]

Gabriel then obtained a position as the new Grand Central Terminal's "official" interpreter, some said with Roosevelt's help. But just a few months after the station opened, the publisher Irving Putnam overheard a foreigner ask at the information booth "if any of the attendants spoke French or German." The negative reply took him aback. Considering what enormous attention to architectural detail went into the magnificent new terminal, he wrote to the *Times*, had no one thought "to provide at least one person on its information staff who could answer questions from puzzled, non-English foreigners?" Maybe Putnam didn't know about Gabriel's employment there, or maybe Gabriel's position was overstated. Considering the scrutiny Williams was prone to, as a Negro who was chief porter, it seems odd that a black polyglot interpreter—an African friend of Roosevelt's, no less—could go unnoticed in such a consequential post. A few days after Putnam's letter, someone took umbrage at the suggestion that Grand Central disregarded its foreign-speaking travelers. "As a matter of fact, the writer of this letter is the official interpreter of the information bureau," Edward Witkowski wrote, "speaking the languages in question, and several others." Perhaps Gabriel's job description was lost in translation.[10]

Indeed, while the New York Central management likely hired George Gabriel on Roosevelt's recommendation, it equally likely assigned him to Chief Williams: the Red Cap force was the only public department then open to black employees. Since distant Africa was a common bond through descent of Chief Williams and his men, the Abyssinian Gabriel was poised to make a powerful impression upon his African-American co-workers. Even a reporter for the *New York Sun* reflected upon "the fact that in his veins flows the blood of those who long before Christ walked the earth did their part in building an empire."[11]

A few years later Gabriel's remarkable linguistic abilities drew attention. In January 1916 Zoe Beckley reported in the *New York Evening Mail* that the stationmaster at Grand Central had been confronted with a distraught woman, sobbing incomprehensibly.[12] The stationmaster summoned the official interpreter, whose impressive arsenal of eleven languages turned out to be as useless as a wet matchbook. "Send for Redcap no. 20!" the stationmaster then ordered. It may have been Williams who fetched Gabriel, whose repertoire, broader than the official interpreter's, included the troubled woman's dialect. If race had disqualified him from taking on this position "officially," he effectively become the de facto interpreter, pressed into service when needed without additional recompense to his porter's earnings.[13]

The romantic incongruity of the Red Cap's past and present circumstances captivated Beckley, who recounted the worldly nomad's singular journey. America impressed Gabriel as "the supreme country of the world except in one thing": it was still a land "where race and color are counted against a man, no matter what he is otherwise." And apparently no matter who recommended him. "That is why George Gabriel is toting grips at the Grand Central," Beckley remarked, "one of the recognized callings a man of brown skin may follow."

Faced with such inherently American obstacles, it's a wonder Gabriel did not return to the British or French, who welcomed his obvious abilities. But he likely had too little means—and maybe too much pride—to return. And perhaps, like many immigrants, he still found something alluring in America's promises, however unfulfilled they were. Gabriel stuck it out and served his adopted country in the First World War. In the fall of 1920, a newly naturalized citizen, Gabriel booked passage to Switzerland to visit his Austrian wife and children, whom he had not seen for years. He visited them again four years later, but at some point his marriage ended. By 1927, he was working as a Pullman porter on the New York Central when he decided to resettle upstate in Buffalo, New York. Gabriel became chief of the Red Caps at the Exchange Street Station and stayed there for some thirty years.[14]

Unlike Gabriel, Chief Williams had not experienced world travel. But the opening of Grand Central Terminal and the growing distinction of black Harlem nonetheless gave him access to a world view. Both enclaves afforded him a singular vantage point, and each would be described as "a city within a city." "Here we have the largest Negro community in the world," the renowned black sociologist Kelly Miller said about Harlem, "a part of and yet apart from the general life of Greater New York."[15] And Grand Central, the "gateway to the American continent," constituted a temple of transportation, with shops, restaurants, galleries, offices, hotels and more that formed a so-called "Terminal City." James Williams had a foot planted firmly in both places.

◈

One way Chief Williams strove to bridge the discrete worlds of Grand Central and Harlem was through athletics. By 1915 America's favorite pastime, baseball, was as evident in Harlem as anywhere else in the country. Local fans crowded to attend semiprofessional Negro League games on uptown fields such as Harlem Oval at 132nd Street and Lenox; Olympic Field at 136th Street and Fifth; and Lenox Oval at 145th Street and Lenox. Indeed, the Chief afforded several young athletes a shortcut to redcapping at Grand Central by positioning the baseball diamond as their point of entry.

In 1916, perhaps still inspired by Wesley's club in Williamsbridge, Chief Williams organized a baseball club among the men at the station. A far more noteworthy outfit than the earlier one, his team garnered fans, particularly at games where the club squared off against the rival Red Cap club from Penn Station. But when the Great War came, the selective draft swept players from Harlem ballfields to European battlefields. Seeing first-class semipro teams lacking star players, Williams sought to make improvements in his own outfit.

In March 1918 a writer in the *Age* commented that "few aggregations of men can boast of a greater number of activities than the Red Caps of Grand Central Station." In light of their splendid mutual benefit organization and active civic interests, it was hardly surprising that the men were "now preparing to seek new laurels in the field of athletics." Not a few lauded Williams for his master stroke in building a team: "Chief Jas. H. Williams, president of the Grand Central Red Caps Base Ball Club Association, and P. F. Webster, better known as 'Specks' Webster, the famous catcher, formally of the Royal Giants, have come to terms. Webster was a hold-out for a larger salary. By signing this star the Red Caps will have one of the fastest teams in the east."[16]

By May, Williams was advertising the Red Caps B.B. Club, his new traveling team, "composed of some of the former stars of the Lincoln and Royal Giants." He called on all of "the best semi-pro teams in the country" to book his men for games directly through their manager, himself, at Grand Central Terminal.[17]

For good measure, Williams assembled his dream team at Lenox Oval, a popular Harlem sandlot at Lenox and 145th, for a photograph. The team's impressive members included captain and center fielder Charles Babcock Earle (whose prowess the white Brooklyn poet Edna Perry Booth extolled in a number of published verses); right fielder Howard "Monk" Johnson; pitcher Smoky Joe McClammy; and Specks Webster. The men were all smartly uniformed in knickers and jerseys, with RED CAPS boldly arced across their chests, and GCT embroidered on their sleeves. Standing in a black tailcoat at the head of the lineup was their manager, James Williams, with his recognizably proud jaw, at the left margin of the photo.

Chief Williams's baseball club made an impressive showing on the diamond. But regardless of the team's good gamesmanship,

In 1918 Chief Williams used the incentive of Red Cap jobs to build a crack baseball team at Grand Central from stars of the Brooklyn Royal Giants (seen at Dexter Park), which rankled powerful owner Nat Strong (top left, with the field's later owner, Max Rosner, top right). *Dr. Bennett Rosner Family Collection.*

the ballfield was also a battleground. As Jim Crow pervaded most American activities and enterprises, it also touched every aspect of baseball, from the players and managers to the designation and regulation of ballfields. The most redoubtable figure in baseball bookings and playing fields was Nathaniel "Nat" Calvin Strong, the executive owner of the World Building. Strong, who was white, had been secretary of the National Association of Colored Baseball Clubs of the United States and Cuba, and he long dominated most of the country's major black teams in the East. Black managers complained that the magnate's control over dozens of amusement places and parks let him negotiate stifling terms that kept their clubs dependent and stagnant. Not a few black managers and players distrusted his alliances with Tammany Hall bosses: the politi-

In 1918, Williams (in a black tailcoat, left margin) proudly shows off his new star lineup of the Grand Central Terminal Red Cap Baseball Club at Harlem's popular Lenox Oval, at Lenox Avenue and 145th Street. *Columbia University Rare Books and Manuscripts Library.*

cal machine, with its decades-long influence over the game, could control a site's leasing terms or its street and transit accessibility. As an enterprising black sportsman, Chief Williams saw Strong as a formidable obstacle.[18]

In June 1918, Williams accused Strong of preventing the Grand Central Red Caps from securing choice dates, and he took his complaint to the press. Lester Walton, in his sports column in the *Age*, noted that some years earlier original Brooklyn Royal Giants owner John W. Connor had made a complaint similar to Williams's and was still convinced that Strong discriminated against him as a colored ball team manager. Walton urged an immediate investiga-

Legendary all-American athlete, artist, and activist Paul Robeson (right, with football coach Fritz Pollard) in 1918, would briefly work as a student Red Cap at Grand Central. *The Crisis.*

tion, saying "the colored fans should rally to the cause of the Red Caps" if Williams's claims were true. Walton was nonplussed at Williams's assertion that "Strong is trying to corner all the colored ball players," opining that it was in the latter's "honorable ambition" to secure the best colored team and the best dates he could muster. But to purposefully shut out colored managers was something else again. Walton ventured no white manager would practice it "if it was thought that the colored public would strongly object."

Indeed, while Lester Walton went to bat for Williams's just complaint, he also took New York's black baseball fans to task for failing to patronize their own, as in Chicago and other towns. He was not averse "to white managers separating the colored fans from their dimes" if in fair play black managers were in the mix, but he opposed an effort to "get the colored public's money but keep out the colored manager." He posited that black ticket-buyers had the power to bring about change. "If the colored fans demand that Manager Williams's nine be given desirable dates their wish will be gratified," Walton wrote. "But it will take more than street-corner, barber-shop and bar-room talk to turn the trick."[19]

Though Chief Williams was the acknowledged creator and manager of the baseball team, Brooklyn papers occasionally wrote of "Charles B. Earle's Grand Central Red Caps, the best colored team in the country." While that attribution was apt to please Williams—for it implicitly acknowledged his coup in obtaining Brooklyn's star player from the Royal Giants—Earle's defection was bound to vex Nat Strong. Walton gave Strong column space in the *Age* to answer Williams's charge that he was discriminating against the Red Caps on playing dates.

Strong claimed that several of his Royal Giants players would have been out of work were it not for him keeping the ailing club in business. He also described how, at various times after the season had closed the previous fall, half a dozen players had asked him for a letter of recommendation to the New York Central—which he wrote. And each man had prophesied aloud about what a great team the Royals would have next year—that being the season now at hand—until mid-March, when they suddenly announced they had decided to play with the Grand Central Red Caps. Strong suspected their strategy was to undermine his ability to muster a team in time.

The controversy put Strong on the defensive to establish his turf boundaries. He professed his ability to secure Royal Giants' games "on my own personal acquaintance with various teams and managers all over the country," but he obviously resented the Chief's peculiar abilities. Williams had somehow influenced his club men to trade in their Royals uniforms for Red Cap jerseys; and he somehow had been able to offer his players steady gainful employment season round. Strong patronizingly disclosed Williams's stated desire (so he claimed) "to get into baseball and make some big money," yet he himself, the white magnate of colored baseball, was that very dream personified. Strong's argument lapsed into condescension as he beseeched Walton to "imagine when all a man has to offer to a player is an opportunity to carry bags at the Grand Central Depot 10 hours a day." But had the fact of his players' acceptance signified nothing? "I am not afraid of my reputation being assailed by such a man as Williams," Strong lashed out.[20]

Yet "such a man as Williams" had not been the first black manager to complain about Strong's monopoly, or to reproach his own race for putting up with it. "The ball players out west follow Rube Foster," read a *Defender* editorial, evoking the black baseball player and manager who founded the Negro National League, "not the white man."[21]

"I know where I stand among the colored folks," Strong wrote assuredly, "aside from Williams and those associated with him who tried to kill colored professional baseball." This was an accusation Walton and his readers knew to be patently untrue, a case in point being Earl Brown, a star student athlete who would join the Chief's team years later.

"We were fresh from the sticks," Brown, a Virginia-born journalist and politician, alluded to his rural origins when recalling how he first met Chief Williams. In the early 1920s, Brown and a schoolmate from Harvard (where he would graduate, class of 1924) had come down from Massachusetts to look for work in New York. An influential friend who knew they were good baseball players sent them to Grand Central to look up Captain Earle—Charles Babcock "C. B." Earle, Williams's assigned head coach of the Red Cap team—to try out for the ball club and "incidentally, to get jobs toting luggage to make money." When Brown met Earle, he boasted of his and his friend's prowess on Harvard's varsity baseball team. Earle heard them out, then located the Chief. Brown recalled feeling intimidated when Chief Williams appeared; his stern look belied the sparkle in his eyes as they nervously repeated their spiels. "What d'ya think, Cap't?" the Chief asked. No harm in trying them out, Earle supposed. "All right," the Chief agreed. "We'll take 'em up to the field with us this afternoon and see what they've got."

Brown and his schoolmate practiced on the diamond with the Red Cap "nine" that afternoon, and their performance convinced the Chief to have them report for work early the next morning. He of course relished getting to play ball with the Chief's Red Cap team. But Brown had ultimately ventured to Grand Central from Harvard for the gainful employment, as the older players had done from Brooklyn during the war.

◈

In August 1914, a year and a half after the terminal opened, armed conflict broke out in Europe. The United States had entered the war in April 1917 to "make the world safe for democracy." But as Williams knew, the American ideal of democracy was at odds with its grimly discordant home front: on July 2, 1917, white mobs went on a rampage in East St. Louis, Illinois, wantonly massacring nearly one hundred black citizens in broad daylight. Many decried the terror as the culmination of some three thousand lynchings and murders committed against American Negroes over the past three decades. The incident pitched the country into expressions of national shame and remorse. In New York, black citizens organized an action in midtown Manhattan to draw attention to the outrage.

On Saturday afternoon, July 28, 1917, some fifteen thousand black men, women, and children, led by the NAACP, marched down Fifth Avenue from 57th Street to Madison Park at 23rd Street. By prior agreement, the participants in the Silent Protest Parade remained profoundly mute as they followed the slow, steady pulse of a muffled drum. They chanted no strident slogans but instead carried bold banners that read MAKE AMERICA SAFE FOR DEMOCRACY; AMERICA HAS LYNCHED WITHOUT TRIAL 2,867 NEGROES IN 31 YEARS AND NOT A SINGLE MURDERER HAS SUFFERED; WE ARE EXCLUDED FROM THE UNIONS AND CONDEMNED FOR NOT JOINING THEM; PUT THE SPIRIT OF CHRIST IN THE MAKING AND EXECUTION OF THE LAWS; and Theodore Roosevelt's stock promise, A SQUARE DEAL FOR EVERY MAN—T.R.

The Silent Protest Parade was purportedly conceived by the Rev. Frederick Asbury Cullen (father of later world-celebrated poet Countee Cullen) of the Salem Methodist Episcopal Church at Seventh Avenue and 132nd Street.[22] On the organizing committee were Dr. W.E.B. Du Bois; the millionaire businesswoman Madame C. J. Walker; and the pastor of Abyssinian Baptist Church, the Rev. Adam Clayton Powell, Sr. Williams's old neighbor from West 134th Street was also on the committee, Dr. Ivison Hoage. The names of Manhattan Lodge Elks on an NAACP list of supporters suggests that Williams's own participation in the Silent Protest Parade was also likely, if maybe tacitly.

Like any social justice organization, the NAACP considered it paramount to engage young members. The previous spring the writer James Weldon Johnson, the NAACP's field secretary at the time, vouched for the College Men's Round Table, saying the students promised to cooperate in any campaign aimed at "increasing the membership of the local branch and arousing general interest in the work of the Association." According to the *Chicago Defender*, its members came from "every leading college of the east, namely, Harvard, Yale, Dartmouth, Columbia, Brown, College of the City of New York, New York University, Fordham College, Cornell University and University of Chicago." Many of the Round Table young men must have needed to earn money for school in the fall. Given the race-barred job market, it was a sure bet that a good number sought Chief Williams to hire them as Red Caps.[23]

The Silent Protest Parade passed near the terminal, and since Red Cap porters were necessarily walking information booths, the Chief might have considered how they might tactfully answer the public's questions. His entirely African-American corps, relegated to work like pack mules, surely felt personally touched by the horror in East St. Louis and no doubt shared the indignation of a protest banner that read WE ARE MALIGNED AS LAZY AND MURDERED WHEN WE WORK. Chief Williams might easily have given a number of the men leave to "staff" the crossing at 42nd Street and Fifth Avenue a block away, where they could contribute to the passing march. "'Red Caps' from the Grand Central Station took delight in telling the curious what it was all about," Lester Walton wrote, "preferring to perform such service for the time being to making tips." Indeed, the opportunity to act as an impromptu speakers bureau for the Silent Protest Parade might have been worth any pecuniary sacrifice that Saturday afternoon.[24]

The Silent Protest gave rise to the Dyer Anti-Lynching Bill, which failed to pass Congress in 1922 and several times after that. Its failure fueled the broad political defection of the nation's black voters from Republican to Democrat, and it set the stage for massive civil rights demonstrations and protests to come.

◈

Williams was well-known for rallying his Red Cap porters to support "racial uplift" causes. In 1913 they had contributed $150 during a twelve-day campaign to raise $4 million to build a Colored YMCA and YWCA in Harlem.[25] In 1916 they participated in raising funds for the Booker T. Washington Memorial Fund, to honor the renowned educator and orator who had died the previous year. For the memorial campaign, Chief Williams's Red Caps and their counterparts at Pennsylvania Station diligently saved "five cents a day for twenty days." At Grand Central, Williams gave three dollars, and each of his men one dollar, to a total contribution of $175 (about $4,247 today). At Penn, Capt. W. H. Robinson gave $1.75, but only a few men (including Chief Williams's son Wesley) gave one dollar, and the others pledged fifty cents, for a total of $75 (about $1,820 today)—a possible indication that Penn was the less lucrative of the two stations for Red Cap porters.[26] The organizers explicitly commended Williams and Robinson, lauding them as "philanthropic knights of the grip" and for showing up the so-called "big Negro" business professionals who conspicuously failed to contribute.[27]

In the spring of 1917, after the United States entered the European war, Williams had reason to take pride in his men's out-of-pocket show of enthusiasm. The New York Central's president, Alfred H. Smith, was also chair of the Liberty Loan Committee of Railroads, which fueled the sale of war bonds systemwide—from executives down to errand boys and porters. One railway trade journal cited the Red Caps as over a third of the roughly 150 various depot attendants who took bond subscriptions, observing that they "in most cases pa[id] cash which was not taken from savings banks."[28]

In the summer of 1918, the government's "work-or-fight" rule mandated an immediate draft of unemployed males. That caused a notable attrition of Grand Central's Red Caps, whose numbers dwindled to only sixty-five men. Chief Williams explained that most of the men inducted were of draft age, and many chose to fight, but a number of others were aliens, some with ten years at the station, whose lack of papers "proved detrimental to them" when the rule went into effect.[29] Yet regardless of the depletion of the workforce (which may have increased by fall), Chief Williams personified the Red Caps' philanthropic zeal, as when he organized 110 Red Caps that October to buy Fourth Liberty Loan war bonds. They "went over the top . . . some buying as much as $500 worth of bonds," outdoing all other terminal groups by collecting $20,000, the *New York Age* reported.

This came on the heels of another recent contribution, that the same item noted: "Three weeks ago Chief Williams and his co-workers contributed $111 to Haywood Unit no. 14 to help further its canteen work."[30] Haywood Unit no. 14, located at 2388 Seventh Avenue, boasted that its canteen had "social rooms, bedrooms, pool and billiard tables, dining rooms and a well-kept back yard." Both "colored and white war workers in large attendance" participated that summer in opening the canteen, which might have infused a degree of optimism about the waning of racial prejudice, especially alongside headlines proclaiming "no color line" for Negro troops in the ranks of our French allies.[31]

More than a dozen Grand Central Red Caps volunteered for service in Europe, And the military recruited from the Red Cap ranks sixteen commissioned officers, three of whom were in France with the 369th Regiment, the "Harlem Hellfighters." Chief Williams rallied his attendants to furnish all manner of clothing and gear to their fellow Red Caps in the army, from socks and scarves to "a pair of army regulation field glasses" and "a wrist watch" and "colored [news]papers." One paper noted that "Chief Williams writes to his former comrades every ten days."[32]

Army Mess Sergeant Chester A. Wilson, who had enlisted in June 1916, was one who wrote back to him.

Dear Chief:

Since I wrote you last I have received two letters, two packages of papers and the precious candy which you sent me. I certainly appreciate your kindness and will always feel obligated to you. Tucker is here with me and helped to enjoy the candy and papers. "Dr." Ransom is stationed at another place, so I will have to tell him about it when I see him.

Well, this is our second attempt on the Germans, and believe me the same old tradition stands good. These boys will all give a good count of themselves every time they have a chance. You can tell them with confidence that this regiment is making good. Wish I could relate some things to you, but the censor will only cut it out. So I will wait and tell you when I return, if I am spared to do so. The weather is very hot today and everything is quiet except the artillery. We can tell that they are near. Battles high up in the air are common sights. Gee, whizz, you should see them.[33]

One aspect of the Chief's diligence at Grand Central suggests his likely affiliation with the Circle for Negro War Relief. Established in November 1917, the circle was a women's initiative dedicated to promoting the welfare of black troops and their families impacted by the war. Its vigorous activities included sending comfort kits and chewing gum to the soldiers overseas. It was spearheaded by the white reformer Emily Bigelow Hapgood, its president, who built up a formidable coterie of white and black activists. According to the writer and activist Alice Dunbar-Nelson, the circle's influence on black participation radiated across the country, similar to the Red Cross.[34]

On November 2, 1918, Chief Williams helped celebrate one of the circle's major public events, in Carnegie Hall. Billed as a "Patriotic Evening," some two thousand citizens, black and white alike, attended the fund-raiser to benefit the Circle for Negro War Relief. W.E.B. Du Bois presided over the program. The evening's star attraction was the war correspondent and humorist Irvin S. Cobb who, despite his southern Confederate stock, had recently written an eyewitness account of the discipline and valor of the Negro fighting troops in France.[35] The two famous regiments—the 367th "Buffalo" Infantry and the 369th Harlem Hellfighters —had shown so much patriotism on the battlefront that the Americans and the French would decorate over a hundred of them. The segregated Hellfighters had trained under French command. Cobb lauded two black soldiers, Henry Johnson and Needham Roberts, who thrashed twenty-odd enemy Huns on their own. France awarded the pair the coveted Croix de Guerre, distinguishing two black soldiers as the first Americans to receive its highest military honor for extraordinary gallantry. The audience greeted Cobb's testimony with riotous bursts of enthusiasm.

The special guest who followed Cobb was Col. Theodore Roosevelt, the former president. Williams knew "Teddy" well: when his son Wesley applied to the city's fire department—the only black applicant out of seventeen hundred—Roosevelt had purportedly written him a character reference. Roosevelt's personal appearance at this "Patriotic Evening" was highly symbolic: in 1906 he had received the Nobel Peace Prize (he was the award's first recipient), and he had recently contributed $4,000 of $45,482.83 in securities and cash to the colored YWCA War Work Council. He explicitly earmarked the purse in support of the Hostess House at Camp Upton, Long Island, "for colored troops and in work among colored women and girls in and about the camps and cantonments."[36] Roosevelt had originally donated his prize to Congress to establish a permanent Industrial Peace Committee to promote "fair dealings between classes of society."[37] But Congress never organized the committee, and the onset of the Great War prompted Roosevelt to petition for the return of the funds.

If "Teddy" was ever a great favorite of African Americans, his personal appeal now on behalf of the Circle for Negro War Relief stood him in good stead as he encouraged the crowd to pledge donations to the circle. Their cheers shook the great concert hall as Roosevelt boomed his own promise to do all he could "to aid you to bring nearer the day of the square deal."[38] He would not realize his mission; he fell ill the following week, rallied, then died two months later, barely a week into the new year.

It had happened that one of the two heroes whom Cobb mentioned was now back home in New York: Needham Roberts. That Roberts's exultant return coincided with the Circle's big New York fund-raiser was timely. The organizers hastened to adjust the program "to have the colored hero introduced to the audience." To that end, Chief Williams must have seemed an obvious liaison to Roberts. The Williams family had been in the news all summer, due to his feud with baseball czar Nat Strong and his son Wesley's auspicious application to the fire department. In October, the NAACP's annual children's issue of the *Crisis* illustrated a verse, "The Black Madonna and Her Babe"—by Lucian B. Watkins, the "Poet Laureate of the New Negro"—with a photo of four generations of Williamses. The image, though captioned incorrectly, was of the senior John Wesley

A miscaptioned photo of senior John Wesley Williams and the Chief—each framing Wesley holding his infant son James II—pairs with a Lucian B. Watkins poem, "The Black Madonna and Her Babe," in the October 1918 issue of the *Crisis*. Crisis, *October 1918*.

On November 2, 1918, Chief Williams accompanied Needham Roberts—American war hero whom France decorated with its Croix de Guerre—to a "Patriotic Evening" at Carnegie Hall. *Robert Langmuir African American Photograph Collection, Emory University, Manuscript, Archives, and Rare Book Library.*

Williams and the Chief, both framing Wesley, who is holding up his infant son James II.[39] Between Harlem and the Terminal City, the Chief was being lauded for his organizing around the Fourth Liberty Loan and other war work, and his rapport with Grand Central's Red Cap doughboys. This timely, favorable attention would have made him suitable for the task of chaperoning Roberts, Harlem's most famous soldier who had escaped the stark hell of Europe's battlefields, to the opulent paradise of Carnegie Hall.

Private Roberts had only to take a step across the stage to steal the thunder from both Roosevelt and Cobb. At the young warrior's appearance, every man and woman in the hall shot to their feet. The celebrities urged him to speak, but the explosive ovation may have stunned him into silence. And he needn't have spoken. The Hellfighter's bearing spoke for itself as he stood onstage before the adoring crowd, "resplendent with distinguished medals and service stripes awarded him by the French for exceptional gallantry in action."

The program's overall mood was optimistic. Lt. Fred Simpson led the Fifteenth Regiment Band; the composer J. Rosamond Johnson, director of the Music School Settlement for Colored People, played piano; Roland Hayes, the race's leading concert tenor was in exceptional voice with the Fisk Jubilee Quartet; and black nurses acting as ushers in the great hall appeared angelic in white uniforms. Cobb, conveying his sense that the war's end was in sight, quipped that anyone wanting to talk of the world war as a present event "will have to hurry." The mood was indeed also one of encouragement. "There were many nice things said last Saturday evening at Carnegie Hall," Lester Walton mused, "but the nicest of all was the statement *that after the war the Negro over here will get more than a sip from the cup of democracy.*" Covering the event, the *Age* ran a long front-page article with a photo showing Pvt. Needham Roberts and his three brothers standing outside, enjoying cigars with "J. H. Williams, Chief of Grand Central Red Caps." All are smiling for the camera, as if to rekindle every dimming heart on the home front.

◈

Having made it to Carnegie Hall, some might have quipped, what was left for the war to do but end? Indeed, it did end, little more than a week after Cobb's prescient quip at the "Patriotic Evening."

In the late 1910s, Chief Williams's parents had moved to a ground-floor Harlem tenement apartment at 19 West 131st Street. *Charles Ford Williams Family Collection.*

Four days before the signing of the armistice on November 11, 1918, a false report had ignited the city into spontaneously jubilant celebration everywhere. Workers and residents poured from buildings, crowds paraded, paper litter was deployed as confetti, and the renowned tenor Enrico Caruso sang from his fifteenth-floor hotel balcony. Chief Williams felt reasonably relieved and proud. The end of the war would soon return his baseball players home, and upon their arrival, he organized potentially "one of the strongest colored teams in the East" to welcome them.[40] At Grand Central, Red Caps went "cake-walking through the concourse behind one porter who was pushing an invalid chair in which was a stuffed figure of the kaiser."[41] Two months after the armistice, on February 17, 1919, some three thousand uniformed black men—Hellfighters of the 369th Infantry—paraded up Harlem's Lenox Avenue to 145th Street.[42] Many would later pin the birth of the Harlem Renaissance on that date.

But in the aftermath of the war, Harlem was not quite finished with Europe. "Harlem is like Paris; indeed, we may aptly call it

Black Paris," a Harlem writer observed, noting that the City of Light had long been slandered as decadent. "What Paris is to Europeans, Harlem is to the American Negro. It is the finest Negro city in the world, with broad, tree-bordered, parked avenues, Negro residential streets such are seen nowhere else, alert, well-dressed, energetic people. Brokers, teachers, preachers, physicians, lawyers, politicians, singers, composers, poets, novelists, editors, musicians—Black Paris indeed!"[43] Across the ocean, some black musicians like Louis Mitchell and his ragtime band the Seven Spades had been the toast of London, and they remained to conquer Paris. Their sojourn would be as influential as that of any ambassador, speaking the common tongue of jazz.[44]

PART III

HARLEM RENAISSANCE

CHAPTER 7

"A Sweet Spot in Harlem Known as Strivers' Row"

And you can have your Broadway, give me Lenox Avenue,
Angels from the skies stroll Seventh, and for that thanks are due,
To Madam Walker's Beauty shops and Poro system, too,
That made them Angels without any doubt.

—W. C. HANDY, "HARLEM BLUES," 1922

In mid-August 1918, a couple of weeks after Chief Williams's fortieth birthday, a small item in the *Chicago Defender* mentioned that he had left for his annual Canadian vacation at the hunting lodge of the ex-governor of Vermont. By sheer coincidence, while Williams was away, the same day's paper announced that Wesley passed the civil service examination for the city's fire department. What was more, as a call from home probably confirmed, "Wesley Williams passed the physical test with 100 per cent." The news spread like a fire itself, igniting the black press and much of the white. Articles made much of Wesley being a devout teetotaler and nonsmoker; some even enumerated every diameter and circumference of this physically perfect he-man. Though the Chief must have missed being home during this momentous news, he was no doubt elated to share it among his angling pals. His son, who had been the only black candidate out of seventeen hundred applicants, was the only one to score perfectly on the physical exam.[1]

Wesley's score surprised few. Now turning twenty-one, he was not only an all-around athlete but the protégé of a white professional exhibition athlete, Charles Ramsey. “He happened to live next to an aunt of mine,” Wesley said of his mentor, who had lived at 32 West 137th Street, a Harlem walkup of predominantly black working-class households. Born a British West Indian in 1886, Ramsey had emigrated to the States in 1904 and become an acolyte of health guru and publisher Bernarr Macfadden, the “Father of Physical Culture.” As Ramsey eyed Wesley during the fire department's physical, he could read the sinews of the lad's weightlifting experience as clearly as a name tag.

While Wesley Williams became the first black fireman in Manhattan, he was not the first in the city: that honor belonged to a little-known Brooklyn fireman named John Woodson. Though the Williamses hadn't met Woodson personally, they knew about him

In 1918 Wesley Williams was the only black applicant out of 1,700 for the New York City Fire Department, and the only one to score perfectly on the physical examination. *Charles Ford Williams Family Collection.*

from the papers. He had been on the force since September 1914, appointed to a hook and ladder company in Greenpoint, and he was the city's only black fireman since the paid department had been established a half a century before. Most of the city was unaware that a Negro fireman even existed on the force. Then on September 12, 1916, almost two years after he had started, Woodson daringly rescued a mother and baby from an early-morning blaze in a Brooklyn tenement. The act finally cinched him recognition: the following summer, Mayor John Purroy Mitchel publicly awarded the obscure pioneer a medal for courage.

The hiring, performance, and public recognition of Woodson–who was described as "a regular Jack Johnson"–fueled the case for racial parity in municipal services. Writing in the *Age*, James Weldon Johnson measuredly praised Commissioner Adamson, the fire chief whose Georgia roots had at first made many blacks apprehensive, for displaying "the sense of fairness and the stiffness of backbone" to give Woodson his post. "If there were more colored men like Fireman Woodson and more high officials like Commissioner Adamson," Johnson challenged, "the race would soon have a fair representation in all the departments of the city." The Woodson affair no doubt prompted Harlem's civic leaders to canvass another likely black fireman candidate, this time for Manhattan.[2] Chief Williams's son Wesley was an obvious choice.

Once Wesley Williams decided to apply, the Chief engaged his influential social connections to intercede on his behalf to the fire commissioner: Vanderbilts, Goulds, and Morgans as well as former Vermont governor E. C. Smith—men who owned and used railroads. Former president Roosevelt wrote a recommendation. Yet of all his father's powerful friends, Wesley felt most grateful to Charles Thorley, the millionaire florist, whom he also recalled as a heavy contributor to Tammany Hall, which ran the city. "He told my father, 'the only thing they got against your son is that he happens to be a black man,'" Wesley said, "'but he will stay there regardless of what [fire department officials] like.'"[3]

Wesley was appointed to start at the fire department on January

10, 1919. As when he was made Chief of the Red Caps ten years before, Williams felt heartened that even strangers offered congratulations to the family on his son's appointment. But despite the Chief's overwhelming pride in his son's achievement, he had good reason to be anxious, too. He remembered how cruelly the white cops had hazed his friend Jesse Battle, a strapping six-foot-three giant, with stony silence.

The death of former president Roosevelt on January 6 cast a pall over the country that the Williamses no doubt felt personally—"Teddy" had championed Wesley's appointment. A few days later, Wesley received a personal letter, also postmarked, with some eerie poignancy, January 6 from Jamaica, Queens: it was from Fireman Woodson, who had read about his appointment. "I know you will be quite surprised to hear from a stranger," Woodson began his touching four-page letter. "I'm going to ask that you will not consider me as one as I feel that it is my duty as a (Race) man to enlighten you as to conditions that exist in the Fire Department." Having spent nearly four and a half years in the ranks, Woodson overflowed with practical advice on how Wesley might deflect a most certain chilly reception: "You'll find quite a lot of *jealous* and *narrow* minded men in the Dep't, and at times you may feel disgusted, but take a tip from me. When you are assigned to a company do your work and do it as near perfect as you can, above all don't listen to other lazy men, do everything the commanding officer tells you to do, no matter what it might be *do it*!"[4]

On January 10, Wesley commenced his assignment at Engine Company 55 at 363 Broome Street, in Little Italy. He had no sooner reported for duty than the rank-and-file firemen ostracized him. Woodson's words echoed again: *"At times you may feel disgusted."* The fire captain himself took his retirement, effective immediately. He walked out "rather than have the stigma of being the captain of the company where the black man was sent," Wesley later recalled. Likewise, every fireman in the company requested transfer, indig-

Wesley Williams (right end of middle row) with his graduation probation class of the Fire Department of New York, 1919. *Charles Ford Williams Family Collection.*

nant at having to work and sleep in the same firehouse with a black man. The department denied each man's request, but that hardly put Wesley at ease. He was relegated to a "black bed," Jim Crow quarters that firehouses infamously contrived for the rare black recruit. "I was assigned to a bed right by the toilet in the rear of the firehouse," Wesley recalled, which put him in earshot of his co-lodgers' vows to "burn this nigger up."[5]

The white firemen soon almost made good on their threat. Within the first six months of Wesley's probationary term, an explosion summoned the company to the Bowery near Kenmare Street (a continuation of Delancey). The lieutenant, the officer duty-bound to be first to go down and last to leave, ordered Wesley to lead the way into the burning basement. "As the flames rolled over my head, everybody else ran out," Wesley said. "That left me down there alone in the cellar." When battalion chief Ben Parker arrived on the scene and asked if all the lieutenant's men were accounted for, the officer responded that Wesley was still down there. But then the colored rookie emerged from the cellar, having finally put the fire out alone. Wesley's stinging eyes slowly cleared to the sight of Chief Parker fixing his white co-workers with a withering stare. Whether the men had planned the blaze or it happened as a near-granted wish, they knew their hazing would have to take a new tack. "You were gonna burn *him* up?" the battalion chief said incredulously. "Looks like he burnt *you* fellas up."[6]

Wesley cited Chief Parker's action that day as giving rise to his reputation as a valiant "smoke-eater." But other skills he brought to the fire department seemed to make him at once essential and unpopular. For the three previous years, from age eighteen to twenty-one, he had driven a parcel truck for the Pelham Post Office. Aside from acquiring a keen sense of city geography, the automotive job gave him an even more decided advantage. Many of his white counterparts "had been trolley car operators and truck drivers and stevedores and so forth," who " only knew about driving horses." Fire department officials had been trying for weeks to train the men in how to drive a motor apparatus, but the Engine Company 55 station house presented a particular handicap due to its orientation. When Wesley's turn came to take out the great steam engine and drive it back in, he knew from experience not to try to back in straight, but to do so on a bias. The monstrous apparatus seemed sweetly obeisant to the intuitive hand of a longtime practitioner. Wesley's effortless performance earned him the appointment of company chauffeur after his three-month probationary period. But though he was naturally qualified to be that engine's regular driver, the assignment "was resented much by the white men."[7]

Wesley came to predict his co-workers' contrariness. "If I went upstairs, they went down," he would recall, yet he admitted that their ostracizing had a benefit. Following Battle's example, Wesley made his solitude constructive. He filled his locker with books by Arthur Schopenhauer, Jack London, Friedrich Nietzsche, William

James, and Carl Van Vechten and used his idle hours to read and study without interference. Being shunned also gave him leeway to reclaim Engine 55's rooftop for himself, adapting the hose tower into a makeshift gym with setups for boxing, weightlifting, and stomach workouts. "They helped to make me a Superman," Wesley remarked, "the prejudice."[8] Indeed, Wesley was nothing short of a Superman before long: six months into his new career, he helped to rescue an Italian mother and her six kids from a three-story house on 213th Street and White Plains Avenue in Williamsbridge. Though the act went unheralded officially—the prejudice was still too prevalent—it possibly contributed to his growing bond with the Italian-American community that surrounded his firehouse down on Broome Street.

Chief Williams was of course as heartened as his son by John Woodson's encouragement and invitation to meet. At some point the Chief and Wesley did meet the other fireman: when occasionally in Manhattan, Woodson planned to greet the Chief as he passed through Grand Central Terminal, and Wesley sometimes dropped by to join them.

⬥

On July 28, 1919, white and black Republicans alike voted unanimously to nominate the black dentist Dr. Charles H. Roberts as the party's candidate for New York alderman for the district encompassing Harlem. Roberts was extremely popular and the first black man to gain the nomination. He was a graduate of Lincoln University; president of the Manhattan Medical Dental and Pharmaceutical Association of New York; and organizer of the Children's Dental Clinic, sponsored by the Children's Aid Society. He had served on the dental staff of the French Army's medical division during the war.

Roberts's platform included advocating for public baths in the district; building an armory for the "Hellfighters" regiment; vigorously prosecuting food profiteers; opposing increases in public transit fares; and establishing a public market in the district.

Chief Williams was named amidst the best-known public figures to endorse Roberts, whose other notable supporters included Lt. Col. Theodore Roosevelt (eldest son of the late president); James Weldon Johnson; W. C. Handy; and Reverend Powell, Sr., of Abyssinian Baptist Church.

Roberts won the election, becoming the first black to serve on the New York board of aldermen. Charles W. Anderson—known as the "Colored Demosthenes" whom President Roosevelt had appointed internal revenue collector for lower Manhattan in 1905—presided over a victory dinner for Roberts at the Libya, one of Harlem's grandest resorts. Chief Williams acted on the celebration's dinner planning committee, whose setup was no doubt impeccable: "Floral decorations for the dining hall were furnished by Thorley, the Fifth avenue florist," the *Age* noted.[9]

◈

In October 1919, for reasons that are not clear, the Williamses quit the house at 823 East 223rd Street in Williamsbridge and returned to Harlem. A few years later Sandy P. Jones moved into the house they vacated.

Chief Williams signed a deed for a row house in Harlem at 226 West 138th Street, in a tranquil tree-lined enclave known as the King's Model Houses. Built in the early 1890s, the exclusive development had refused to sell to blacks, but after three decades it was opening up, and as new black homeowners moved in, it was fast becoming known as Strivers' Row, a flippant allusion to their middle-class aspirations. Perhaps the new house also harbored his daughter Gertrude's youthful longings.

Some weeks earlier, on August 22, 1919, Gertrude Williams turned twenty-one. If everybody's attention had hung on her brother Wesley's accomplishments for the past year, she now got her time in the family spotlight: two weeks after her birthday, the radiant young woman married William Nehemiah, a jobbing musician of considerable ability.[10] Nehemiah (called by his surname for clarity) had worked at Grand Central as one of the Chief's boys on the marble concourse, but left for the battle trenches in France. A violinist, he played with the "Hellfighters" Fifteenth Infantry NYC Band, organized by the influential bandleader Lt. James Reese Europe and the composer Noble Sissle.

The Harlem Hellfighters returned from war with the taste of champagne. But as a song recorded by Europe's band asked, "How ya gonna keep 'em down on the farm after they've seen Paree?" Parisians in turn were intoxicated by the ragtime and jazz that had crossed the Atlantic and were ravenous for more. "Having fallen willing victims to the melody dispensed by race military bands," the columnist Lester Walton wrote, "the music-loving public of the French capital is eager to hear a colored orchestra from the States."[11] Parisian club owners gave black American musicians carte blanche. The dashing veteran Nehemiah might well have stoked the young hairdresser Gertrude with notions of living in Paris.

The owner of the Casino de Paris, that city's most popular music hall, retained Louis A. Mitchell—a well-known New York bandleader and drummer—to assemble an orchestra of fifty American Negro men for his Paris club. Mitchell was arguably the first great bandleader to carry jazz abroad (at the suggestion of composer Irving Berlin, it was said). He had introduced the new music first to London in 1914, and then to Paris in 1916.

The new orchestra, Mitchell's Jazz Band, was to feature the bandolin, mandolin, guitar, and other stringed instruments that black musicians were known to master, and it was invited to display its versatility in both operatic and ragtime repertoires. Mitchell likely knew Nehemiah's playing from the Hellfighters band, and recruited him.

Black American musicians responded to Mitchell's invitation from Paris enthusiastically—it was a chance to win over a welcoming and appreciative international audience, and at the same time to raise the esteem of American Negro musicians for their original talent and craft. It was a grand plan. Mitchell booked passage for his troupe on the *SS Espagne* on May 6.

But the U.S. State Department, unswayed by the importance of entertainment, denied the musicians' passports. Passport agent Ira

F. Hoyt attached a note to Nehemiah's application: "Claims to be in 15th Inf. N.Y.C. Band. Does the above fact necessitate applicants getting permission from the Secretary of War?" Mitchell tried to expedite Nehemiah's and others' applications, but Hoyt serially rejected them.

This situation shattered Mitchell's ambitious plan for the fifty-man orchestra. He sailed back to Paris with only seven bandmen, to form Mitchell's Jazz Kings, who performed at the Casino de Paris for the next few years. Meanwhile "even [white] theatrical managers of prominence and stars of the footlights find themselves marooned in New York," Walton noted.[12] And perhaps a few sweethearts like Gertrude felt marooned, too.

Gertrude and William Nehemiah wed on September 3, 1919, at the Municipal Building downtown near City Hall. The marriage certificate was peculiarly without witness signatures, and the society columns were oddly mute. Indeed, the couple's civil marriage seemed as much an elopement as had her parents', whose Strivers' Row house the newlyweds moved into.

The following spring Gertrude often enjoyed dancing at the new Rose's Hotel on West 135th Street, where Nehemiah was one of the musical trio, on Saturday evenings. The invitational dances were sponsored by the venerable Aurora Social Club for "the younger element of New York's exclusive set."

Rose's, which had opened in October 1919, was a grand affair. J. W. Rose was a businessman whose Colored Dairy Lunch system had made him a fortune—a local songwriter had dubbed him the "hash and egg king of Harlem."[13] Rose took exception to the Hotel Theresa that loomed over Harlem at Seventh Avenue and 125th Street—it was a citadel of exclusion to Negroes. In response, he bought and renovated three townhouses comprising 246-248-250 West 135th Street and combined them into a palatial race hotel. Though smaller than the Theresa, Rose's New Transient Hotel, as it was fully called, was Harlem's—and perhaps all New York's—first full-scale swank hotel for a black clientele, boasting modern amenities and convenience to all Harlem surface transit lines.

The new hotel started accommodating guests even before its grand opening: white Broadway producer Charles B. Dillingham arranged for "a group of musical artists from Louisville, Ky." to lodge at Rose's.[14] In January 1920 the National Urban League held a dinner there to formally recognize its local New York branch "as a separately incorporated body."[15] A women's police reserve feted Lincoln's Birthday with a tribute to S. Elizabeth Frazier, an auxiliary organizer who was the city's first black teacher (who once taught at Williams's grammar school) assigned to a mixed school.[16] In April over three hundred guests filled the Rose's dining room for the grandest banquet to date of the Knights of Pythias Masonic lodge in honor of John M. Royall, a black realtor who had brokered many transactions between white property owners and black buyers and renters in Harlem. Musicians of the Clef Club entertained, so Nehemiah might have played the gig there on his violin, fulfilling the Rose's promise of "good music day and night" as his best girl danced. Unfortunately, J. W. Rose's poor health forced him to abandon his successful hotel venture. In late September 1920, all of the Rose's furnishings were sold at public auction; the police department adapted the building for a temporary station, then razed it ten years later to erect a customized precinct building on the site.

While the closing of the hotel was a loss for black American society, Nehemiah landed on his feet. By September, he was a member of the house trio for the Garden of Joy, a new open-air cabaret at the swank Libya on Seventh Avenue at 139th Street. (And he was probably the same "Willie Neemeyer" who, forty years later, blues singer Lucille Hegamin recollected had accompanied her on violin.) Clarence Muse, a beloved actor from Harlem's Lafayette Players, emceed the cabaret, which drew crowds of out-of-town visitors.[17]

◈

"At the Grand Central station is a colored man who probably knows more people than any other Negro in New York," began a front-page article in the *New York Age* in the summer of 1923. It featured a photo of James Williams just below the banner, describing him as "head of the Red Caps of the Grand Central station."[18] Barely two weeks later, the death of an American statesman lent the observation a case a point.

On August 2, 1923, President Warren G. Harding died, thrusting Williams's service into the spotlight. In the late afternoon of August 10, about five thousand mourners pressed into Grand Central's upper concourse. Col. Miles Bronson, superintendent of the terminal's electric division, had organized a memorial service there. At five o'clock, the crowd of thousands hushed to the sound of taps emanating from the west gallery. Men bared their heads. The railroad's choral society sang the late president's favorite hymns. Another somber tribute had already started ten minutes before in the east gallery, where a relic of the antebellum New York Central station house had been set up. The old stationmaster's bell had been mute since 1871, but on this day Williams "tolled the bell at half-minute intervals" for the late president.[19]

In the fall of 1923, Chief Williams was back in the newspapers in his own right. He had announced his latest sports venture: a basketball team. The Grand Central Red Caps were "a first-class traveling attraction and are desirous of booking games with all first-class teams with home courts."[20] The promotion echoed his recruitment of athletic porters into the semiprofessional Grand Central Red Caps baseball club. Some of the West Indian Red Caps were kicking around a plan for a cricket club—as Williams heard out such plans, the media kept abreast of his latest competitive interest. This time it was basketball, a game Williams knew well. Years earlier Wesley had been one of the hardest players of the local Alpha Club, and James had since become an ardent fan of the sport.[21]

It was basketball's Black Fives era, referring to the number of starting players, at a time when the game was still racially segregated.[22] By 1923, a multitude of the city's amateur basketball clubs—outfits of various churches, businesses, colored Y's, fraternal organizations, and other groups—were caught up in a "professional craze" as scores of star-quality recreational players were seemingly

Wesley Williams (kneeling at left), with Bill Mitchell's Manhattan Athletic Association team, the later St. Mark's Bears. *Schomburg/NYPL.*

raptured up to play-for-pay basketball nirvana. Harlem was an incubator for many new basketball teams.

Chief Williams figured noticeably in the game's evolution from amateur to professional. The news of the new professional Renaissance Five playing at the Renaissance Casino coincided with the news of Chief Williams promoting his new Grand Central Red Caps Five. While the "Rens" had imported well-known players, the Chief recruited Red Cap players with impressive reputations, too. He tapped such stars as Ardeneze Dash, a former CCNY and Spartan Club forward; Howard "Monk" Johnson (a veteran of Williams's 1918 Red Caps baseball team) of the Puritan Club, in Orange, New Jersey; Henderson Huggins, of the Incorporators and Chicago Defender Five; the "sensational" Lester Fial, of the Brooklyn Royal

Giants baseball team; and especially Ferdinand Accooe. Fans knew Accooe as the former captain of the Borough A. C. Five and from the Carlton Avenue Colored YMCA (and who was a sports editor for the *New York News* and *Inter-State Tattler*).

Through ardent advertising, Williams secured the team's first out-of-town games in Westchester County.[23] The Grand Central Red Caps opened their season in New Rochelle, where they did not disappoint: they vanquished the Orientals on their home court. "Ferdinand Accooe was the outstanding star of the game," the *Chicago Defender* wrote. W. Rollo Wilson, sports columnist for the *Pittsburgh Courier,* echoed praise for the popular "Ferdie Accooe" who shone as the Red Caps "handed Louis Garcia's New Rochelle Orientals a sweet licking 33-19."[24]

Despite their bold debut, the Chief's fives were not infallible. That same month on Harlem's Commonwealth Casino court, perhaps they were overconfident, but the "Red Caps did not play together as a team." The Silent Separates, a formidable deaf Jewish basketball club, easily beat them 26–18.[25] (One might wonder if Lucy, the Chief's wife, acculturated to the deaf world, didn't wink for the other side.) But generally the Chief's crack squad made an auspicious showing, making good on one sports writer's earlier observation that the veteran players of the Red Caps basketball club "give promise of being even better than the Renaissance Five," a capable Harlem club.[26] The sentiment was soon echoed. The Renaissance Big Five, the Commonwealth Big Five, and Pittsburgh's Loendi teams held the spotlight for some time, but the Grand Central Red Caps "came upon the basketball horizon demanding attention," another writer admitted, "and they received some, too."[27]

Chief Williams's visibility was rising on the social horizon as well. At high noon on Saturday, November 24, 1923, Harlem arts patron A'Lelia Walker—a businesswoman who had assumed the helm of her late mother's beauty-product empire, the Madame C.J. Walker Manufacturing Company—held a resplendent "million-dollar wedding" for her daughter Mae. Nine hundred guests were invited, and thousands more people, undeterred by the rain, filled the streets just to catch envious glimpses of the elegant pageant arriving at St. Philip's Episcopal Church (which had moved up to 134th Street). The Williamses' youngest child, five-year-old Katherine, was one of the three flower girls in that sumptuous affair. The Chief and Lucy beamed as little Kay and her two companions clutched tiny baskets decorated with rosebuds and bright tulle bows. Their heads laureled with flowers, the three girls resembled blossoms themselves in loose-draping white georgette frocks with fluted lace ruffles and handmade rosebuds. The trio preceded the bride, paving the path of the church's center aisle with tiny fistfuls of flower petals as they passed.

From Harlem, the Williamses joined the subsequent wedding reception at Madame Walker's own magnificent Westchester estate, Villa Lewaro, in Irvington-on-Hudson.[28] An unrelated item in that

On November 24, 1923, Chief Williams's youngest child Katherine (left) was a flower girl in A'Lelia Walker's storied "million-dollar wedding."
Madam Walker Family Archives.

same morning's *New York Age* also brought A'Lelia Walker and Chief Williams together, and it perhaps suggested an inkling of the former's invitational who's who. The paper reported on the formation of a campaign committee to establish a permanent headquarters for the New York Urban League on West 136th Street. The article cited her brother-in-law Edward H. Wilson, owner of the Hotel Olga—which, since the demise of Rose's, had emerged as Harlem's now preeminent race hotel—on Lenox Avenue and 145th Street, where Walker housed the wedding's groomsmen. There was Lillian Dean, best known as "Pig Foot Mary," whose business acumen at cooking and selling a certain porcine delicacy from a repurposed baby carriage brought her wealth, fame, and Harlem real estate. And the list included Fred R. Moore, editor of the *Age*, and father-in-law of journalist and politician Lester Walton, who was also on the committee.[29]

Chief Williams not only counted among Harlem's multifarious movers and shakers, but drew from them a source of strength that he must invariably have needed from time to time. In the early morning of June 21, 1924, a junket of Missouri Democrats arrived at Grand Central Terminal, to an official reception and fanfare. Williams's full army of Red Caps, now 350 strong, joined dozens of other terminal employees to flank Mayor John J. Hylan and his retinue on the platform. Police reserves pressed back the crowd, and the municipal band struck up the "Missouri March" as ninety-six delegates from that state clambered out of the *Houn' Dawg Special* to a boisterous welcome.[30] The southerners had come for the Democratic National Convention at Madison Square Garden, an event destined to be remembered infamously as the "Klanbake." On the Fourth of July, the convention prompted a local Ku Klux Klan rally in New Jersey, where some 20,000 people railed against a Catholic presidential prospect, Al Smith, whom they decried as governor of "Jew" York. The rally culminated with a cross burning—the likes of which was even closer to home for Williams only three months before.[31]

In midsummer 1924 Chief Williams attended the monthly gathering of the Red Caps Literary Club in Chicago. The theme of the meeting is not clear, but the weight of a summit conference prevailed amid the dense throng of attendees, prominent speakers, and musical interludes. Robert Sengstacke Abbott, founder and editor of the *Chicago Defender* and a local NAACP official, delivered a keynote that was "forceful and well received." Williams was introduced as an honored guest in the august company. Afterward the Chicago clubmen whisked him away to a luncheon at the Ideal Tea Room, where he was introduced to Red Cap organizers from the Northwestern, Dearborn, and Illinois Central stations. Their invitation to the "chief usher at the Grand Central Station, New York City" not only helped the Red Caps of Chicago to accomplish "one of the most encouraging and enthusiastic meetings since their beginning." It also signified Chief Williams's status as a principal arbiter of "race" men on the railroads.[32]

The Williams house on 138th Street was not dormant during his sojourn in Chicago. James and Lucy's elder daughter Gertrude turned twenty-six that August and took the month off from her job as a dental nurse at Dr. Booth's in Harlem. She spent her carefree respite in Saratoga Springs and Atlantic City, playing tennis, golfing, and swimming.[33] Nehemiah, her husband of five years before, was no longer in the house nor, apparently, in her life.

Gertrude's theatrical interests were evident that summer: she performed as a principal in a dance and song exhibition at the new Ethiopian Art Theater School.[34] The program was staged by Jesse Shipp, Gertrude's former next-door neighbor from West 134th Street. Amid the social whirl of the theater crowd, Shipp may have indirectly ushered her into a romantic foray with David "Chink" Watkins, a musician friend and pallbearer for the recently deceased Jesse Shipp, Jr.

For the next few years, Gertrude and David kept fast company, palling with some of the highest of Harlem society and brightest of Broadway. That first summer Gert would have been the envy of any young girl entertaining her own stage ambitions: she found herself in the company of Florence Mills, the recent singing sensation of the Broadway shows *Shuffle Along* and *The Plantation Revue*. During the three-day out-of-town tryouts for *Dixie to Broadway* at Asbury Park, New Jersey, the troupe stayed at Laster Cottage at nearby Spring Lake Beach; Gertrude and David joined them there and "spent much time on the beach enjoying surf bathing."[35] The seaside, as essential a social corridor as Harlem's Lenox or Seventh Avenue, clearly seemed Gertrude's medium.

That same summer Gertrude did several modeling stints and beauty pageants, revealing that she possessed a beauty to be reckoned with. She won some local contests (notably for hair bobbing) and was featured in ads for Dr. Fred Palmer's skin product that promised "Bewitching Beauty for any Complexion . . . in 10 days."[36] She posed for Randolph "Mac" McDougall, a noted black photographer for Underwood & Underwood.

Later, in April 1925 Gertrude modeled in a benefit fashion show for a children's recreation center, wearing a blond bengaline "Mildred hat," a creation of Mildred Blount, Harlem's rising millinery star, who would have an auspicious future in Hollywood. Later that day Gert posed in the same hat for Edward Elcha, a prolific chronicler of Harlem's vibrant theater and fashion world—and the preeminent black photographer of the Great White Way. Doubtless Gertrude was keenly aware that such legends as Florence Mills and Bessie Smith had preceded her before his camera.

In the summer of 1925 Gert returned to the shore, where she was keenly observed: "Miss Gertrude Williams of New York looked exceedingly well in her style bob. She was very attractively dressed as usual."[37] And during a Labor Day Weekend at Atlantic City, "her bandanna was red, which was so becoming to her tanned complexion," a columnist observed. "She wore a black one-piece bathing suit and was stockingless."[38]

In the late fall of 1926, Gert quit her dental nursing job and went to work as a manicurist for Marcia Louise Lansing, whose posh salon was just steps away, in a townhouse at 2305 Seventh Avenue.

In April 1925, Gertrude Williams modeled a hat designed by Mildred Blount, who was yet to become a pioneer black milliner in Hollywood, for prestigious black Broadway photographer Edward Elcha. *Charles Ford Williams Family Collection.*

The building also housed the New York bureau of the *Pittsburgh Courier*, which so frequently reported on Gertrude's activities. "Who Wouldn't Like Her to Work on Their Hands?" read the caption to a featured photo of her.[39] Chief Williams could have smiled as he saw the photo, perhaps recalling that she had practiced on her mother and little sister's hands.

In December 1926, the Brotherhood of Sleeping Car Porters that

By 1926 Gertrude Williams, noted for her signature bobbed hair, was a sought-after manicurist at a posh Harlem salon steps away from the Williams's Strivers' Row home. *Charles Ford Williams Family Collection.*

was recently organized by A. Philip Randolph staged a huge carnival at the Manhattan Casino. The highlight was a bobbed-hair contest whose presiding judges were celebrity newsmen Lester Walton (writing for the *New York World*); Floyd Calvin (the *Pittsburgh Courier*); Lincoln Davis (the *New York News*); Benny Butler (the *Interstate Tattler*); and Romeo L. Dougherty (the *New York Amsterdam News*). "Among the three prizewinners we could not help but taking notice of the winner of the first prize, who happened to be Miss Gertrude

Williams," Dougherty wrote of her triumph among thirty women. "This young lady is the daughter of Chief Williams of the Grand Central Station, and perhaps it was appropriate that first honors should go to her. My dear, aside from wearing a bob one should know how to carry the head to get the real effect, and this young lady stepped out with an assurance which could not be denied."[40]

By now bobbed hair had become Gertrude's signature, and this particular victory drew recognition beyond the black press. The *New York Daily News* ran a photograph of Gertrude flanked by her second- and third-place co-winners in the contest. "White papers heretofore have refrained from printing pictures of pretty colored girls except when they figured sensationally in the news," the *Courier* remarked, regarding the coverage as a surprising first.[41]

Her carefree 1920s flapper persona aside, Gertrude was one of a growing number of independent enterprising women in Harlem's beauty, fashion and event-planning professions. Being a manicurist also kept her in the loop of Harlem's theatrical world and community network into the 1930s.

◈

In 1924 James Williams was forty-six to his son Wesley's twenty-seven. They had a tight-knit father-son relationship. Wesley was fanatically peripatetic: he even spoke of occasionally walking from his home in Williamsbridge to the firehouse on Broome Street, then back again. The Chief frequently enjoyed keeping pace with him for a few miles when his son headed for duty. Indeed, his son's celebrity on the street was perhaps overtaking his own: that spring Harlemites read how Wesley had "thrillingly rescued a white woman and two children in a big fire" down on the Lower East Side.[42]

On October 19, Wesley picked his dad up at home on 138th Street, and they walked down St. Nicholas Avenue, enjoying the usual greetings from friends they passed by. The Chief probably never imagined he would see his son in action, but at around 118th Street they came upon a building ablaze. Nineteen-year-old William

Thompson was hanging perilously from an open window. The crew extended an aerial ladder toward Thompson, and fireman Patrick Russell scrambled up. Meanwhile a thirty-foot hand ladder also raised a few feet away, and fireman Wesley Williams clambered up that one. Just as Wesley reached his ladder's top rung, Thompson jumped to the nearby aerial ladder. Thompson clung momentarily, then started to collapse. "Williams, by a daring jump from his own ladder to the aerial, caught Thompson as he seemed ready to fall and carried him to safety," the *Times* reported.[43]

Wesley's typical heroism inspired other men in the ranks. Indeed Monk Johnson, former shortstop on the Red Caps baseball team, had named a newborn in the family Wesley Williams Johnson, after the Chief's son the year before.[44]

◈

Prohibition was in full swing at this time, and it of course profoundly influenced the Williams's lives. Wesley had many social connections at Grand Central—aside from his father and three paternal Red Cap uncles, Joshua, Apollos, and Richard—and at Pennsylvania Station, where he himself had redcapped a few years before. "People, the dining car men and Pullman porters and all, wanted whiskey," he later recalled. Wesley also "became very close with the Italians in the area—Lucianos, the Tony Rizzos, the Cusumanos—who were on my side because they hated the Irish." Wesley's Italian connections entrusted him with a truck and a driver, and a doctor's prescription, which privileged him to withdraw cases of alcohol from a warehouse. With the diligence of Florence Nightingale, Wesley made runs up to Grand Central and Penn Station to unload his "medicinal" supplies of Green River, Canadian Club, or whatever whiskey. "I was making three, four five hundred dollars a day, which is a whole lotta money!"

One of Wesley's regular customers was Conrad Immerman, the bootlegger owner of the new Harlem speakeasy Connie's Inn, on Seventh Avenue and 131st Street. In a campaign to expose illegal "hooch joints" in Harlem, the *New York Age* often sized up tipsy patrons leaving the nightclub as evidence that liquor was amply flowing inside. Maybe the paper couldn't yet tell how the club got its alcohol supply, but the Williamses might have known. While Wesley's white co-workers at Engine 55 were still shunning him down on Broome Street, Immerman was welcoming him. He occasionally ordered twenty-five gallons of alcohol to "cut" into something else. "I was running with a truck up here and delivering it in full uniform," Wesley said. "[Prohibition] was a stupid law."[45]

Although Wesley got through Prohibition unscathed, his driver was less fortunate and was later deported back to Italy. The driver opened a restaurant outside Rome, where years later some white fire chiefs from New York on a family vacation happened to stop in to eat. Overhearing them, the Italian restaurant owner asked if maybe they knew "a color fella name a Wesley Williams?" What a small world, because sure they knew Wesley! Or so they thought. "Boy," the Italian guy told them, "he was the biggest bootlegger down there!"[46]

◆

Despite Williams's subordinate status at Grand Central, his recurring contact with some travelers often gave rise to mutually profound interpersonal relationships. He got to know many young people this way, often students returning home on summer vacation from private schools: their headmasters or parents or servants wired to apprise him in advance of their scheduled arrival at the terminal, and he shepherded them from their train and into a taxi home. He watched out for former Vermont governor Edward C. Smith's grandchildren this way, as he had once watched out for their mother when she was a young girl. Julian Street, the novelist and humorist, had an invalid niece who frequently visited the city: she would only have "Chief Jim" lift her out of the car into her wheelchair. It touched him and also thrilled him when one day she walked into the terminal of her own accord. Through her, Williams formed a close friendship with Street and his son, Julian Street, Jr.,

A 1921 magazine cover depicts a Red Cap porter, typically charged with all manner of a traveler's bundles—even a cranky toddler. *Illustration by William Clifford Hoople,* American Legion Weekly, *October 7, 1921.*

a reporter. And sometimes a few young overpartied sons of celebrities needed to borrow cash from him to get back home.

Williams got to know Anne Stillman through such contacts. The daughter of Anne Urquhart Potter and financier James A. Stillman was about his own daughter Gertrude's age. On October 18, 1924, he boarded a train to Westchester, where he would go on to Mondanne, the Stillman family estate in Pleasantville. Chief Williams was "among the few friends" invited to the wedding of heiress Anne Stillman to financier Henry P. Davison of J. P. Morgan, where her father worked.

"It became known today," reported the *Daily Argus*, "that Miss Stillman had invited George [sic] Williams, the porter, to be present at the ceremony because of the attentive courtesies he has shown her during the long period she has passed through the New York Depot in going to and from Pleasantville."[47] The *New York Post* also referred to him as George: "James H. Williams, more familiarly known as 'George,' head attendant at Grand Central Station, set out for Pleasantville today to attend the wedding of Miss Anne Stillman and H. P. Davison. He was a specially invited guest of Miss Stillman, whose baggage he has carried on numerous occasions. Williams is a Negro and has been at Grand Central for twenty years. He lives at 226 West 138th street." If that didn't just beat all, the paper threw in for good measure that another invited guest was John Cane, for many years the Stillman chauffeur.[48] The condescension may have aimed to cut the eccentric Stillman household down to size as much as to put some uppity Negroes in their place.

Quite commonly, whites liberally referred to any sleeping car porter, Red Cap, or other black service worker as "George," irrespective of whether they knew him personally. It was an age-old practice, assumed to date from the time when one of industrialist George Pullman's new railroad sleeping cars carried the remains of assassinated President Abraham Lincoln from Washington, D.C., to Springfield, Illinois. Journeying through seven states and 180 cities, the stately and stylish train intrigued thousands of mourners along the funeral route. Pullman, who hastened to meet the expectations of middle-class luxury-seeking white passengers, had a surfeit of newly freed Negro men to provide obsequious service on his "hotel on wheels"—many called them "George's boys."

Later the blanket "George" moniker for black porters might have gained traction around 1903, when the New York Central's General Passenger Agent George Daniels admitted Williams to Grand Central's staff of white Red Caps he had organized earlier. By the time the new terminal opened in 1913, its use was widespread enough that lumber baron George W. Dulany founded the Society for the Prevention of Calling Sleeping Car Porters "George" (SPCSCPG). The sardonically named club aimed more to spare its white members the indignity of being taken for a mere porter than

A 1922 advertisement for the Grand Central Terminal's operative hardware evokes fluidity of passenger service through the conspicuous toil of the station's Red Caps. *Author's collection.*

to promote racial justice—yet it oddly impacted all porters beneficially: in 1926 the Pullman company agreed to display the given name of the porter on duty in each car. It was said that of Pullman's twelve thousand porters and waiters, "only 362 turned out to be named George."

Needless to say, many porters (including the rare few actually named George) hated it. "Tell you this, I have to come when these fellas yell for George," a porter admitted, "but I don't come with some such alacrity as I do for them that calls me just plain porter."[49] Perhaps snarking back at SPCSCPG, porters at Penn Station had organized a new union, it was said, with a chief objective of discouraging the traveling public from "calling every man who wears a red cap, 'George.'"[50]

It seems doubtful that Anne Stillman addressed Chief Williams by anything but his real name. By their initiative and insistent dignity, Williams and other Red Caps frequently transcended traditional ethnic castes and economic stations.

CHAPTER 8

The Black Decade

Thomas Beer's "Mauve Decade" seems to have set a fashion in associating decades and colors. . . . Some enterprising person should write the history of the present epoch under the caption of "The Black Decade."

—EDEN BLISS, 1926[1]

Given the often mean reception that black college boys could expect at northern colleges, it was no wonder that so many sought refuge under the Williams roof on Strivers' Row. In 1924 at Columbia University, a campus-bodied Ku Klux Klan group actually burned a cross in front of the Furnald Hall dormitory to drive out a black law student. Frederick W. Wells, the targeted youth, refused to vacate, for which he had the university's support, as one newspaper tersely reported: "The boy was brave, and so was the dean, and the attack failed."[2]

However the following year, no doubt hoping to avoid another outburst, Columbia's more cautious solution was a dormitory segregation policy. Students filling out the dorm room application had to mark a space for "race." Whether to assuage befuddlement or avoid controversy, the application explained that the question "is desired in order to assist in congenial grouping in the halls." One black student—who had already lived three summer sessions in campus rooms without incident—applied for a 1925 residence assignment this way:

Dear Sir:

Enclosed you will please find my application for room in residence halls filled out to the best of my knowledge. The space where you ask for designation of race I have filled as specifically as possible. Like a very large percentage of the population of America (perhaps a majority) I am not a member of any one race, but of several races.[3]

By responding to the "race" question by writing in "American," this renewing student apparently failed "to apply in the regular way" that the Committee on Men's Residence Halls deemed satisfactory. Refused a dormitory assignment, the student lodged at nearby International House instead.

How college students in similar situations came to find a refuge in the Williams home is a mystery, but the entire student debating team of the New York chapter of Omega Psi Phi (the first African-American fraternity founded by Howard University in 1911) was living at 226 West 138th Street—Williams's address. And Lucy Williams's philanthropic Harlem social club, Semper Fidelis (Ever Loyal), offered a fifty-dollar stipend "to any woman student of excellent scholarship, morally worthy, and in need of assistance who wishes to continue her studies beyond high school." That Thanksgiving the regally beautiful Gertrude—nominated by a student-led Negro Youth Movement—was crowned Queen of the Annual Howard-Lincoln Football Classic Day.[4] Indeed, student life and matters permeated the Williams household.

At Grand Central, the labyrinthine terminal was too vast and kinetic for the Chief to monitor alone. He assigned captains to keep a vigilant eye on key entrances and platforms. But of course he had to answer for any laxity. "We choose them carefully," Chief Williams told a reporter. "They must give references going back for five years, and these are carefully investigated before they are given employment."[5]

Ads for the Cafe Savarin across the street from the terminal advised travelers to "ask the Red Cap" to direct them. Spur, *November 15, 1924.*

In the mid-1920s, the Chief had no regular formula for procuring new Red Cap workers, because numerous methods suited the purpose. Present Red Caps commonly vouched for a friend or family member as a fine hard worker—like Sam Boyd, who brought his future son-in-law Samuel Delany into the workforce. Many young men sought out Williams, perhaps with a letter of recommendation in hand (or perhaps not) from a community leader, a school dean or professor, or a cleric. Williams's sisters Ella and Lena, who ran the Colored Mission, which was also an employment agency, probably referred men occasionally to their well-positioned brother. In addition, the Chief could readily recruit young job seekers on the northeast corner of the intersection of Seventh Avenue and 135th Street—called the "Campus," this was the effective commons of Harlem's college youth. They emerged on late summer afternoons especially, as shadows began to stretch from the City College hill. For a young student looking to work, everyone seemed to agree, "you would always be able to find him on the Campus."

The Campus quad was the generous sidewalk that traced the curved redbrick facade of the Chelsea Bank. Two doors to the left of the bank's Seventh Avenue entrance was Jackson's Pharmacy, which the students used as an ad hoc communication and business headquarters. To the right of the bank, a few yards east, was the stoop of the Y, a dormitory for numberless collegians. The curbside abounded with young men who came up from Howard, Hampton, Lincoln, Morehouse, Morgan, Tuskegee, and many other black colleges and met, for the first time, the rare blacks in northern white colleges like Columbia, Princeton, Harvard, Yale, Dartmouth, and so on. The students also met socially at baseball games between the two Red Caps teams, or at the Howard-Lincoln football classic.

On the Campus, the young men emerged to solve the ills of the world. "Most of our present outstanding professional men, teachers, and leaders used to argue and debate and joke and 'clown' on the campus," the educator Arthur P. Davis later wrote.[6] Enduring friendships formed here as well. Elliott Hoffman had come north to earn money for school and spent the summer working at Grand Central. Two days after he quit, as he left the College Station Branch

Brooklynite Gus Moore, a Boys High School track and field star, saved for college as a Grand Central Red Cap. During St. Bonaventure's 1927–28 track season, Moore (right end of front row) roomed with Vincent "Roi" Ottley (top row, third from left), well-known journalist and author. *St. Bonaventure University Archives.*

post office with $229—his entire summer savings—crooks robbed him. His friends rallied to raise the money for his carfare and entrance fees.[7]

The students were not here on leisure vacations. Though they commiserated with each other over jobs for which they were infinitely overqualified, they dutifully disposed themselves to work. Both Grand Central and Penn Station required additional summer hands, so Chief Williams could rely on the Campus to fill shortages at the terminal with college men, who were conspicuous.

A writer at the Baltimore *Afro* encountered myriad teachers and students, who were purportedly attending Columbia's summer school, well off campus in the city. "I am led to believe that that noble seat of learning has moved from the venerable old hill and is now holding classes in the Grand Central Station," he wrote, "where many of the alleged students are wearing the regular college regulation outfit of red cap and blue jumper with a number on the sleeve."[8] One who worked as a Red Cap was a medical student at Meharry College in Nashville, Tennessee. Walter Dawkins was lauded as "an example of the colored youth who is trying to attain his goal by his own bootstraps."[9]

Lester Granger was another such exemplary student. After graduating from Dartmouth in 1918, he served in France, then returned to resume his education. Williams hired him as a Red Cap at Grand Central: the veteran doughboy studied social work at New York University. "In the summers of 1920 and '21, and through the winter of 1922, I roamed the paved stretches of the station's labyrinths," Granger later recalled, praising Williams for opening up these lucrative "vacation" jobs to college students. He confessed, however, that "most of us were scared half to death of him." One particular night when he should have been at the station, Granger was in Williams's own home on Strivers' Row, visiting the beautiful Gertrude. His boss caught him. "I sat paralyzed," Granger remembered, until the Chief "nodded briefly, said 'Good evening, Granger,' and passed down the hall." The Chief never mentioned the incident afterward, and Gertrude's recollection is unknown.[10]

Between 1920 and 1922, Lieut. Lester B. Granger worked as a Grand Central Red Cap while studying social work at New York University, and later became a well-known civic leader of the National Urban League.
Robert Langmuir African American Photograph Collection, Emory University, Manuscript, Archives, and Rare Book Library.

◈

Mary White Ovington had once recollected Frederick Douglass claiming toward the end of the previous century that his color had become "an unfashionable one." But in the fall of 1925, Chief Williams was now observing the race soaring into vogue and prominence. Clarence Darrow, the lawyer famous for the "Scopes Monkey Trial," had also won the acquittal of Dr. Ossian Sweet, a black doctor who shot and killed a white man in self-defense. And the popular general interest magazine *Survey Graphic* devoted an entire issue called "Harlem: Mecca of the New Negro." The Harlem Renaissance was an especially salient topic in 1925.

However that fall the Grand Central School of Art, on the seventh floor of the terminal, emerged as the site of intense discrimination. The art school wasn't part of the Chief's rounds, but when it opened two and a half years earlier, in the spring of 1923, he rode upstairs for a special reception to familiarize the Red Cap porters so they could direct travelers there. The American painters Walter Leighton Clark, John Singer Sargent, Edmund Greacen, and others had launched the art school concurrently with the sixth-floor Grand Central Art Galleries. The school's enrollment of over four hundred students that first year soon more than doubled, making the Grand Central School of Art one of the city's largest art schools. Many of the noted instructors were a draw for students.

Frank Smalls was one aspiring artist who applied. He had finished a private school curriculum in portrait painting and for the past two years had studied at the Brooklyn Art Institute. The only black student there, he enjoyed "equal instructions & courtesy as the white pupils." Yet despite his promising résumé, the Grand Central School of Art denied his application. The school's secretary assured Smalls that, while the school had no colored people in its classes, it had "no personal objection" to them. "We think, however, that you would be more comfortable at the Art Students' League," she wrote, "where they have quite a few of your race enrolled." (Six years later the same secretary would reject two black artists, Elba Lightfoot and Zell Ingram, a close friend of Langston Hughes, citing the school's "racial quota.") Frustrated, Smalls wrote to W.E.B. Du Bois at the NAACP, enclosing the rejection letter. Though Du Bois promised Smalls he would try to follow up on the matter, the outcome isn't clear.[11]

Smalls turned from artistic pursuits to freelance writing for the black press. While taking evening degree courses at City College and Columbia University, he took a job as one of the first black station agents (later promoted to dispatcher) when the new Eighth Avenue subway system opened in 1932.

Another young man, Richard Huey, applied to Chief Williams

for a job at Grand Central. He had been a student at Virginia's Hampton Institute until a hunch that the school aimed to make him a farmer sent him fleeing west to law school. In Los Angeles, he had fairly stumbled into performing in W.E.B. Du Bois's historical pageant *Star of Ethiopia*, cast as King Solomon. Afterward Huey returned east—he arrived in New York and inevitably settled in Harlem. He started a course in social sciences at City College, but needing some interim grunt work to make ends meet, he headed to Grand Central.

Chief Williams turned Huey down at first, but the young man's personal letter of recommendation got his attention:

> *To Whom It May Concern:*
>
> *I have known Richard James Huey personally for about a year, but he was introduced to me by close friends in Los Angeles, Dr. and Mrs. John Somerville, who have known him for a long time and who vouched for his good character and ability. I shall be glad of any favors shown him.*[12]

It was signed by W.E.B. Du Bois himself.

While redcapping, Huey landed his first New York acting job, in Paul Green's Pulitzer Prize–winning drama *In Abraham's Bosom*, co-starring Jules Bledsoe, Abbie Mitchell, and Rose McClendon. Though the production was on Broadway, it paid too little for him to quit his Red Cap job. Williams let Huey work around his theater schedule.

Huey said that Williams was "always lenient on boys he knows are trying to do something worthwhile on the outside." Williams told Red Caps that the work was "only something temporary until they can do better." Huey would recall, "I made contacts and moved up in the world to be a Red Cap in Grand Central Station. Make no mistake, that was movin' up."[13] For indeed, redcapping enabled him to keep his sights on Broadway—and to conquer it.

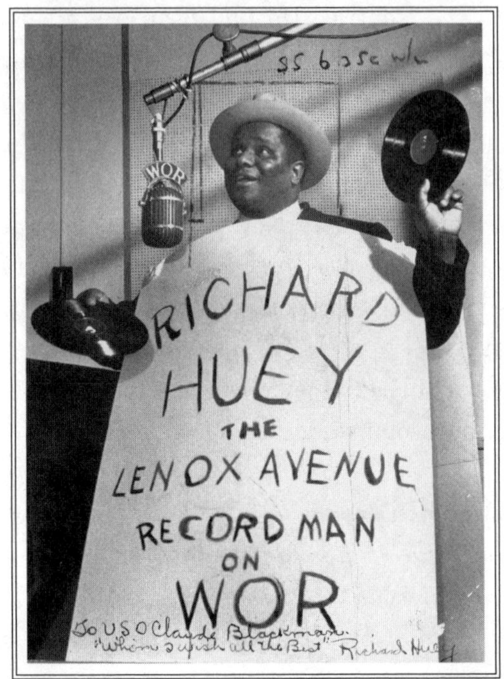

With a reference from W. E. B. Du Bois, Richard Huey got a Red Cap job in 1925, from which he emerged an influential Broadway actor, restaurateur, booking agent, and radio moderator. *Robert Langmuir African American Photograph Collection, Emory University, Manuscript, Archives, and Rare Book Library. Photo: Erich Kastan.*

In 1914 writer Charles Searle wrote an article about the history of American livery, or uniformed service. He imagined the predicament of a bewildered couple, Mr. and Mrs. Jones, alighting at Grand Central Terminal: they immediately faced the prospect of navigating their unwieldy luggage down the long platform toward the concourse, then to a taxi stand. But then a Red Cap magically appeared. At a signal from Mr. Jones, the smiling African under the crimson headgear gathered the baggage and led the way. Once he set them up in a taxi, Mr. Jones fished out "the small gratuity which he drops into the dark palm," grateful to whatever unknown genius thought up that conspicuous red cap, "the chief object of livery—identification."[14] But in fact livery had two focal points, not only the conspicuous crimson headwear but the "smiling African" and the "dark palm."

From the late nineteenth century through the mid-twentieth, the visual culture of American railway travel included the presence of black workers. Perhaps most saliently romanticized was the folk hero John Henry, a mythically strong "steel-drivin' man" who pounded metal stakes into rocks to construct railroad tracks. But by and large, the traveling public typically recognized service workers within the setting of a rail terminal, platform, or train car: the legion of black male Pullman train porters and Red Cap station porters. Even to nontravelers, they were iconic and familiar through media, whose stereotypical depictions of them ranged from the subliminal to the grotesque.

One artist's model for magazine advertisements and book illustrations portrayed anonymous porters with remarkable humanity: Maurice Hunter. For several decades starting about 1920, he was ubiquitous in commercial print illustrations, on the covers and pages of the *Saturday Evening Post*, *Collier's*, *Liberty,* and other national magazines. And he appeared in advertisements promoting everything from soft drinks to hard liquor, from holiday virtues to civic works.

Artists and sculptors praised Hunter for his perfect physique—he stood five-eleven and weighed 165 pounds—and for his sense of drama that inspirited his poses with character. He was described as the "prototype of Pullman porter" and, more widely, as "Harlem's man of a thousand faces." He deployed "unusual powers of facial expression," Lester Walton noted, that, enhanced by his often self-made costumes and adept pantomime, made him the country's foremost Negro artist's model.[15] A 1932 profile in the *Brooklyn Daily Eagle* even described him as a "Super Model," saying, "He brings to the artist the power of character creation unequaled by any model in America."[16]

Hunter sat for some of the most illustrious artists of the time. In 1925, when the renowned sculptor Daniel Chester French created a monumental war memorial, *In Flanders Field*, in Milton, Massachusetts, he used the eloquent template of Hunter's black nude figure "for its magnificent proportions, adding a Caucasian head."[17] In addition, Hunter posed for illustrators J. C. Leyendecker, F. X. Leyendecker, and Charles Dana Gibson. He modeled at the Art Students League (where he sometimes lived), the Corcoran Art School, the Pratt Institute, the Yale School of Fine Arts, and the Pennsylvania Academy of Fine Arts.

Chief Williams likely crossed paths with Hunter in the Grand Central concourse, as the latter was heading to artist Ezra Winter's studio in the art school upstairs. But the Chief's daughter Gertrude more likely encountered Hunter uptown. Hunter fueled many of Harlem's young colored set with modeling aspirations. At the close of 1929, Gertrude and Hunter were guests at the same New Year's Eve party: she was by then likely too experienced to be starstruck, however the presence of a black model of Hunter's caliber was not something a fashion plate like Gertrude would likely take for granted.

Though Hunter was not actually a Red Cap, he once briefly worked as a porter, and Chief Williams likely surmised that Jim Crow attitudes subjected the artist to the same fiscal uncertainty and hustle of those very uniformed porters he portrayed. Despite the model's prolific output and his reputation as the consummate professional, Williams could readily glean from the papers that Hunter was pursuing his remarkable career without fair representation or compensation from his industry. "If I had to do it all over again, I'd be a porter or an elevator man," the artist's model once confessed wistfully. The sentiment was all too familiar to the Chief.[18]

◈

Grand Central Terminal lay fairly dormant at night but roused itself with the early-morning arrival of sleeping car trains. Then between eight and nine o'clock its pulse quickened as trains arrived practically every minute on three of the four tracks in the Park Avenue tunnel. Waves of commuters poured out in quick succession onto the platforms and diverged in straggling columns up the ramps.

Some hastened through mazes of marble passages toward adjacent office or hotel buildings. Others redescended to reach subway lines, or exited the station to a taxi, bus, or trolley, or disappeared on foot onto the bustling sidewalks.

But at 9:40 the rush hour stilled itself, and a restive hush filled the cavernous temple of transportation, signaling the arrival of the *20th Century Limited.* This train excited the New York Central men with singular adulation or an almost religious fervor. “To them it symbolizes their railroad,” wrote one observer. “Its arrival must be made an event of superlative ceremony.”[19]

It was a ceremony at which Chief Williams often officiated. At the blast of his whistle, the Red Caps would aggregate toward the Biltmore Room—a small waiting room known more descriptively as the “Kissing Gallery”—under the terminal’s Vanderbilt Avenue side. Lording over this room was the great arrivals blackboard, upon which a trainman wrote in bold white script with a stub of chalk. The Red Cap porters rushed in like secular acolytes, knowing they were needed, and fell into military files. Then they were marshaled in a body down a ramp to the platform where they would meet the incoming *Century.*

A character in Fannie Hurst’s 1921 novel *Star-Dust* describes “the marble vastness of Grand Central Terminal” as she observes “the run of ‘red caps’ and the slow disgorging of passengers,” a scene soon followed by an uncle “struggling to save his luggage from the fiery piracy of a ‘red cap,’” which soon culminated as “a ‘red cap,’ wild for fee, made for one of the brand-new leather cases.”[20] The scene, more literary than literal, described a basic truth: a Red Cap practically had to run if he hoped to make a buck.

While some contended that a porter’s thanks grew in accordance with the size of the tip, others saw it as less about venality than sustenance. “Their salaries are nominal. They live on the tips,” literary critic Burton Rascoe wrote, defending their honor in a syndicated column. “They are efficient, willing, courteous and genuinely helpful. Each one of them performs a hundred services a day for passengers, for which they get nothing. People, for some reason, who will give a half dollar to a cloak room attendant at a nightclub or hotel concession owned by a profitable syndicate, the head of which [is] a millionaire, often neglect to give even a dime to a red-cap for carrying their grips."[21]

In a letter to New York Central president A. H. Smith, Mrs. S. R. Kaufman praised the Red Caps at Grand Central: "Chief Williams certainly has a gift in getting from his men what he wants, and a stranger would never suspect that he was 'Chief,' so willing to serve himself is he."[22]

One day in November 1926, word spread around Grand Central that Frances Heenan Browning was boarding the 7:49 for White Plains. Peaches Browning, as she was better known, was the teenage bride of "the rich but fatuous middle-aged New York realty broker," Edward West "Daddy" Browning. The previous spring, when the sensational May-December newlyweds arrived in the city after their wedding, "Grand Central Station was packed to overflowing with men and women who craned necks to view them, screaming with excitement the while."[23] The passing months had not abated the fascination, and the lapse in decorum was equally spectacular. From every recess of the station spilled "redcaps, gatemen, baggage hustlers, car cleaners and every unofficial [employee] who wasn't tied to his work" to ogle the young woman. "It was a good wager that Mr. James Williams . . . was not around. For being a strict disciplinarian, he would not have countenanced such ill-mannered actions from his personnel."[24]

Indeed, Williams was not likely to make such a wager lightly, having to answer for lapses in his staff's comportment. A rare reproof of the Chief appeared in the *New York Age* on November 2, 1929, when railroad news columnist James H. Hogans reported on a business traveler's recently lost baggage. The passenger, detraining at Grand Central, had an important engagement with the head of his business firm. In the bag he carried were papers that were very necessary to the conference. The passenger arrived at six o'clock in the evening; the appointment was for seven o'clock, exactly an hour later. But it was nine o'clock before the traveler could transact his business because a fellow passenger took his bag.

Williams must have cringed to read this account in the newspaper. Though Hogans conceded that such mix-ups occurred frequently in all large railroad terminals, he pointed up the impossible conundrum: "the porter blames the redcap; the redcap faults the passenger, and the passenger reproaches both the redcap and the porter." Unless timely action was undertaken to eradicating the problem—by a proactive collaboration between Chief Williams, his captains, and the [Pullman] porters—"someone is going to be affected by these constant complaints," Hogans cautioned. "And, as every redcap and every porter knows, that someone is not going to be the railroads nor is it going to be the Pullman Company."[25] If the public airing of this story in the black press stung, it likely hinted at how strongly the race generally felt implicated in the Chief's predicament and invested in his success.

But Chief Williams more often seemed every bit the "Big Boss" as a newspaper photomontage dubbed him.[26] As a supervisor, he toted baggage far less frequently than did his three to five hundred men, however special passengers warranted his personal attention and drew him down to the tracks. One morning in 1927 as the *20th Century Limited* from Chicago pulled into Grand Central amid the din of tunnel bells, he was standing with a telegram. The man he was waiting for soon stepped out of the sleeper: it was Alfred E. Smith, the governor of New York, who had wired in advance of his arrival. The two men greeted each other familiarly as "Al" and "Jim." The writer John R. Tunis witnessed their warm reception. "No one else except the Chief was permitted or has been permitted for eighteen years to handle Al Smith's baggage," Tunis would later write. The sixty-some other Red Caps stationed down the platform gave due deference to "Al's Red Cap."[27]

Many travelers on the *20th Century Limited* began or ended a trip with Chief Williams as a frame of reference. Hailing him as "Chief," "Jimmy," or "Jim" or even just making a visual connection, mutual or one-sided, could feel essential to the traveling experience. "We make the first and last impression," the Chief would say. That mindfulness had made him the favorite of such notables as former

Vermont governor Edward Smith, heavyweight boxer Joe Louis, both Presidents Roosevelt, and Archbishop Patrick Joseph Hayes. "No Grand Central passenger can consider himself a big shot until Jim has personally met him," Tunis said.[28]

One young psychologist, who had paid for school thanks to working several seasons as a Pullman porter, recalled that a certain "grandiose" industrialist always called the Chief the day he meant to leave town. Williams duly made boarding preparations on the *Century* for the rich, hypochondriacal traveler (left unnamed), his constant valet, and his personal physician. For the day of the departure, the Chief cast several tall Red Caps—in a *coup de théâtre* that assured a big tip—to appear minutes before the train's scheduled departure, giving the tycoon the "psychological moment" that he desired. "Then the Chief Red Cap would lead the procession to the train, on his arm reposing the overcoat of the famous captain of industry."

The eight or so statuesque Red Caps followed single file behind Williams, this one carrying a bag, that one an umbrella, another a coat, all setting the stage for the pompous gentleman to fall in line behind them, trailed by his manservant and doctor. The already boarded passengers who saw this vignette through their windows were mystified as to who this man was, "so great that even the chief red cap, another exalted being, would deign to stoop and carry his coat." They might have half expected (or hoped) the men to break out into an impromptu chorus of "The Charleston," like the Red Caps who had introduced the song behind Elizabeth Welch on Broadway a few years before. After the men set down his luggage in the train's stateroom, the famous industrialist made the charade worth their while, grandly flashing a wad of bills in front and giving "each red cap a new five-dollar note and the chief red cap a twenty-dollar note."[29]

However lucrative such indulgences might be, Chief Williams knew them to be worth more than coin. It heartened him that the former first lady, Edith Roosevelt, always contacted him personally from Oyster Bay before she left home. According to one magazine, "no subordinate is allowed to touch the bags of any member of the Roosevelt family if Williams knows anything about it."[30]

Earl Brown, the former baseball-playing Harvard student, recalled making such a gaffe as a novice Red Cap: he grabbed two elegant pieces of luggage from a *Century* Pullman porter, reasoning that their owner would certainly be good for a dollar tip. His hunch was right. He was content that the "stoutish woman" they belonged to gave him what he had guessed, until he'd done putting them all into a taxi: "As I turned to leave the scene I saw the Chief looking at me with a steely glint in his eye."

"How come you so smart?" he asked Brown.

"What have I done? I didn't do anything," Brown said defensively.

"Well, that was Madame [Ernestine] Schumann-Heink, the great opera singer, and I had an appointment to meet her at the train. A fresh kid like you had to go and grab her bags of all others. Don't be so fresh the next time."

Brown regretted beating the Chief out of Madame Schumann-Heink's usual ten-dollar tip, though admitted he was delighted in having "made a quick buck."[31]

◈

Chief Williams was a rigid disciplinarian, insisting that the Red Caps maintain their personal appearance meticulously. He made daily rounds to inspect them—"and woe to the culprit who is not up to the standard," one let on.[32]

In March 1927 *The World*, a newsmagazine, exalted the four living generations of the Williams family as a remarkable triumph over adversity in an article called "Up from Slavery," echoing the famous title of Booker T. Washington's autobiography. It spotlighted the family patriarch, the runaway slave John Wesley Williams; his son, the Chief of Grand Central Terminal's Red Caps and consort of statesmen; his grandson Wesley, the first Negro in the city's fire department—cited for acts of heroism, whose imminent promotion to lieutenant in September would make him the city's first black fire officer of rank; and a fourth generation of great-grandchildren.[33]

But in October a series of three articles purportedly penned "by a former Red Cap" equated Grand Central's porters to mere slaves.[34]

Allan S. A. Titley's purported exposé, called "Slaves of Grand Central Terminal," cited widespread dissatisfaction in the porters' ranks. While he did not attack Williams personally, he seemed poised to take the esteemed Chief down a peg.

"Pure bunk," Williams shot back, dismissing the claim as "propaganda on the part of some disgruntled person who . . . lost his job through his own machinations." But was it merely this, or did Williams's defensiveness reveal some naïveté? Titley's argument—that the Red Caps' unorganized state accounted for their unfortunate lot—was not preposterous. In fact, given the Red Caps' job definition, it was even reasonable. Titley's articles did not induce immediate dissent. But nor did they endear him to those who believed an outside organization was agitating to form a station porters union, like the Brotherhood of Sleeping Car Porters, organized two years before, that was at once cherished and controversial.

CHAPTER 9

Testaments in Transit

The father of the new Lieutenant is James H. Williams, chief porter at the Grand Central Terminal who of course enjoys the acquaintance of Governor Smith, Mayor Walker and other celebrities.

—*NEW YORK SUN*, 1927[1]

In August 1925, Wesley's name appeared on the city's new list of firemen eligible for promotion to lieutenant. He pored over the stats: 3,010 men had competed, 1,200 had failed, and 920 withdrew. He scored a final percentage of 89.12. "A difference of one point," he explained in a letter to the *New York Age*, "would mean a difference of about 100 names in the standing on the list." He had taken the two-day examination a year earlier, having studied three years at the Delehanty Institute for Civil Service at Fifteenth Street and Fourth Avenue. He was only five years on the force when he took the test, whereas many of the men had it over him in seniority and points. Now Wesley's name was 189th on the list. "I am in the money, as they say," he wrote, overjoyed that his score qualified him.

Still, Wesley was wary of being overconfident. "Now will they promote me when my turn arrives?" he wrote to the *Age*.

"I believe in preparedness, so I am notifying the Negro Press now as I expect a fight about it later on. Although they will not reach my name for a year to eighteen months; don't you think I am right in getting prepared now?"[2]

Wesley surely took after his father when it came to preemptive

In 1925, Mayor John F. Hylan ended his seven-year term by finally honoring Wesley Williams—still Manhattan's only black firefighter on New York's force. Left to right at City Hall were Wesley, his grandfather, the mayor, his father, and his son James II. *Charles Ford Williams Family Collection.*

planning. Chief Williams set himself to advancing his boy's promotion, and one of his most potent tools was small talk. Wesley's past achievements gave him ample things to mention in passing to whomever might make a difference over the next two years.

On September 16, 1927, Fire Commissioner Dorman indeed promoted Wesley to lieutenant. Negro firemen and officers were already common enough in Chicago, Washington, and Baltimore, so their breakthrough was overdue in New York. Nevertheless, the delayed occasion was glorious. As with Wesley's initial appointment to the fire department nine years before, papers across the country reported that he was the first colored fireman promoted to an officer's rank in the department. The Chief was unreservedly proud: "I guess he's about as fine a boy as you'll find," he responded to a reporter's question. "The only trouble we ever had with him when

In 1927, Wesley Williams's promotion to lieutenant made him New York's first black fireman citywide in the rank of officer. *Charles Ford Williams Family Collection.*

he was a kid was that when it came to his turn to do the chores, you'd always find Wesley with his nose in some book. He sure loves to read."[3]

But an unsettling rumor had it that Wesley would be assigned a desk job after his promotion, shunted to another station. A Brooklyn daily acknowledged there was "much speculation around headquarters" that he might be assigned as company chauffeur for Chief John Kenlon, "the Fire Czar." Notwithstanding Kenlon's professed abiding affection for Negroes—in earlier days as a sailor, when he was about to drown, a black cook had plucked him from the brine to a drifting raft—the tactic was doubtless aimed to usher Wesley out of sight and thereby avoid giving a black officer "command over a unit of [white] firemen."

Wesley was not happy about the prospect of reassignment, which would deflate his public triumph. It might also have economic consequences: if moonlighting in moonshine was truly bringing in "a whole lotta money," as Wesley had said, he needed to remain at Broome Street.

The rumor troubled Chief Williams enough that he approached Robert F. Wagner, a U.S. senator from New York and a noted advocate of worker's rights and collective bargaining, as well as a strong proponent of federal antilynching laws. Williams told him about Wesley's impending promotion and his concerns about being displaced from Engine Co. 55 on Broome Street, where he had made his name and wished to stay. Williams found him a good listener.

Wagner told the Chief that Wesley "should continue on active service in a fire company as this was right and also necessary if the proper pattern was to be established for the future Negro members of the New York City fire department," as Wesley later recounted the story. The senator urged Williams to write to Patrick Joseph Cardinal Hayes, Archbishop of New York, who he was confident would be sympathetic. A word from such an exalted religious leader should prove invaluable.[4]

Chief Williams surely knew Cardinal Hayes as a dyed-in-the-wool New Yorker: the prelate was born downtown in Dickensian poverty in the old Five Points slum, and he opposed Prohibition. The Chief had also presumably made his acquaintance now and then in the station. Considering the stakes, he unhesitatingly punched above his weight. On September 9, 1927, in his capacity as an official at Grand Central, he appealed to Cardinal Hayes:

> *Your Eminence:—*
>
> *My son Wesley Williams, a member of the New York Fire Department is shortly to be appointed to a Lieutenancy and as he especially desires to continue his labors at his present location (Engine Co. 55—363 Broome St.) may I take the liberty of appealing to you to intercede with Commissioner Dorman on his behalf so that he continue there.*
>
> *A word from Your Eminence would be the determining say so hoping that you will condescend to help me, I remain.*

Respectfully & gratefully,
Your humble servant.
James H. Williams
Chief Porter, Grand Central Station[5]

The Cardinal's response to the Chief's plea is lost to history, but Wesley did remain nearly a quarter-century longer at the Broome Street firehouse—conspicuously, and through further promotions. Many years later, in 1962, when a black fire department officer, Act-

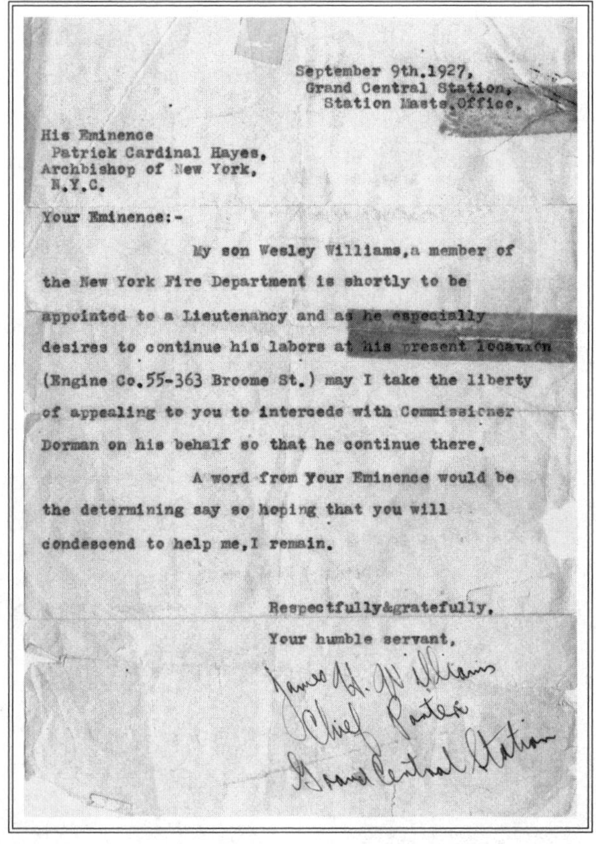

September 9th.1927,
Grand Central Station,
Station Masts.Office.

His Eminence
Patrick Cardinal Hayes,
Archbishop of New York,
N.Y.C.

Your Eminence:-

My son Wesley Williams,a member of the New York Fire Department is shortly to be appointed to a Lieutenancy and as he especially desires to continue his labors at his present location (Engine Co.55-363 Broome St.) may I take the liberty of appealing to you to intercede with Commissioner Dorman on his behalf so that he continue there.

A word from Your Eminence would be the determining say so hoping that you will condescend to help me,I remain.

Respectfully&gratefully,
Your humble servant,
James H. Williams
Chief Porter
Grand Central Station

On September 9, 1927, Chief Williams beseeched Patrick Joseph Cardinal Hayes, Archbishop of New York, to intercede with the New York Fire Department Commissioner on his son Wesley's behalf. *Schomburg/NYPL.*

ing Lt. Robert O. Lowery, was up for promotion to deputy fire commissioner, Wesley, echoing his father's example, wrote to Francis Joseph Cardinal Spellman to enlist his endorsement for the Lowery promotion.

Now with apprehension over Wesley's promotion and assignment vanquished, the Williams household celebrated with ease. On Sunday evening, October 16, 1927, James and Lucy Williams hosted a reception. Invited friends, mostly couples, filtered up the steps of their Strivers' Row brownstone at 226 West 138th Street. Among the family members attending were the Chief's brother Charles and their elderly parents John Wesley and Lucy; as well as his children Gertrude, Pierre, and Katherine. Also attending were extended family members including Police Sgt. Jesse and Florence Battle (who lived across the street), and Grand Central men C. B. Earle (who was also Williams's lodger) and John Holder. Other guests came from as far off as Illinois and Vermont.

And still others attested not only to the importance of Wesley's achievement but also to the Chief's influence. Here was Lester Walton, the eminent columnist, who had covered Williams's earliest sports management venture, the Grand Central Red Caps baseball

James H. Williams and Lucy A. Williams. *Charles Ford Williams Family Collection.*

club. A few months after the new terminal opened in 1913, Walton persuaded the Associated Press to henceforth capitalize the word *Negro* as a noun in print and to desist altogether from using the obnoxious term *Negress*. In the mid-1930s, President Franklin D. Roosevelt would appoint him U.S. minister to Liberia.

The Williamses hired vaudevillian star Tom Fletcher to entertain. One of the highest-ranking stage men of the day, Fletcher's later autobiography, *100 Years of the Negro in Show Business,* would be regarded as an essential eyewitness source for musical theater historians.

As the Williamses welcomed their guests, each congratulatory handshake increased their flush of pride. Perhaps the most notable was Col. Charles W. Anderson, the late Teddy Roosevelt's internal revenue appointee; that he had come to honor Wesley must have moved the entire Williams household.

A much more elaborate ceremonial dinner took place a few months later. On January 28, 1928, Chief Williams climbed the ten brownstone steps of the E Flat Banquet Hall at 56 West 135th Street. The hall was filled with distinguished men—businessmen, physicians, an army major, at least two aldermen—to whom the waiters served a lavish dinner that included shrimp cocktail, chicken, scallops with tartar sauce, filet mignon with mushrooms, and potatoes rissole. Eventually, with the service of fancy ices, cakes, demitasse, cigars, and cigarettes, the banquet hushed, and Williams's old protégé Jesse Battle presided as toastmaster over the after-dinner speeches. All the guests cheered the Chief's boy as a native son of the sidewalks of New York and exalted him for his temperance and self-discipline. "He does not smoke, he does not drink, a gentleman as well as an officer," one reporter wrote. The Chief smiled broadly when Wesley credited his success to the guidance of his mother and father.[6]

Then the tribute committee of Red Caps, from both Grand Central and Penn Station, presented Wesley with "a beautiful Tiffany watch and chain, with a small gold knife attached"[7] as well as "a huge mantel clock."[8] The Red Caps' extravagant offerings to Wesley—the

Tiffany gift alone was reputedly valued at $350—also demonstrated their affectionate loyalty for his father.[9] They all grasped the deference due to the "chief of the more than 500 Red Caps employed at the Grand Central station," where he enabled many of them to pay their way through school.

◈

Throughout the 1920s, the Chief's older children, Wesley and Gertrude, clearly caught the limelight much more than the younger three: Roy (whose full name was James Leroy), Pierre, and Katherine. In 1920, Roy was eighteen, living in the family's Strivers' Row home and working as a Red Cap porter, although it's not known if it was at Grand Central or at Penn Station. On April 9, 1923, twenty-one-year-old Leroy married seventeen-year-old Lula Ledbetter, who was about two months pregnant with their first child, Gloria. The couple had a difficult marriage, perhaps further strained by the birth of a second child, June, in the spring of 1925. When June died at less than a year old, the couple separated.[10]

Lula, estranged from Roy, was inconsolable over losing her baby June and absorbed in caring for toddler Gloria; Lula was also struggling to support her mother, who lived with them. She joined the chorus line of "beautiful creole girls"[11] downtown at the Club Alabam, one of the toniest Broadway cabarets in Times Square that featured black revues.

The dancing was arduous, as athletic as it was exuberant. A wave of chorus girls around the city fell in step to form a union: a particular sore point was the issue of salaries, which were not uniform in the Broadway cabarets. At the popular Plantation Club, a few entertainers had balked at making only $30 or $35 per week and left to join better-paying revues, prompting other clubs to negotiate wages. Ciro's reportedly offered $45 weekly, and Club Alabam reportedly promised to match it; both seemed higher than Lula could hope to earn closer to home, since "Connie's Inn in Harlem tops the uptown places with $35 per [night]."[12] Jazzy black uptown shows had become lucrative ventures for white downtown nightclubs, which earned them cachet; indeed, as a chorus girl in the Alabam's "all-colored" revue, Lula likely did well for herself.

Lula's gig at the Alabam rocketed her professional reputation. In early July the club announced the extension of its immensely popular cabaret revue, *Alabam Fantasies*, through the summer. "Ethel Moses, out," columnist Floyd Calvin reported. "Lula Ledbetter, in." Some called the radiant Moses the "sepia" Jean Harlow, though Gertrude Williams actually outshone her in a beauty pageant the previous fall. Anyway, Moses was off to pursue a new opportunity toward stardom, and the revue's producer clearly had confidence in Lula's own star potential.[13]

Her companions in the fourth edition of *Alabam Fantasies* were a redoubtable troupe. Some were already internationally known, like the venerable soprano Abbie Mitchell and the eccentric pantomimist Johnny Hudgins; future film actress Fredi Washington; and two veterans of the musical hit *Runnin' Wild*, monologuist George Stamper and dancer Lyda Webb, whose choreography "introduced the Charleston to Broadway." "The stepping and dancing of these performers far exceeds any show of its kind we have yet seen," a reviewer wrote, adding, "They are all born entertainers." A few months later, on April 30, 1927, the *Pittsburgh Courier* cameoed Lula's face on its front page, featuring her as "Miss Personality Plus," a reigning cast member of the fashionable Times Square nightclub.[14]

Barely a month later, however, the public learned that the renowned Club Alabam, "which has hitherto employed a colored floor show, dismissed the revue last week and has put in an all-white aggregation, including band."[15] Jazz was still the rage, but even the progenitors of the "Jazz Age"—so delightfully percolating into mainstream culture—were not exempt from the American color line.

Lula's unexpected loss of work may have brought her closer to her in-laws, the Williamses, who she remained on good terms with despite her separation from Roy. As she picked up new jobs here and there, their house on Strivers' Row would have been a convenient place for her to leave Gloria from time to time. As a society column remarked one day in June, "We regret to learn of the illness of Mrs.

James H. Williams 226 W. 138th St. and baby daughter. We wish them both a speedy recovery."[16]

As Lucy Williams's youngest daughter was ten at the time, more likely this "baby daughter" was Gloria, indicating that the elder Williamses continued to protect their daughter-in-law and grandchild. Though Katherine may have been affectionately called the baby of the family, the reference seems to better fit little Gloria, who was three.

The fall theatrical season of 1927 saw several new productions that drew from Dixieland settings. In white productions like the Theater Guild's *Porgy* and David Belasco's *Lulu Belle*, as well as in black ones, the trend looked to be an unusual boon for out-of-work race actors. And like these other companies, Florenz Ziegfeld's new Broadway show, *Show Boat*—a musical staging of Edna Ferber's best-selling saga of the year before—required a sizable cast of black players to authenticate its southern setting.

Ziegfeld called on Will Vodery, one of the most influential black musicians in New York theatrical circles and long one of the producer's steadfast associates in various capacities as composer, arranger, and music director. Vodery had played a key role in brokering greater Broadway employment to some "of the prettiest colored chorus girls in town"—a corps of whom had drawn largely white audiences to the successful all-black revue *Shuffle Along*. He hired over a dozen dancers for *Ziegfeld Follies of 1922*, offering them "the highest salaries ever paid Negro choristers."[17] Now for *Show Boat*, Ziegfeld mandated the procurement of the show's black talent to Vodery, the show's choral director. Vodery needed forty black actors and invited Lula to join the company. Lula didn't pass it up.

In December 1927, *Show Boat* opened two days after Christmas at the new Ziegfeld Theater on West 54th Street, and Lula Williams was in the cast as one of the dozen Dahomey Jubilee Dancers. The historic production employed numerous black talents including Jules Bledsoe; stars of the show's future stage and screen incarnations would include Paul Robeson, Hattie McDaniel, and Alberta Hunter, some of whom were Williams's friends.

Vodery also likely acted as paymaster, dispensing $600 as the highest weekly salary. As a member of the chorus, Lula earned $50 a week. It was somewhat more than what the Club Alabam had paid two years before, but Lula was possibly living beyond her means in Sugar Hill, on Edgecombe Avenue near her in-laws. It was said that Sugar Hill became fashionable after Jules Bledsoe, a co-star of *Show Boat*, moved up to the neighborhood. That the Red Caps nicknamed Grand Central's Vanderbilt Avenue entrance "Sugar Hill" suggested that once-exclusive Strivers' Row now had a worthy competitor. To keep up appearances, Lula Williams was competing with herself to maintain a prestigious address for her daughter and her mother.

The result was tragic. On July 22, 1928, an awful headline appeared in the papers: "Gas Kills Negro Dancer." Lula's mother, Cassie Ledbetter, had found her daughter in their gas-filled apartment on Edgecombe Avenue. Overcome, she explained to the police that the landlord had given her daughter an eviction notice two days earlier. "The scant furnishings were mute evidence of their poverty," a reporter observed. Lula left three notes in three separate envelopes: one to Gloria and Mama; one to "Roy, address unknown"; and one to Willie. She sealed the back of each with a fresh lipstick kiss. To her mother, Lula had written, "I've tried hard to keep things going, but I am a complete failure and know it. Giving up my home is more than I can bear. I want to die. . . . Nobody is to blame for this but me." She expressed her concern for Gloria's upbringing, "as she is the only person that loves mother and thinks I'm wonderful," and specified her wish that Gloria "be placed in custody of the child's grandparents, Mr. and Mrs. Jas. H. Williams."[18]

The awful scenario was sadly familiar to James Williams. Five years earlier it had been Oscar Gant, a Red Cap with him at Grand Central since '08. The man's mother woke to find her son locked in the bathroom, lying in the tub with the gas jet turned on full force. Some said he had had a nervous breakdown, that working in a war munitions factory broke him. Others said he never stopped brooding over his breakup from his wife.[19] But supposings were all after the fact. There was Gant, here was Lula. What could anyone say to make up for this loss of young life?

Lula's note to "Willie" revealed a love affair. "Good-bye, man of my heart," she wrote. 'I love you and only you. . . . I have done wrong to your wife, but couldn't help it—Love is bigger than me." That afternoon Lula's mother had left her daughter at home "in the company of her friend, Singleton," as she took little Gloria out. Willie Singleton owned a prominent billiard parlor nearby on 135th Street. Soon after the incident, Walter White would hire Singleton to cater the NAACP's historic "buffet smoker" for attorney Clarence Darrow to meet over a hundred of Harlem's foremost businessmen.

Lula's letter for her husband Roy, "address unknown," was the most enigmatic; it simply read: "Good-bye, Roy. I hope you marry Sip." But who Sip was, was anyone's guess.

Will Vodery, who had brought Lula to Broadway, took charge of her funeral arrangements. Lucy and the Chief, who was approaching his fiftieth birthday, took charge of their granddaughter, Gloria.

◈

On a brighter occasion for the Chief a year later, the Campus was the point of departure for one of Harlem and Grand Central's most unlikely envoys. On Sunday afternoon, June 16, 1929, a crowd of well-wishers in Harlem cheered William Theodore Davis as he set off on "a journey around the world from Seventh Avenue and 135th Street" on a motorcycle. He was riding an Indian Chief, model number 74, its fuel tank good for 150 to 200 miles. His traveling essentials included a "blanket, cooking utensils, a few books, diary, ukulele, tennis racquet, camera, field glasses and a change of clothing," he later wrote. "And, quite important, $2,000."[20]

Davis called himself the "Lone Wolf." Though only twenty-four, he was no novice to this sort of adventure; three years earlier he rode from New York to Los Angeles, demonstrating "grit and endurance." Then in 1927 slack-jawed fans watched Davis make history with a trip from Harlem to Halifax, Nova Scotia—"in the phenomenal time of 48 hours," an enthusiast noted in the *American Motorcyclist*, a feat in itself. The American Motorcyclist Association, organized in 1924, had an official "whites only" policy and barred Davis from membership, but its magazine reported that some 2,000 Haligonians lavished fellowship on the black roadster, whom they "carried through the streets amid cheering, throwing of hats and waving of handkerchiefs."[21]

Now Harlemites exalted the endurance champion Davis as he revved his engine in the Campus intersection. It isn't known if Chief Williams was on the scene, but the salon where Gertrude worked had a window that gave fully on the spectacle of the departing "Lone Wolf" Davis and the colored Cyclone Motorcycle Club in formation to escort his departure. Disregarding Davis's self-adopted nickname, many in the crowd cheered him as "Lindy of the Ground," after Charles Lindbergh, who made the first transatlantic solo flight from New York to Paris.

This time the Lone Wolf would ride from Harlem to San Francisco, where he had booked passage on a Japanese steamer to Hawaii—whose islands gave him his "first taste of the foreign . . . greatly Americanized"—that continued on to Japan. Doing exhibition riding along the way, his circuitous journey carried him to Hong Kong and Shanghai in China, and then to Korea, and to Manila.[22] He would continue across Asia on his trusty bike. He would then drive through the Middle East and Europe. Backers and promoters flocked to sponsor white riders like Erwin "Cannon Ball" Baker (namesake of later Cannonball Run races), some of whose records the Lone Wolf aimed to break. Lacking such support, Davis covered his own costs by bell-hopping at hotels and portering at rail stations. For this around-the-world escapade, Davis planned "to foot all the bills from his earnings last winter at Grand Central Station," the *Defender* noted.[23]

What Davis did not foresee, as he set out in June 1929 on his Indian, was the imminent stock market crash. Once the dark cloud of the Great Depression rolled in, his family and friends surely welcomed any word of his exploits as diversion. The *Amsterdam News* sports editor Romeo Dougherty—whom black press colleagues esteemed as the "Dean of the East"—shared with his readers a letter Davis had written him from Yokohama, Japan, on April 12, 1930:

> *Having traveled thus far in safety from New York City without encountering any unusual difficulties, I am quite sure that the remainder of my journey will be successful.*
>
> *Traveling, in my mind, is the surest and the highest education. It is the golden experience whose fragrant memory neither time nor adversity can take away. . . .*
>
> *I am leaving for China and Africa next week.*
>
> *Kindly extend my greetings to the people of Harlem.*
>
> *Yours truly,*
>
> *"The Lone Wolf Motorcyclist of New York City."*
>
> *William T. Davis.*[24]

COMPLETES WORLD TOUR ON MOTORCYCLE

WILLIAM T. DAVIS, Harlem boy, who returned home on July 2 after trip around the world on his motorcycle.

Round-the-World Motorcyclist Back In New York After Little More Than Year's Riding, Circling the Globe

Fueled by Red Cap tips, on June 16, 1929, William T. "Lone Wolf" Davis set off from Harlem on an Indian Chief 74 motorcycle to circle the globe, returning from the endurance trip a year later. New York Age, *July 12, 1930.*

The Lone Wolf returned to New York on July 2, 1930. Perhaps wishing to leave neither stone nor cloud unturned, he went on to train as a pilot at the American School of Aviation and flew with race aviators of the Negro Flying School Aviation Club. His acute sense of wonder, underpinned by his mechanical knowledge, gave wings to descriptive travelogs he occasionally wrote for the *Philadelphia Tribune* and other papers.

It would be surprising if Chief Williams felt anything but pride over Davis, who, like his son Wesley, seized opportunities with an abandon that was at once confident and philosophical. The young man's remarkable feat personified the "New Negro" that the race hoped to push to the fore. His broad interests, both mundane and extraordinary, pointed up other leisurely pastimes that blacks pursued just as ardently or apathetically as whites: convivial ukulele playing, competitive tennis and baseball, organized biking, and aviation. And seeing that his roles as teacher and learner were inextricably linked, Davis aimed "to continue his education both on the road and in the confines of educational institutions."[25]

One woman was moved enough by Davis's pluck and resourcefulness to encourage her grandsons to emulate him. But she was wary of backhanded flattery: "Please do not feel that the nickname 'Lindy of the Ground' is an asset to the race," she advised. "Would Lindy feel it an honor to be called 'Davis of the air'?"[26] This caveat, in light of Davis's fall into obscurity, was a sentiment Williams might often have considered, too.

PART IV

CELEBRITY HOUSE

CHAPTER 10

Bandwidths

Red Cap, Red Cap,
Save the tips you get, for if you do,
Then, Red Cap, ol' chap,
Perhaps someday you will be calling, "Red Cap!" too.

—LOUIS ARMSTRONG/BEN HECHT, "RED CAP," 1937[1]

Throughout the 1920s, the social whirl of Harlem coincided with the functional ballet of Grand Central Terminal. Chief Williams was expertly attuned to the rhythms of both. Indeed, his intimate awareness of Harlem's numerous society orchestras perhaps convinced him that his palatial railroad station should have its own. Around February 1929—as a sixty-year-old colossal statue of Commodore Vanderbilt was being relocated to the terminal's south exterior—the Chief actively set out to create a band. As several of his porters played instruments, he readily mustered a group to form the Grand Central Red Cap Orchestra. He put them under the baton of Leslie Davis, a Red Cap captain experienced as an assistant bandleader in France during the Great War. The versatile Harlem-based band soon was in demand for record, radio, dancehall, and concert dates that called for jazz, classical, choral, or a cappella repertoires.

As with his previous athletic ventures, Chief Williams's impulse to organize a band took cues from his social activism. That February and March, Williams, an active NAACP member at least since the war, threw himself into selling fifty dollars' worth of tickets among his men for the organization's annual dance at the Renaissance, this one for its twentieth anniversary celebration. The affair on March 15, 1929, netted over $2,000, and Williams's diligence in making it the association's most successful ever did not go unnoticed by committeewoman Grace Nail Johnson, wife of the NAACP's executive secretary. Two days prior to the event, the Chief found James Weldon Johnson's letter from the national office in his mailbox on Strivers' Row: "Mrs. Johnson has told me how you have followed up the interest which you have shown for so many years in the work of the Association by disposing of twenty-five tickets for the Twentieth Anniversary Dance to be given by our Women's Committee next Friday night."[2]

Johnson's personal thanks were echoed in the press: "Much credit is given Chief Williams of the Grand Central for the fine co-operation given in selling tickets among his men at the station," society writer Bessye Bearden (whose teenage son became the famous artist Romare Bearden) wrote the day after the event.[3] Such commendations and a theatrical setting may soon have crystallized Williams's idea for a band into an actual plan. On the evening of May 12, 1929, he was invited to Lexington Hall, where Broadway producer Lew Leslie was hosting a banquet to celebrate the first anniversary of *Blackbirds of 1928*, the latest in a musical revue series that had been a triumphant vehicle for its late star Florence Mills.

Williams's dinner companion was his thirty-year-old daughter, Gertrude, the marcelled, statuesque flapper who was the face behind a recent Dr. Fred Palmer's ad. One writer's assessment of the evening as "the outstanding social event of the theatrical season" was not altogether hyperbolic, given its attendance and program. The evening's most noted guest was New York's flamboyant mayor James J. Walker. The self-dubbed "Night Mayor" paid his usual good-natured gibes to old friends, then sobered to claim that "for the first time in any public speech, I will make reference to race or color." He assured the honored *Blackbirds* company that their success came as a result of their unselfish service. "People will take what you have to give no matter where it comes from," the mayor averred, calling attention to an episode from the previous Novem-

Chief Jimmy Williams enjoys a jovial exchange outside of Grand Central with the famously wise-cracking Jimmy Walker, mayor of New York City from 1926 until his ouster in 1932. *Schomburg/NYPL.*

ber, the sinking of the ship *SS Vestris*. The ship's black quartermaster, Lionel Licorish, had personally saved some twenty passengers from shark-infested waters off Virginia. His bravery was still making headlines. Mayor Walker lauded the sailor: "When he was rescuing those white people from the water nobody asked him to hold up his hands to find out what color they were," he told the diners. "The cruelty, the unfairness of it all, is that if he were in their position some discrimination might come in somewhere."

Alderman Fred R. Moore, the powerful editor of the *New York Age*, proclaimed it "a fine thing to see Mayor Walker so outspoken against intolerance." The evening's tribute to the current *Blackbirds* cast took a calculated moment to acknowledge the late great Florence Mills, whose untimely death in November 1927 was still felt as a palpable absence in the theater world. The Chief and Gertrude rose in concert with the entire banquet gathering—which included Florence's mother, sister, and Ulysses "Slow Kid" Thompson, Mills's widowed husband and co-star—and stood silently for two long minutes. Then the evening's gaiety revived. Dorothy Fields and Jimmy McHugh, the show's lyricist and composer, raptly beamed as Aida Ward crooned their composition, "I Can't Give You Anything But Love." She was followed by the nimble one-legged dancer "Peg Leg" Bates, the baritone and bandleader Lois Deppe, and the lyricist Andy Razaf, all of whom would soon have a role in the musical scheme the Chief was formulating.[4]

Russell Wooding, the music arranger for *Blackbirds*, drew a good share of the crowd's attention. Wooding had been a principal bandleader in D.C., where he'd given some early professional gigs to another young Washingtonian commanding attention in Harlem's music scene: Duke Ellington. Since moving to New York City in the summer of 1924—to be a manager at the Clarence Williams Publishing House—Wooding had been constantly mentioned in the same breath as other top arrangers on the city's Broadway and dancehall scene like Vodery for Ziegfeld; J. Rosamond Johnson for Hammerstein; Harry Burleigh, the father of concert spiritual arrangements; and William Grant Still for W. C. Handy. The Chief knew Wooding was a talent worth watching.[5]

Several weeks later, on July 3, "Jimmy and His Gang"—as Harlemites affectionately nicknamed the reception personae of the Chief and his station porters—"tossed a yachting party of huge proportions on the Hudson River." The new Grand Central Red Cap Orchestra "played the hottest of dance music" as guests boarded, armed "with lunch baskets and bottles and proceeded to make whoopee in no uncertain terms." The Chief's wife Lucy was aboard, as well as his daughter Gertrude, his son Wesley, and his older brother and sister-in-law Charles and Jennie Williams. Although Wooding was not seen, other show and society folk who had attended Leslie's *Blackbirds* party were there, including the

Ford Dabneys, the Bill "Bojangles" Robinsons, Ulysses Thompson, and Wilhelmina Adams.[6]

In the fall of 1929, the Chief's new enterprise was generating interest and exposure. Booked for October 4, the Red Cap Orchestra appeared on the billing for the Harlem's Renaissance Casino below the bold letters of Vernon Andrade's Orchestra, the house band.[7] The Chief had good reason to feel optimistic about the band's career, and some encouraging possibilities took root soon enough. A tiny, but significant, notice in a Baltimore paper reported that the Red Cap Orchestra "under the direction of Leslie Davis, who plays three trumpets simultaneously," was preparing for a number of recording, broadcasting, and dance tour dates.

Despite the crash of the stock market on October 29, 1929, Chief Williams didn't appear to break his stride. The Red Cap Orchestra enjoyed warm receptions both uptown and down during the bustling Christmas holidays, when they were in great demand. On December

Chief Williams and his Red Cap orchestra forsake the thousand and one duties which fall to their lot in Grand Central Terminal to turn to jazz for relaxation. This organization, which has been banded together by the Chief under the baton of Captain Leslie Davis, after three months rehearsal has gained a city-wide reputation. The musicians have already made their radio debut over station WABC during the Negro Achievement Hour and have appeared before several clubs for dances and concerts. Mr. Davis was an assistant band leader in France during the World War.

By the spring of 1929, Chief Williams was inspired to organize musical porters into the Grand Central Terminal Red Cap Orchestra. New York Central Lines, *Terry Link Collection.*

27, 1929, they furnished music for a "holiday circus" to benefit the Boys' Club of New York City. The event, which NBC Radio broadcast live from Grand Central, featured circus-clown-turned-radio-artist Bob Sherwood portraying the legendary showman P. T. Barnum, with "incarnations" of the "Swedish Nightingale" Jenny Lind, and "'Major Tom Thumb.'"[8] The public appeared to want more from the Red Cap Orchestra, and by late December, the Chief was seizing every opportunity to step up.

A big opportunity came in January 1930: word arrived that Freeman Gosden and Charles Correll would be coming in from Chicago early one morning on the *20th Century Limited.* The two white "blackface comedians" were better known as their famous radio show characters, Amos and Andy. Their celebrity was just the ticket.

Blacks in some quarters winced at *Amos 'n' Andy.* An Arkansas preacher, the Rev. Arthur D. Williams, railed at the radio program's white actors, complaining that "the characters they portray are lazy, shiftless and drifting." The *Pittsburgh Courier* canvassed a million signatures demanding the program's ouster from the airwaves, but the petition came shy of its goal.[9] Even a white writer who disliked *Amos 'n' Andy* confessed he nevertheless found them intriguing "for the same reason that Rudy Vallee is—anyone who attracts so much popularity, regardless of merit, is an important sociological phenomenon, and should be treated as such."[10]

But in fact, *Amos 'n' Andy* had avid black fans in New York. On Dean Street in Brooklyn, "the Amos and Andy Whist Club gave a very successful party." On NBC Radio, Bill Robinson hosted an all-star *Harlem Salute to Amos and Andy on Radio* featuring several fellow Broadway stars and the bandleader Cab Calloway.[11] And the Chief knew fanfare for the radio celebrities would easily lend free publicity to both the Grand Central Red Cap Orchestra and the terminal.

Anticipating their arrival at Grand Central, Chief Williams summoned a few of his Red Cap musicians to welcome

Gosden and Correll—and bring their instruments. Though the men were not due to report for work until three p.m., a handful "gladly complied with the chief's request." As if by chance (though doubtlessly orchestrated), a photographer from the *New York Central Lines Magazine* captured the Red Cap band greeting the two comedians on the platform at the moment of arrival. In the published photo, Chief Williams is flanked by the two stars, who themselves are flanked by the ad hoc fanfare. One writer noted the scene as "a great ad for the Red Cap outfit, who plan a concert shortly in Boston."[12]

Only a few weeks into 1930, Harlemites were eyeing their social calendars for the imminent masquerades, Mardi Gras, and other pre-Lenten affairs that traditionally took place in the early months of each year. "Having always been wows of the first order," one experienced reveler wrote of the free formals, "we are looking forward to another night of nights."[13]

On Friday night, February 14, Valentine's Day, James and Lucy Williams paid $1.50 admission for a St. Valentine's night that promised phenomenal entertainment and free souvenirs. The Rockland Palace (formerly Manhattan Casino) at West 155th Street and Eighth Avenue was holding its 62nd annual Masquerade and Civic Ball, sponsored by the Hamilton Lodge no. 710. It was a costume ball, specifically a drag ball, ensconced in black Gotham's tradition of festive abandon.

As far back as 1887, when Williams was a boy—though too young to attend, he probably heard about it—the Hamilton Lodge's famous masquerade in the Tenderloin had attracted an "assemblage of very queer people," according to the *Herald*, who included a good number of high-costumed and scantily clad whites as well: "The Hamiltons congratulate themselves upon their ability to bring such a jovial and motley crowd together, and as one of them remarked to the reporter, 'the *crème de la crème*, too.'"

At this year's Masquerade and Civic Ball, in Harlem, about seven thousand people filled the hall, to be part of, or to cheer, the spectacle of men decked in gorgeous feminine costumes "which, for their sheer magnificence, would make a Follies beauty envious." Many of them were hard pressed to contain their "muscular bodies in their dainty French evening gowns." Pianist Gladys Bentley, famous for her naughty "double-entendre" songs and her white cutaway tuxedo, was there, and John C. Smith's Modern Dance Orchestra presided over the dance music for this fabulously risqué demimonde. The ball was a serious costume competition, drawing some judges from as far away as Chicago. The spectators were "some of Harlem's most prominent lawyers, physicians, artists, writers and teachers," who included A'Lelia Walker, hostess of the Dark Tower, Harlem's most prestigious social salon; Lucille Randolph, wife of A. Philip Randolph, head of the Brotherhood of Sleeping Car Porters; singer Alberta Hunter; Wilhelmina "Willy" Adams, beauty queen and redoubtable civic leader; Wallace Thurman, novelist and literary gadfly; Nora Holt, composer and music critic; Edward G. Perry, acclaimed party planner (called "Harlem's male Elsa Maxwell"); and the "Chief Williamses."[14]

There was also collective anticipation for Williams's next "Jimmy and His Gang" soirée. The Williamses hosted their own ball just a few days after Hamilton Lodge's. On Wednesday evening, February 19, bandleader Sam Patterson (who formerly headed the Ziegfeld Roof Garden Orchestra atop the New Amsterdam Theater at Times Square) was now in Harlem, poised for his Syncopated Orchestra to heat up the Renaissance Casino. The "Renny," Harlem's most effervescent reception hall, on the southeast corner of West 138th Street at Seventh Avenue, was just down the block from Chief Williams's home. Williams okayed Patterson to strike up the band, and the doors opened.

The guests poured into the banquet hosted by "umpteen swell fellows, who have thoroughly mastered the art of tossing a party": Jimmy and His Gang. The hosts handed their guests little bronze elephants and dogs as party favors. Their prearranged boxes and loges throughout the hall were already laid out with "an inexhaustible supply of viands and liquids." Lucy Williams and Gertrude were stately in complementary ballgowns of emerald green and white satin, respectively. Irene Jordan, wife of ragtime composer Joe Jordan, shimmered in a dress of canary satin. Martha Dabney, wife of composer Ford Dabney, was "stunning in coffee colored lace." Dr. Gertrude Curtis, New York's first African-American dentist, wore an "important silver and blue sequin gown." From her apartment just across the street, the sensational blues singer and composer Alberta Hunter cut a figure in red velvet, and Lottie Tyler (Hunter's longtime companion, niece of the late star Bert Williams) wore a gown of white hand-painted satin.

The Chief signaled an intermission in the festivities and introduced his Gang to the guests, as cheers flooded the Renaissance's ornate hall. Then he pulled out a telegram from someone who was unable to attend but "nevertheless, wanted some part in the great celebration of Jimmy and His Gang." It was from Gosden and Correll, the radio stars Amos and Andy. The Chief's party was a hit. "We came early, we danced late and even then we complained," one guest said, "because eventually they had to put us out to air the casino for a Thursday night dance."[15]

Summer brought a new occasion for the Chief to prove himself a winsome host. His was one of two back-to-back events on the same day, setting many of Harlem's fashionable set abuzz. The first was an afternoon tea party at the home of the celebrated heiress A'Lelia Walker, the renowned Joy Goddess of Harlem (as the poet Langston Hughes dubbed her). Walker wound up her tea party early, perhaps because she herself did not want to miss the second lavish event, an annual moonlight sail up the Hudson River. "There are sails and sails," one observer wrote, "but you have never been on a sail until you are the guest of Jimmy and His Gang."

On that evening, at the foot of West 132nd Street, the natty Chief and his men lined the gangplank to welcome illustrious guests aboard the *Myles Standish.* Dr. "Hap" Delany (brother of the centenarian Delany Sisters, and uncle of award-winning writer Samuel R. Delany, Jr.) was on board. So were the jazz singers and entertainers Adelaide Hall and Alberta Hunter; Hunter, along with cabaret performer Jimmie Daniels and schoolteacher Harold Jackman ("the handsomest man in Harlem"), would become iconic gay figures of the Harlem Renaissance. The Chief's dear friend Jesse Battle was on hand. And of course A'Lelia Walker, Harlem's premier hostess, bringing several guests in tow from her weekly "at home" tea.[16] Having their pleasure entrusted to his hands, Chief "Jimmy" deployed two orchestras aboard the vessel.

◈

Williams took "great interest and pride" in the Red Cap Orchestra and was confident in the men's professional potential. Their demonstrable talent that summer may have made him more eager than ever to approach Russell Wooding, whose name as an arranger and composer was gaining traction in New York. Though cornetist Leslie Davis had been the band's very qualified organizer, he was also a working Red Cap, which cramped the band's ability to flourish. They needed a dedicated musical director. Unlike Davis, Wooding was a free agent, and better connected. The Chief wanted Wooding to sharpen up his musical porters into a truly reputable orchestra.

By 1930, the Chief was making a wise choice in Wooding, who was much in demand.[17] For *Blackbirds of 1928*, his adept choral handling of W. C. Handy's "St. Louis Blues" prompted Handy himself to state that Wooding "created a demand for choral arrangements."[18] For the revue of *Hot Chocolates* (1929), Wooding had winningly orchestrated Fats Waller and Andy Razaf's classic song "Ain't Misbehavin'"; the trumpet deity Louis Armstrong made his Broadway debut in that show, performing in the ensemble.

Sometime in early November 1930, Williams and Wooding powwowed about prospects for the Red Cap Orchestra. Ultimately, the porters must have convinced Wooding they had the chops, for he granted the Chief's wish that he take charge of the band. By mid-November, word of their new affiliation was out and about.

On November 23 a Big Midnight Benefit was to be held, to kick off the Harlem Cooperating Committee on Relief and Unemployment, an ambitious early Depression-era initiative. The benefit would be held at the Lafayette Theatre, Harlem's most famous entertainment stage; the theater's general manager, Frank Schiffman, donated the house. The benefit show was being adapted from Lew Leslie's current Broadway hit, *Blackbirds of 1928*, but Marty Forkins's hit, *Brown Buddies*, would also bring its stars Bill Robinson, Adelaide Hall, and Ada Brown uptown to treat Harlem locals. The collaboration of big producers Leslie and Forkins, and their stellar performers, promised "to make sure that the night will be even bigger than originally planned."[19]

The announcement also noted that the evening's added attraction would be the first-time appearance "of that much spoken of array of musicians known as the Grand Central Red Caps Concert Orchestra, an organization which had the support of Chief Williams from the start." And the Chief and the maestro both must have been thrilled to read that it was "under the personal leadership of the popular and well known Russell Wooding."[20]

The Grand Central Red Cap Orchestra opened the second half of the evening's bill, which was constellated with such outstanding stars as Ethel Waters, Flournoy Miller, Aubrey Lyles, and Eubie Blake, as well as actors Richard B. Harrison and Leigh Whipper. For Chief Williams, Wooding, and the Red Cap Orchestra, the Lafayette Theatre benefit show appearance was most auspicious.

> Opening the second part [of the concert] the Grand Central Red Cap Orchestra under the leadership of Russell Wooding made their bow. Lovers of good music who failed to be at the Lafayette when these gentlemen offered their numbers missed a treat, and it is with a great deal of satisfaction and pleasure to be able to extend congratulations to Mr. Wooding, one of the finest men on and off the stage it has ever been the good fortune of this writer to meet. A splendid array of men he has to lead, and the orchestra should be heard on some specially arranged occasion right here in Harlem.[21]

Meanwhile at Grand Central itself, passengers entering the main concourse—to buy a ticket, to catch a train, or to adjust a watch against the opal-faced clock—suddenly might hear strains of "Swing Low, Sweet Chariot," or some other familiar Americana. The source was often Chief Williams's "office," the balcony above Track 30. Music columnist Cora Gary Illidge, who was a black graduate of the New York Institute of Music and Art (a forerunner of the Juilliard School), offered mystified travelers two explanations: if the music was from an orchestra, "some thirty earnest Red Caps"—organized by Leslie Davis and directed by Russell Wooding—"may have been rehearsing for an appearance that afternoon at a tea dance, or at a formal banquet the next evening, or perhaps at a fraternity dance at a nearby hotel." However, if they heard a quartet, the music was from "four men who do double duty—sing and play in the orchestra."[22]

The Chief, who did not play an instrument, was the founder and president of both the Grand Central Red Cap Orchestra and the a cappella Grand Central Red Cap Quartet. His drive behind the orchestra's gaining popular momentum was more apparent, and notwithstanding Wooding's role as maestro, many often referred to the group as Chief Williams's Red Cap Orchestra—especially in its smaller, band-size aggregation.

If the Chief could trace their route by train, then generally nowhere was too far out of town to deploy his musical men. On December 29, 1930, they performed upstate, at a dance "to purchase fire fighting equipment for the new truck" that the Hillside Protective Association had bought from funds "raised at a clambake early in the fall." Though the orchestra went only as a nine-piece band, one of them, who is unknown, "proved to be a singer and a tap dancer" whose skill halted the dancing couples and drew them around the stage.[23]

The Chief also did well in establishing a corollary vocal group. The Red Cap Quartet comprised Eric Adams, William Robinson, Coyal McMahan (a later Broadway musical performer and recording artist), and Percy Robinson (who was also a reputable drummer and the brother of the Chief's friend, dance lion Bill Robinson). The men executed a four-part close-harmony repertoire, both gospel and secular, in an African-American tradition, the a cappella style that had become popularly known as "barbershop quartet" singing. They frequently performed on the radio and at private concerts, and, as Illidge alluded, they might reach unwitting audiences from the tunnels or mezzanines of Grand Central. Indeed, the quartet's success reflected the influence of Chief Williams's singular musical hire, Robert H. Cloud, a composer-arranger, saxophonist, and pianist who trained and managed the singers.

Chief Williams met Robert Cloud at about the same time as he met Russell Wooding, or possibly a few months earlier: some discographies have Cloud recording in New York City as early as February 1929.[24] It isn't known if he became a Red Cap at Grand Central around that time—or was perhaps in the earliest formation of the Chief's new orchestra. As with Wooding, the Chief met Cloud in Harlem. But while Cloud's professional reputation preceded him as an orchestra leader, the jazzman was an enigmatic figure.

Cloud hailed from Fort Wayne, Indiana, where as early as 1922 he advertised his services as a music arranger in *Billboard*. "Broadway" Jackson later reported the musician's offer "to join the staff of the Clarence Williams publishing house" in New York—an offer possibly brokered by Wooding.[25] In 1927 Cloud was in Florida, performing variously as composer, arranger, pianist, and saxophonist, with a black Jacksonville jazz band called the Ross De Luxe Syncopators. Victor recorded two of Cloud's original dance numbers, the "sizzling" foxtrots, as *Variety* praised the songs, "Mary Belle" and "Lady Mine"—"played as only native Ethiops can play 'em."[26] New York was clearly next on Cloud's horizon.

If the Chief did not meet Cloud in early 1929, he was likely aware of him by summer. On August 25 a big dance event at the Renaissance Casino featured Cloud's fifteen-piece Orquestra Casi Latina—including "ten Latin-American musicians"—an eruption of Cuban-flavored rhythms.[27] If the Chief saw Cloud in action here, he understandably wanted to work with him—but he may already have set his sights on Wooding, whose social circles strongly overlapped with Williams's own.

At any rate, over the next year, both of Chief Williams's musical directors would noticeably enhance the traveling public's experience in the terminal. And maybe that of the Red Cap porters themselves at Grand Central, Penn Station and stations elsewhere across the country. "These men, who are now Red Caps, deserve unstinted praise for remaining musicians," posited Illidge. "The canned music of the present day sound pictures has thrown scores of them out of employment, so these men have had to seek other means of livelihood."[28] Indeed, the men in the Chief's Red Cap musical associations were finding Grand Central's acoustic tunnels to be ready gateways toward achieving material advancement.

The year 1931 opened jubilantly for the orchestra Chief Williams had put in Russell Wooding's capable hands. On January 3, a theater column in the *New York Age* commended Wooding for organizing "a jazz band from amongst the hundreds of colored musicians" who worked at Grand Central. Wooding had ramped up the Chief's

Leonard Harper, Harlem's master spirit of rhythm-pulsed nightclub revues, staged the *Red Cap Follies* at the Lafayette Theatre. *Robert Langmuir African American Photograph Collection, Emory University, Manuscript, Archives, and Rare Book Library.*

musical porters into a top-flight forty-piece outfit, "as fine a band as one would want to hear," the columnist wrote. They would now "render all of the music for next week's show at the Lafayette Theatre, which will be called *Red Cap Follies*."[29]

More impressively, the weeklong *Red Cap Follies* would be staged by Leonard Harper, the master spirit of Harlem's rhythm-chocked nightclub revues. At least two stars of Lew Leslie's *Blackbirds* would appear in the show: the lovely soprano Aida Ward, also of Connie's Inn and Cotton Club fame, and "Peg Leg" Bates, "the marvelous one-legged dancer." A Harlem newcomer would also appear: young movie actress Mildred Washington, who was gaining stage fame as a "colored Oriental dancer," a popular category of pseudo-Eastern exotic movement and bare midriff. Another projected cast member was Lois Deppe, from Vincent Youmans's show *Great Day!*, whose

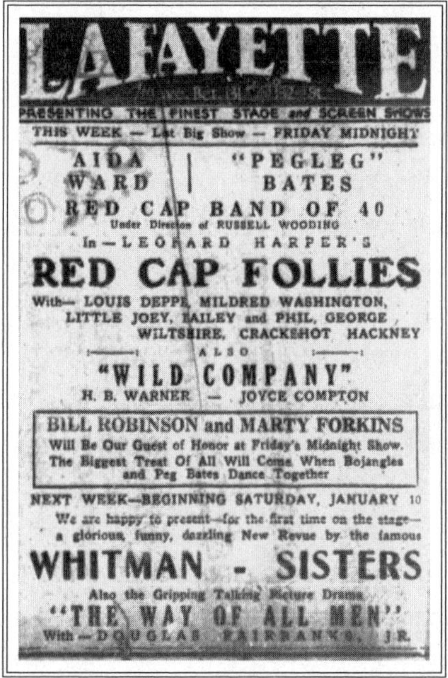

In January 1931, Leonard Harper's weeklong *Red Cap Follies* at the Lafayette Theatre featured Grand Central's forty-man band under Russell Wooding, Broadway jazz soprano Aida Ward, and neophyte tap dance legend Peg Leg Bates. *New York Age, January 10, 1931.*

character introduced the show's title song and another, "Without a Song," which would both become American standards. The Lafayette paired the live performance of *Red Cap Follies* with showings of the 1930 movie *Wild Company*, starring H. B. Warner and Joyce Compton, a combination aimed to guarantee full houses.[30]

February 17 was the eve of Lent, and as befit Mardi Gras, Chief Williams performed "with colors flying and trumpets in full blast." Jimmy and His Gang again took over the Renaissance Casino. Unlike last year's trinketry of bronze party favors, this time the Gang treated guests to "the new, long, slender fountain pens and stands right from Paris." Vernon Andrade stirred the Renny's house orchestra, but he gave the stage in alternate turns to the Grand Central Red Cap Orchestra, still charged up from wowing audiences at the Lafayette's Big Midnight Benefit and the *Red Cap Follies*. Here at the Renny, the Red Caps wore black tuxedos—as was their wont when performing away from the terminal—as did the male guests. The women supplied the color—from peach crepe to colored chiffons, taffetas, velvets, lace, and jewels. At the intermission, the Gang's grand march stoked deafening cheers from the guests as Chief Williams appeared "at the psychological moment . . . borne on the shoulders of his loyal and devoted men."[31]

That same week the Red Caps band was on the agenda of an NAACP committee meeting. On February 24, the acting secretary Walter White sat with members Mary White Ovington; literary critic and civil rights activist Joel Elias Spingarn; and Philadelphia NAACP branch president Isadore Martin. Their first matter to discuss was the Grand Central Red Cap Orchestra.

White informed the committee that conductor Russell Wooding proposed "to have the orchestra play for dances under the auspices of the Branches of the Association, for the two-fold purpose of helping to raise money for the Association and to help build a reputation for the orchestra." The orchestra, being made up wholly of Red Caps, could travel the states by railway free of charge. Moreover, Col. Miles Bronson, the Grand Central Terminal manager, appeared to be interested in the orchestra's success. To gain the

NAACP's approval, Wooding arranged for the committee to attend a special audition in the terminal, on Sunday afternoon, March 1, at three-thirty.[32]

The next day White briefed W.E.B. Du Bois, then the NAACP communications director, about Wooding's invitation and half-hour audition appointment. "We would be very happy to have you and Mrs. Du Bois come and pass judgment upon the orchestra," White wrote.[33] The NAACP was sympathetic to the proposal and agreed to send its representatives to hear the band. The prospect of Du Bois tapping his feet to the Red Caps might have reasonably excited Chief Williams, though he was ultimately disappointed. "Dr. Du Bois will be unable to hear the Grand Central Red Cap Orchestra Sunday, as he will be out of town," Du Bois's secretary Daisy Wilson wrote to White on February 27. As an alternative, she sent White's letter "to Mrs. Du Bois, who may be able to attend."[34]

It's unclear if Nina Du Bois attended the audition on March 1, but apparently Walter White did, as the following day he wrote excitedly to Miguel Covarrubias, a Mexican artist who was well known in Harlem. White wanted his friend to hear "solo numbers by [the] Grand Central Red Caps Orchestra, which plays the 'St. Louis Blues' as you have never heard it played before," and invited him to the NAACP's spring dance on March 16, at the Savoy Ballroom.[35] The upcoming gala, organized annually by the Women's Auxiliary Committee, was the NAACP's major fund-raiser. The event would now serve as White's formal launch of Wooding and the Grand Central Red Cap Orchestra's impending fund-raising tour for the NAACP—which was counting on them to play two solo numbers on the important evening.

Williams knew the significance of his band appearing at this high-profile showcase. For the event, White went over the program details with lawyer Eunice Hunton Carter, the chair of the advisory board (who would soon gain notoriety for bringing down mob boss Lucky Luciano). He reiterated that the orchestra would perform two solo numbers—which were "not for dancing." He asked Carter to convey the information to Bill Robinson, the slated master of ceremonies.[36]

On March 16, liveried ushers fanned open car doors to admit the elegant guests, black and white, to the Savoy. The lively inpouring of reservations had forced the event's ticket handler to draw up a new table chart to accommodate more celebrity subscribers. Carl Van Vechten was arguably Harlem's most recognizable white habitué, but most of the evening's smiles were aimed at James Weldon Johnson, who was stepping down from fourteen years as the NAACP's secretary in order to teach literature at Fisk University in Nashville.[37]

Noël Coward attended, fresh from the Times Square Theater on Broadway, where he was starring in his own play, *Private Lives.* At the Savoy, he found himself "being introduced to the town's sepia society by the brilliant Eslanda Goode Robeson"—the wife of Paul Robeson—"and the adorable A'Lelia Walker." Among the other notables present were the author and poet Dorothy Parker; the journalist Heywood Broun; the prolific Harlem society columnist Bessye Bearden; the novelist Dorothy West; the philanthropist Julius Rosenwald; the novelist Blair Niles (whose *Strange Brother*, a gay-themed tale set in the Harlem Renaissance, appeared that year); and the ubiquitous Alberta Hunter.[38]

Both of the Savoy's own orchestras furnished the evening's dance music, while Cab Calloway's Cotton Club Orchestra headlined the entertainment. The gala also featured a midnight dancing exhibition by the national champions of the Lindy Hoppers contest, a group that was in great demand at the city's leading night clubs.[39] Promptly at twelve-thirty, the Savoy's hall dimmed and hushed as if for a concert. The Grand Central Red Cap Orchestra was ushered into the Savoy, flanked by Russell Wooding and Walter White, and masterfully executed "Body and Soul" and the "The St. Louis Blues."

In fact, the orchestra played several variations of "The St. Louis Blues."[40] Mr. Handy himself might have been all smiles. A Baltimore paper praised the renditions of "some grand solo music of popular songs"[41] played by the Grand Central Red Cap Orchestra.

The event's success was no doubt timely as well for Wooding, whose mother-in-law died a week later.[42]

There's no doubt Chief Williams was jubilantly aware that this accolade enhanced the Red Caps' image. The orchestra's disciplined artistry under Wooding's leadership, and its contribution to the NAACP dance, earned his attendants, as a whole, great cachet, which may well have impressed Colonel Bronson and other terminal officials.

In April the New York Central permitted the Harlem Cooperating Committee on Relief and Unemployment to open a booth in the terminal to sell tickets for an upcoming charity costume ball. The emergency relief group had grown rapidly since November, when the Red Cap band had played for its kick-off benefit at the Lafayette Theatre. The ball was to take place on May 1 at Harlem's 369th Regiment Armory—the base of the Harlem Hellfighters, many of them former Red Caps who had distinguished themselves in World War I—and prizes would be awarded "for the most original, most beautiful, most grotesque costumes." However, the opening of the ticket booth itself on April 17, two weeks before the ball, generated much fanfare. Chief Williams's old friend Wilhelmina Adams, the ball committee chair, was to run the prominent booth. While it isn't known if he played a role in arranging it, the site procurement was considered a unique privilege that was said to be "usually reserved solely for the use of Red Cross and American Legion representatives." The booth's opening would feature several theatrical stars and "a parade of Red Caps and music by the Red Caps orchestra."[43]

On May 13, Russell Wooding and the Grand Central Red Cap Orchestra traveled out to the RCA Victor Recording Studio in Camden, New Jersey. They recorded four songs, several of them behind white artists. Frank Luther, a popular country music and dance-band singer, sang "I Can't Get Enough of You," an original, upbeat foxtrot with words by Joe Goodwin and music by Larry Shay. The band also backed Dick Robertson, who sang "That's My Desire"—its first of many recordings—with words by Carroll Loveday and music by Irving Berlin's principal transcriber, Helmy Kresa. "Niagara Falls," with words and music by Walter Brown, was sung by Willie Jackson, who also sang "Nina," with words by Andy Razaf and music by Wooding and Edgar Dowell. This last title (pronounced to rhyme with *Dinah*), might well have been a tribute to the actress Nina Mae McKinney, a rising "race" movie star and sex symbol, or to Nina Du Bois, who possibly approved the Red Cap Orchestra's appearance at the NAACP gala.[44]

Five days after the Victor recording session, the *Philadelphia Tribune* featured a photo of Russell Wooding standing magisterially in front of the Red Cap Orchestra, whose assembly loomed around him three tiers high. The caption said the band was heading "on a countrywide tour, under the auspices of the NAACP."[45] In mid-June, the *Pittsburgh Courier* commended the New York Central Lines for hiring Wooding, "undoubtedly one of the outstanding musicians of the race," and for "giving these men a chance to earn some additional money during the present time." It noted the release of the orchestra's first record on July 3.[46]

Williams basked in the artistic cachet that Wooding brought to the orchestra. These musical porters were now bona-fide Victor recording artists, and their success was recognized even inside the terminal. On the east balcony, a transportation exhibit displayed a replica of their first recording, mounted against an ornate wrought-iron frame on a floor stand. Upon it the words GRAND CENTRAL RED CAPS DIRECTED BY RUSSELL WOODING were emblazoned around the iconic Victor logo. Below were the titles of two foxtrots, "I Can't Get Enough of You" and "That's My Desire."[47]

But two weeks after the Red Cap Orchestra's record came out, Russell Wooding left the band. Perhaps he and Williams had previously agreed on only a short collaboration. Wooding was probably compensated on contract—either by a terminal authority, or by Chief Williams, or by the musicians collectively—or perhaps he saw it as worthwhile to work pro bono. Wooding had given the band exposure around town and beyond to New Haven and Boston. "He also took the aggregation to the Lafayette Theatre and furnished the complete show for the usual week's run," Percival Outram wrote in his regular musicians' union column. "This, I believe, was the premiere achievement of Mr. Wooding."[48]

Indeed, the achievement was mutually beneficial for Wooding, the band, and the Chief. For Wooding, the affiliation had bolstered his standing as a proficient orchestrator: he was soon being sought out for Broadway productions with renowned song stylist Ethel Waters, composer Irving Berlin, and director Vincente Minnelli. For the Red Caps, it gave them stronger candidacy as a top-flight band, which would afford many of them greater autonomy as individual artists. For Chief Williams, building up the reputation of the orchestra elevated the estimation of his Red Caps corps in general. His association with Wooding, the Red Cap Orchestra, and the NAACP combined to affirm his own position as a cultural arbiter both in Harlem and at Grand Central.

The orchestra continued to perform after Wooding's departure, but it's not clear who took up the baton. Nor do we know why the Chief did not hand it to the able Cloud. Concurrent with Wooding's leadership of the orchestra, Cloud's impressive artistry had been transforming the Red Cap Quartet into Sunday radio regulars on WMCA, WPCH, and other national broadcasts. Later Cloud's quartet expanded to a score of men, as the Red Cap Choir, to appear on Phillips Lord's weekly show, *We, the People.*[49] They also performed at schools and at church and secular socials. Indeed, their overheard rehearsals at work were transforming a grand transit hub into a holiday destination: in December 1930, New Yorkers filled the Grand Central concourse "to hear the chorus of Red Caps sing their annual carols from the balcony of the mighty depot," popular syndicated columnist Alice Hughes wistfully noted, adding, "and a rich experience it is."[50] The singers drew crowds every December for years. Although the Chief's reasons for not putting Cloud at the helm of the Red Cap Orchestra are unknown, Wooding's departure in the summer of 1931 may have prompted Cloud to get back in a recording studio.

On August 14, 1931, the Red Cap Quartet with Cloud recorded four tracks at Columbia Studio, most notably Cloud's own "They Kicked the Devil Out of Heaven," and his "My Little Dixie Home," co-written with black theatrical manager Harrison G. Smith ("the man who owns Broadway," whose influence had boosted the careers of Josephine Baker, Duke Ellington, and child star Sunshine Sammy).[51]

On August 17, three days after the quartet's recording session, Cloud called on Walter White to propose that the NAACP sponsor a tour for the quartet, as the association had done for the orchestra under Wooding. Whatever transpired during their meeting, it apparently inspired Cloud to write a letter to White reiterating his impatient hopes. He enclosed a reference letter attesting to his musical activities before he became a Red Cap porter—or as he archly put it, "before I became associated with the Red Cap Personnel here at Grand Central Terminal"—his effusive lines bursting into caprices of uppercase type:

> *Mr. White:*
>
> *. . . Am sending the printed letter head herein that you may see what my activities consisted of before. . . . THE ONLY REASON I BECAME A RED CAP was my firm belief that I could do more along the lines I have tried to explain to you by being one of them. . . . It is my hope, though, that I can thoroughly impress upon you the fact that, WITH THE THINGS I AM DOING AND INTEND TO DO WITH THESE FOUR, I CAN INSPIRE AND HELP MANY MORE.*

Returning to plans for the quartet's "experimental trip," Cloud reminded White that he had connections in Boston and was eager to make more in New Haven, Hartford, Springfield, and Providence. "Any assistance that you can give me in this matter will be very gratefully received," Cloud wrote. He asked White for an audition, as Wooding had done earlier that year. But White's response is unknown.[52]

Cloud's artistic temperament may have prevented him from realizing it, but people indeed loved his songs and arrangements. His musical talents were unassailable. In the mid-1930s, praise was lavished on his artistry: "a New York Negro, who is a lyric composer of talent, with more than a score of songs to his credit, for which he has written both words and music. His regular job, however, is that of 'red cap' at the Grand Central Station," making him an "odd case of versatility."[53] Gossip commentator Walter Winchell observed "that Robert Cloud, a sepia red cap at the Grand Central Station . . . has written words and tunes to 30 ditties."[54] Cloud was known to withdraw if he sensed condescension toward his Red Cap vocation. "I write songs, good songs," he once insisted to a snooty reporter. "There is heart and feeling in them and someday people are going to like them."[55]

But even if Cloud didn't readily feel it, Chief Williams surely noticed how much the catchy beat of his musical notion was spreading infectiously beyond Grand Central. "It was bound to happen," the *Age*'s music reviewer wrote in 1931. "Not to be out-done by the Grand Central Red Caps, the Pennsylvania Red Caps have organized an orchestra."[56]

◈

In the spring of 1932, the Chief's orchestra performed at the fifteenth reunion of the Princeton University class of 1917—the "War Babies," as they dubbed themselves. F. Scott Fitzgerald would have been a member had he not delayed getting his diploma to join the military. Fitzgerald's school friend Ludlow "Lud" Fowler (who inspired the 1926 short story "The Rich Boy") presided over the reunion dinner, followed by top-drawer musical entertainment, "not the third-rate vaudeville variety . . . but a Grade A show." Fowler introduced the Grand Central Red Cap Orchestra, "the jazziest aggregation of wind and brass acrobats this side of Nome."[57]

And downtown in Little Italy, the Red Cap Orchestra performed regularly at the annual Feast of San Gennaro. Amid the neighborhood's colorful-bunting-clad tenement fire escapes and displays of sacred effigies, the black musicians from Grand Central held sway on a makeshift bandstand. They "blare[d] the familiar notes of a tuneful Italian opera," a 1932 New York guidebook noted, enlightening the sightseer that "for some reason, the darky porters and redcaps have a monopoly on fiesta music."[58] Notwithstanding the racial slur, it's fair to speculate that the band's appearances were influenced by Wesley, who had a considerable foothold in Little Italy. Another writer hailed their sets as "plenty Harlem at times!"[59]

But while such gigs gave the musicians some extra income, they didn't preclude their regular duties at the station. Passing through Grand Central early one morning, writer James Aswell was puzzled to come upon a group of Red Caps moving instrument cases around. A newsstand attendant explained that they were musicians and had been playing all night at an Italian event on Mulberry Street: "Now they are going to put their instruments away and work here all day."[60]

◈

Of course, musical diversions coincided with the Red Caps' interest in sports. As segregation was the norm in baseball, basketball, football, and other organized athletics, tennis was no different. In 1916 some black tennis players, rebuffed by the whites-only policy of the U.S. Lawn Tennis Association (USLTA), formed the American Tennis Association (ATA). In 1929 the white organization barred two young black players from its National Junior Indoor Tennis Tournament. The players, Reginald Weir and Gerald L. Norman, Jr.—of the City College and Flushing High School teams, respectively—had already paid their entrance fees before the USLTA head explicitly stated that it did not permit colored players in national tennis tournaments.

The NAACP protested. On Christmas Eve, associate secretary Robert W. Bagnall wrote to Edward Moss of the USLTA: "The irony of the present situation will become more pointed when it is known that Mr. Norman [Sr.] is himself tennis coach at the Bryant High School [in Long Island City] and that some of the white boys he has coached have been admitted and will play in the tournament." Bagnall said he would give copies of this letter to the press "in order that the question of the color and race bar in a sport supposed to draw from the best . . . may be made a matter of open and public discussion."[61]

Moss dug in his heels:

> *December 26, 1929*
>
> *Dear Sir:*
>
> *Answering your letter of December 24, the policy of the United States Lawn Tennis Association has been to decline the entry of colored players in our Championships.*
>
> *In pursuing this policy we make no reflection upon the colored race, but we believe that as a practical matter, the present method of separate Associations for the administration of the affairs and Championships of colored and white players should be continued.*
>
> *Yours sincerely,*
>
> *E. B. Moss*
>
> *Executive Secretary*[62]

The ATA president at the time was Dr. D. Ivison Hoage, who could not avoid seeing the "reflection upon the colored race" in this contentious volleying. Hoage was also the ATA's tournament organizer. Esteemed as an "implacable, hard-boiled, just" referee, he was the venerable arbiter of state opens and nationals since time immemorial—admired as "frequently amusing, occasionally alarming, always incisive."[63]

The ATA would hold its national championship tournament during the week of August 17–22, 1931, on the clay courts of the Tuskegee Institute in Alabama—its first tournament in the Deep South. One of the most highly anticipated events was the intercollegiate championship match between Norman Jr. (the New Yorkers' favorite), now studying at Howard University, and Tuskegee's Nathaniel

Jackson. Norman was the current champion of the Colored Intercollegiate Athletic Association (CIAA, founded in 1912), and Jackson of the Southern Intercollegiate Athletic Association (SIAA, founded in 1913).[64] Dr. Hoage wanted to offer a prize that exalted their tennis prowess as well as their academic ambition.

And that was when he looked up Williams. Hoage and Williams were old friends for twenty-five years—they had been neighbors back on West 134th Street and now on Strivers' Row. In the first week of August 1930, Chief Williams called together a few of his Red Cap captains to think of a possible prize. They pitched in $800 to buy a sterling silver "loving cup" that stood about two feet tall, perched on a curved wooden base. Known as the Williams Cup, it would become the highest in value and stature of all the ATA trophies. The very name of the prize for the intercollegiate champion reflected the unconventional range of Chief Williams's influence. The winner's college would hold the trophy for the ensuing year.

Arthur E. Francis, president of the New York Tennis Association, wrote in his sports column: "This cup was bestowed as a permanent symbol to the growth and development of tennis as a competitive sport among our group in the colleges, and through Chief James Williams and his fellow porters of the Grand Central Station in New York, the cup was bought and presented through Dr. Hoage to the American Tennis Association."[65]

Francis emphasized the importance of the August 1931 intercollegiate championship match. It revealed black colleges as the setting for advancing young black talent in the American tennis world. Tuskegee's nineteen-year-old Nathaniel Jackson pointed up an increasing trend of college youngsters to assume the forefront of Negro tennis. For such young talent, Francis wrote, the Williams Cup was "favorable with any trophy of the white race for that event."[66]

A busload of New York tennis celebrities, including Francis and Hoage (who carried the Williams Cup), departed on August 13 for Tuskegee. Williams didn't join them, as the Red Cap Orchestra had played for a moonlight sail up the Hudson River the night before.

Two summers later, at the Hampton Institute in Virginia, athletic

In 1937, Tuskegee University president Dr. Frederick Douglass Patterson presented student champion Ernest McCampbell with the esteemed Williams Cup trophy, the American Tennis Association's top prize for three decades from the Grand Central Red Caps. *Tuskegee University Archives.*

director Charles H. Williams spoke effusively about how the Williams Cup had inspirited the ATA's mission to promote the formation of tennis clubs in historically black colleges nationwide. "James Williams of New York City was instrumental in getting the employees of the New York Central Railroad to give the trophy," he said.[67] For nearly three more decades the Williams Cup remained a symbol of wholesome tennis competition, while advancing the game's popularity in middle-class black recreational and social life. Duly inspired, the Chief's younger daughter Kay had a tennis pass for the city parks in the 1940s, and she may have met her husband Hal on the courts.

As with tennis, the bridge world of card players was racially segregated. Black bridge enthusiasts across the country had been enjoying the recreation just as long as their tennis-loving friends and were often one and the same. Chief Williams himself led the "crack contract bridge team of the Terminal,"[68] and Florence Battle hosted at least one "ladies-only" bridge party on Strivers' Row (that the Chief, Jesse, and other husbands playfully "crashed" with food). It was perhaps inevitable that the ATA would be instrumental in fostering a black bridge league.

In 1932, world-renowned bridge guru Ely Culbertson observed that "the tremendous popularity of bridge is due almost entirely to American and English women."[69] He extended an uncommon invitation to the Mu-So-Lit Club, a black social association in Washington, D.C., to take part in a countrywide American Bridge Olympic tournament that October. The card maven was no doubt aware that numerous black players across the country had qualified as certified teachers of his own rigorous Culbertson contract bridge system. That same year a white woman in Lynchburg, Virginia, complained indignantly upon discovering he had recommended a local black woman as her instructor. Culbertson, a Russian Jewish immigrant, reportedly replied: "Dear Madam, Contract Bridge knows no color line."[70]

Culbertson's view proved to be more idealistic than popular: black bridge players instinctively formed their own national league. In August 1933 the American Bridge Association (ABA) held its first national championships to coincide with the ATA's national tennis championships in Hampton, Virginia. The venue was the Bay Shore Hotel ballroom at Buckroe Beach, a tidewater neighborhood on Chesapeake Bay. The elaborate preparations included an awards ceremony: one top honor was Culbertson's silver *Bridge World* trophy, named for the magazine he had founded, offered as an incentive to winners in the contract bridge division.[71]

The Chief's friends Jesse and Florence Battle played in that first

ABA "nationals." Following the example of his Williams Cup for tennis, they sponsored the silver Battle Trophy, "the gift of Lieutenant and Mrs. Samuel J. Battle," to go to the auction bridge winners.[72] The ABA also held elections at that same session, at which Jesse Battle was voted a league officer.[73]

Despite his interest in both activities, personal events unfortunately made the court and card tournaments untimely for Chief Williams to attend.

CHAPTER 11

Moving to the Dunbar

One of the worst tragedies imaginable is an individual trained to do a specific thing and not in a position to do it.

—GEORGE S. SCHUYLER[1]

Despite the economic depression, Chief Williams still had his Harlem townhouse on West 138th Street. The U.S. Census taken in the spring of 1930 recorded its value as $30,000, higher than almost any other on Strivers' Row. However, the deepening financial crisis induced him to sell, and sometime the next year he moved into a fairly new complex on Seventh Avenue and 149th Street popularly called the Dunbar, and later colloquially, "Celebrity House."

The financier and philanthropist John D. Rockefeller, Jr., son of the Standard Oil co-founder, built the Paul Laurence Dunbar Apartments in 1927 as a quality residence for Negroes. The relatively unknown architect, Andrew J. Thomas, was keenly interested in using charitable and state funds for projects that would eradicate city slums. News of Rockefeller's purchase of the Harlem ground for Negro cooperative housing attracted other philanthropic interests. "This is one of the most needed operations that I know of in the City," Walter Stabler, comptroller for the Metropolitan Life Insurance company, wrote enthusiastically to Rockefeller, expressing the hope that the complex might obtain tax exemption toward offering a savings to tenants. "The colored people do not have a fair chance in this, as in many other ways. I know that congestion is very serious there and that they are living under conditions which are not sanitary or moral."[2] The walk-up cooperative complex was the first large-scale residential project of its kind in Manhattan and filled a full, irregularly oblong city block bounded by West 149th and West 150th streets, Seventh and Eighth avenues, and Macombs Place.

What to call Rockefeller's utopian housing project aroused widespread interest. Such an unprecedented venture called for a distinctive name. Several individuals and institutions suggested names of distinguished blacks for the project. John D. Rockefeller thought the Abraham Lincoln Garden Apartments would be fitting, and specified distinct names for individual buildings: the Eighth Avenue building he called the Booker T. Washington; the Seventh Avenue building, the Frederick Douglass; the two 149th Street buildings would be the Paul Laurence Dunbar and the Alexander Pushkin; and the two 150th Street buildings, the Sojourner Truth and the Toussaint L'Ouverture.[3]

By February 1928, when the development opened, a single name had been decided upon for the entire full-block complex: the Paul Laurence Dunbar Apartments, after the esteemed African-American poet (1872–1906). With 512 units, the Dunbar could house over 2,000 tenants in suites varying from three to seven rooms. Sales prices ranged between $3,600 and $9,800, for which purchasers made a down payment of $50 per room and a monthly charge from $11.50 to $17.50 per room. In the papers, Williams would have read of the stern residency requirements of the Dunbar Apartments. Applicants to live in this Rockefeller housing experiment had to provide three solid references.[4]

The Dunbar's all-black staff answered to Roscoe Conkling Bruce, a Phi Beta Kappa Harvard man who was formerly the assistant superintendent of colored schools in Washington, D.C. Bruce's wife Clara Burrell Bruce, an honors law graduate from Boston University, was an assistant manager and legal adviser. "The sporting fraternity, daughters of joy, and the criminal element are not wanted in the Dunbar Apartments," Bruce emphasized to a women's city club. Some found it both sobering and risible that neighbors of one tenant—vexed by another's impatience to just wait for the iceman—reported her for setting out a milk bottle on her windowsill. A writer's observation that the Dunbar was inhabited by intellectuals piqued another's curiosity. "We perused the honors list and failed to find a single undertaker," he wrote. "Maybe the undertakers don't care to bury intellectuals."[5] But despite some occasionally irresistible lampooning, the Dunbar Apartments experiment was taken seriously.

The Dunbar's commercial spaces included a doctor's suite, a dentist's suite, and ten shops.[6] One business that opened on April 17, 1928, broadcast the height of luxury, its name in gold letters emblazoning the windows of the prominent corner at Seventh Avenue and 149th Street: THE MADAM C. J. WALKER BEAUTY SALON NO. 2. A secondary showplace to the company's A'Lelia College, at 110 West 136th Street, the salon fulfilled its $10,000 investment. Three French dolls sat in the show windows, two of them black and one white, surrounded by Madame Walker hair preparations. A thousand visitors inspected the shop the first two days after it opened and found a plush interior. Light-colored mohair draperies with interwoven black fringe punctuated the color scheme of orchid green and orange amid wicker furniture. The floor was green inlaid linoleum. The eight booths were scientifically equipped with beauty apparatuses and products. In May, architect Thomas gave the city's mayor a personal thirty-minute tour of the Dunbar: "Mayor James J. Walker himself spent 10 minutes by the clock inspecting [the beauty salon]," the *Pittsburgh Courier* gleefully reported, adding, "and remarked the place would do Park Avenue credit."[7] While Williams was not yet looking to move, he must have been taking it all in.

The most conspicuous commercial occupant of the cooperative complex was to be its "colored bank" component, at the corner of Eighth Avenue and 149th Street. The prospect had sparked considerable enthusiasm months earlier. Though Harlem's celebrated bibliophile Arturo Schomburg personally recommended several black businessmen with "whole hearted interest in the establishing of such an institution," none were heeded. Rockefeller chartered the Dunbar National Bank in September, under the direction of the

Dunbar's resident manager Roscoe Bruce—the rest of the board of directors being white.[8]

By 1931, given the Depression-troubled housing market, the columnist T. R. Poston found it ironic "that there were at least a dozen vacancies ushered into the Paul Lawrence [*sic*] Dunbar apartments with the new year—although the corporation speaks often of a waiting list that runs into the hundreds."[9]

The Williamses appear to have moved there sometime in 1931. Regardless of the Dunbar's prestige, it was as likely as not Gloria Williams, the Chief and Lucy's granddaughter, who swayed their move to the apartment complex, whose amenities included accommodations for child care and recreation. Though the Williamses were not among the initial cooperative tenants before the crash, they were surely the kind of renting tenant that the selective Dunbar management was eager to cultivate.

The Williamses were indeed part of one of the most important experiments in improved housing conditions for low- to middle-income black workers. Years later, the *Baltimore Afro-American* would point to New York's Dunbar as "unquestionably a precursor of the low-rent housing projects which have been built in cities all over the country through the United States Housing Authority and local housing authorities."[10] Unfortunately, the comforts of Williams's new home were short-lived.

Considering that Lucy Williams was the wife and mother of a celebrity husband and children, she had long escaped the spotlight. Nevertheless, she was usually active, praised by friends as an attentive matron and hostess. On the afternoon of September 30, 1932, she was on a characteristically charitable errand, to visit a friend's dying mother. But upon her arrival, she suddenly collapsed. Some speculated the shocking sight of her friend's condition brought on a stroke. An ambulance came and returned her to her new home at the Dunbar. Someone called for Dr. James L. Wilson, a prominent physician and an old family friend: the Chief hired Wilson as a Red Cap when he was in medical school.

Lucy Williams died at home the next afternoon, Saturday, October 1, seven days shy of her fifty-first birthday, surrounded by her family.[11] One can only surmise their disquiet and sorrow, their anguish being lost to history. Perhaps Dr. Wilson, who pronounced Lucy's death as brought on by a cerebral hemorrhage, fought to conceal his own pain from them. Lucy's service took place three days later at Grace Congregational Church on West 139th Street. Chief Williams sat with his five children: Gertrude, Pierre and Kay, who were living in the Dunbar; Wesley, who had stayed in the Bronx; and Roy, who was lodging in a place nearby. Of course James's parents, Lucy's sisters, and their grandchildren were present as well. Chief Williams was at once composed and undone: Lucy, with whom he had eloped in their teens, his constant companion, was gone. After thirty-five years of marriage, the Chief was now a widower.[12]

In the fall of 1932, the Rev. Richard Manuel Bolden decided to write a weekly series for the *New York Age*, profiling some of Harlem's most outstanding race citizens. Bolden was a natural pick to write the series. Originally from North Carolina, he became pastor of Mother AME Zion Church when it was on West 89th Street. He had been spirited and sometimes controversial. He had spearheaded the church's move to Harlem in 1914 and the same year set off a congregational schism when he refused to accept the bishop's appointment to the Institutional Church at Yonkers. A clerical court tried and expelled him for "insubordination and conduct prejudicial to the peace and harmony of the Church," and his subsequent expulsion prompted him and several followers to establish an independent church movement.[13] "R.M." Bolden was still one of Harlem's most influential voices in matters both sacred and civic.

To debut the series, Bolden decided to feature his old friends James Williams and Jesse Battle. He had met them both some three decades earlier when his former classmate, the Rev. William D. Battle, asked him to look up his brother Jesse at Grand Central Terminal in New York, where he was working as a Red Cap. Bolden had tried to steer Battle toward the ministry, in vain. But after Bolden became pastor at Mother AME Zion, Battle joined the congregation. Bolden recalled it was about then that he, Elks attorney J. Frank Wheaton, and others induced Jesse Battle, "this big, husky fellow, to take an examination to become a member of the police force, the first Negro to make such an attempt."

Battle had been able to study for and pass the exam while working at Grand Central, which moved Bolden. "My interest in Red Caps . . . has greatly increased since Jesse Battle became a policeman," he wrote in the profile. Battle had gone on to earn subsequent promotions. Bolden perceived that race men could use a low-status job, such as a Red Cap, as a leg up toward achieving higher goals.

He also discovered his new appreciation for race men in influential positions, fraught with scrutiny and temptation, who chose to be of service to others—namely, Chief Williams: "He saw his duty clearly, and the performance of that duty, nobly and honorably, has resulted in a great number of Negro professional men realizing their life's ambition. They now hold prominent, and in some cases indispensable, positions of service to their race and to mankind."[14]

Being a Red Cap had been propitious. Wesley (once a Penn Station Red Cap) was his other case in point: "It is to the everlasting credit of Chief Williams that he raised a son to stalwart manhood, in whom he instilled the pride of accomplishment. That son is Lieutenant Wesley Williams, of the Fire Department of the City of New York, the first Negro to attain this honor."[15]

When Wesley was promoted again some months later, Battle sent congratulations for his "very high rating on the Captains List in the Fire Department," adding "kindest regards to your dear family and also your good father."[16] Others often congratulated his father directly: the noted pediatrician T. W. Kilmer (also a renowned portrait photographer whom Williams may have sat for) telegrammed: CHIEF WILLIAMS, CARE RED CAPS / GRAND CENTRAL STATION / CONGRATULATIONS ON WESLEYS ADVANCEMENT KINDEST REGARDS TO YOU BOTH / DR T W KILMER.[17]

Bolden valued that redcapping had enabled many Harlem men to make remarkable inroads into the middle class. Yet others noted that in fiscally dismal and societally prejudiced times, even established middle-class men relied on Red Cap jobs to sustain themselves. News columnist T. R. Poston wrote of a young Red Cap doctor's journey to disillusionment in a poem, "Harlem Healer":

Dr. So and So, M.D.
Dr. So and So, A.B.C.
Dr. So and So, X.Y.Z.
Office Hours, 11 to 3.

Harlem is young—
So are its doctors . . .

Gold lettered window pane,
Proud M.D. behind the name,
Office on the Avenue—
(Two months rent long overdue)—
Disdainful of the smaller town
Where needless Death always abounds.
For this he waged his six year fight—
"Doc" by day, "Redcap" by night.

Where do young Harlem doctors go when they die?
Ask the Pennsylvania Railroad!
Ask the New York Central!
Ask your White God![18]

One could also ask Walter White, as many friends did, for assistance. The NAACP head might write in turn to Chief Williams for a favor, as he did in 1933: Dr. Guy Thomas was an old friend, now in New York, whose dental practice had collapsed in the Detroit banking crisis that year.

Dear Chief:

This will introduce Dr. Guy Thomas who has come to me to ask aid in that most difficult of tasks—finding employment.

Dr. Thomas has not only his wife and himself to support, but an eight-year-old daughter. I know how many appeals are made to you but if you can possibly give employment to Dr. Thomas I will be most grateful.

With cordial personal greetings, I am

Ever sincerely,

Walter White[19]

With a different objective, NAACP field secretary William Pickens wrote to introduce Helen Boardman, "the person who investigated the Mississippi Flood Control situation for us." Boardman, a white former Red Cross relief worker and longtime NAACP staffer, had recently exposed a brutal Negro "peonage" system in a major federally funded works project. Her objective at Grand Central concerned the NAACP's New York membership and financial campaign, for which Chief Williams was a known resource. "The members of your force have taken a good part in our previous efforts to support the Association in New York City," Pickens wrote, hopeful Williams would rally their participation again.[20]

It's unclear if Williams replied. Pickens followed up with a letter to another worker a week later, care of the stationmaster's office (which oversaw the Red Caps), to confirm receipt of information about the NAACP's Harlem campaign: "We would like to get the Redcaps and porters of Grand Central Station interested in our work," Pickens wrote Rudolph Foster (possibly a black office worker), adding, "Kindly let me hear from you, and someday soon I hope to drop in to see you."[21] The field secretary might have been reaching out to a contact at random, perhaps on Williams's recommendation, or maybe was just casting a wide net.

But the Chief might also have been preoccupied with a personal crisis: a year after losing his wife Lucy, his mother Lucy died. On November 19 she succumbed to a cerebral embolism, dying in her ground-floor tenement apartment at 19 West 131st Street. Lucy Ellen Spady Williams, the matriarch of fifteen children, was buried at the Evergreens Cemetery in Brooklyn. Sometime afterward the Chief's sisters Ella and Lena moved their father in with them at the Colored Mission, directly across the street at 8 West 131st Street.

In late January 1934 Pickens invited the Chief to attend the NAACP's twenty-fifth anniversary dinner on March 18, at International House on Riverside Drive. The association was also conducting a campaign called "A Penny for Every Negro," striving to raise $120,000 by collecting 12 million pennies from that number of America's black citizens. For this major campaign to mark the organization's milestone anniversary, Pickens wanted to post uniformed girls with coin canisters and informational handouts at the terminal entrances on February 12—Lincoln's and the NAACP's shared birthday—to collect donations from whomever wished to contribute:

> *My dear Mr. Williams: . . .*
>
> *An organization does not have a 25th anniversary but once during its existence. . . . Can you tell me how we can go about it—to secure the privilege of having some of our workers at the station for this one day? . . .*
>
> *Very truly yours,*
>
> *William Pickens*[22]

Considering the earlier participation of Grand Central's Red Caps during the Silent Protest Parade, one could see what value the NAACP placed on them in its mission to address the country's race crisis. The terminal's conspicuously trunk-laden black men were a deceptively learned bunch of able communicators and masters of discretion. "It looks awfully easy, toting baggage in and out of the train platforms but it isn't," Chief Williams once said. "It takes a man with tact and tact is a rare quality, I'll tell the world."[23] Tact, indeed, was the operative, relevant lesson to the utility of portering that he had no doubt taught his children. Indeed, it was a lesson he now had occasion to see being passed on to his grandchildren. Wesley, to gain summer jobs for his teenage boys, James and Charles, was finessing their introduction to Penn Station by way of the company president, William Atterbury: "Mr. President I once had the honor of handling your luggage, but that was way back in 1916. Now would you be so kind as to give my boys employment as Red Cap Porters, thereby giving them the chance to learn discipline, diplomacy and the ability to give service to the Public under the most trying conditions, just as I learnt to do?"[24]

President Atterbury promptly replied that he was "doubtful . . . if much encouragement can be given them at this time," the midst of the Depression. But perhaps the official warmed to the idea, for which he expressed gratification, that Wesley attributed some of the achievement in the New York fire department to his turn as a Penn Station Red Cap. Atterbury complimented Wesley on his "splendid record" on the force, and, despite his initial doubts, he influenced a favorable outcome for Wesley's request through the Penn Railroad channels.

Pursuing his mission "to help the young man who is trying to help himself," Chief Williams might well have authored the image of the erudite porter, in contrast to the dull, biddable attendant sometimes caricatured by blacks and whites alike. Years before, the satirist Bert Williams had portrayed a hapless, illiterate Red Cap assigned to staff the Grand Central information booth, hilariously rendering a travel system dependent upon infallible directions and timetables into a house of cards. But Chief Williams strove fervently to correct this impression for years.

The real Grand Central Red Caps were hardly unread. "I think I am safe in saying," the Chief observed, "that we give work to more men who are going through college than any other department of the Terminal."[25] They were a paradox: so ubiquitous as to be taken for granted, yet so overqualified for their duties as to be curiosities. In fact, their curious learnedness was frequently the grist of magazine articles nationwide: a writer in *The New Yorker* counted "five graduate students (one an honor student at Harvard), several lawyers, singers, teachers of music, and other persons of some erudition and attainment" among the men staffing Sugar Hill (the terminal's Vanderbilt Avenue taxi entrance).[26]

Student Red Cap was a familiar term in casual social parlance, as when writer Dorothy West described an eclectic Prohibition-era cocktail gathering of "two Negro government officials, two librarians, a judge's daughter, a student-red-cap, a Communist organizer, an artist, an actress."[27] Writing in the short-lived political newsmagazine *Ken* in 1938, writer Ann Ford's provocatively titled article, "Ph.D. Carries Your Bags," emphasized the paradox that typically 40 percent of Red Caps (about every third man in a regiment of hundreds) had college training. "The white man who works as a porter can do nothing else, as a rule," she wrote; "the Negro almost invariably can do something else but can't get it to do."[28]

For decades images of black Red Cap porters toting baggage, such as a 1921 Kuppenheimer clothing ad by noted illustrator J.C. Leyendecker, or an urbane 1934 *New Yorker* magazine cover by Rea Irvin, were ubiquitous in the visual culture of American railroad travel. *Ephemera advertisement; Molly Rea/Molly Rea Trust, Christie Fernandez and Marie Noehren.*

Sadly, this was old news. Chief Williams had commented nearly two decades earlier, "We have a fine class of men here. The men who carry your suitcases are not mere porters. They are artists in their line of work. Why, we have several law students, several dentists and at least one doctor and a preacher in the organization. As for writers and editors, we have any number of them. Only a short time ago one of our men, John Robinson, resigned to become editor of a newspaper. I'm telling you this because I want you to know that it takes education to 'carry on' here at the Grand Central."[29]

Among the numerous educated Red Caps was John Robinson (Williams's earliest profiler in 1909), who went on to manage the *Amsterdam News*; he was also president of St. Mark's Lyceum and active in the antilynching movement. There was Dr. Guy Thomas, Walter White's dentist friend from Detroit, and Rev. John M. Coleman, who in 1933 became rector of Brooklyn St. Philip's Episcopal Church; in 1946 Mayor O'Dwyer would appoint him to the city's Board of Higher Education, the first black board member. Also Emanuel Kline, onetime Red Cap, was a police officer who in 1947 would be promoted to captain, attaining another "first" for a black of that rank. Paul Robeson, the internationally famous singer and football all-American, redcapped at Grand Central to pay for law school at New York University. There was Raymond Pace Alexander, a noted Philadelphia judge and civil rights leader. And Antonio Maceo Smith would become an advertising and insurance executive and help establish the NAACP in Dallas, Texas.

These were just some of the many notable achievers from the ranks and ramps of Grand Central. Relatively few might boast an intimate friendship with Chief Williams, but all would likely acknowledge him as helping them attain prominence. Writer George Schuyler observed with wry grimness: "Turn a machine gun on a crowd of red caps at a big railroad terminal and you would slaughter a score or more of Bachelors of Arts, Doctors of Law, Doctors of Medicine, Doctors of Dental Surgery, etc."[30]

Williams himself had not gone past grade school, but he was fond of likening Grand Central to an institution of higher learning, "The University of Human Nature": he was its president, his dozen or so captains its professors, and the hundreds of Red Caps its student body.

All became skilled at a peculiar diplomacy that strained physicality and equability: "In good times or bad, the Red Cap greets the patron. He knows a little bit of everything. They must be walking booths of information. The questions he is asked vary from the time of departure of the Trans-Atlantic steamers to the time the baseball game begins, and how far is the nearest eating place. He must look out for crooks and pickpockets who infest the city Terminal. He has to walk about ten miles a day in all sorts of weather. He has to keep his temper. He must be a good deal of a mind reader."[31]

A mind-reading porter was indeed one for the books.

Chief Williams appears to have been the prototype for a fictional chief of Grand Central's Red Caps. In the short story "A Woman with a Mission" by Arna Bontemps, he is Ezra High,—"an old West Indian mulatto." In the story, Mrs. Eulalie Rainwater, a white dowager philanthropist, is on a Grand Central platform anxiously awaiting her train for Larchmont. Suddenly a silvery tenor voice emanates from the Red Cap before her: the porter is nonchalantly singing Schubert's "*Du bist die Ruh*," in the original German! She is quite certain that she has just "discovered the strange genius" of a Negro artist. She duly informs Leander Holly, her "treasure from the jungle," that she knows his boss, Ezra High. "Will you tell him Mrs. Rainwater said to telephone her tonight?" she asks. Holly does so when he encounters the chief:

> "Did you see her?" [the Chief] asked. . . .
>
> "See her!. . . . She heard me and asked my number. Then she told me to have you call her tonight."
>
> "She'll see you through if she takes a fancy to you," the chief said. "That's all she's been doing for thirty years. I worked for her husband. . . . And I mean he left her plenty. She's sponsored

> hundreds of young college folks. This Negro fever is something new, though. . . ."
>
> "Lordy, it ain't true," Leander said. . . ."You don't mean she might see me through the conservatory—Music lessons and all that?"
>
> "She always allowed the others about two hundred a month outside of extras, trips, presents, and whatnot."
>
> Leander put his hand on the old fellow's shoulder.
>
> "I can't tote no more leather today, chief. I got castles to build."
>
> That night the plot was completed, and the next evening Leander went to Larchmont to sing for Mrs. Rainwater.[32]

Bontemps's characters point to real-life personalities. Leander Holly evokes the Harlem Renaissance writer Langston Hughes, while Mrs. Rainwater suggests Charlotte Osgood Mason, Hughes's generous patron. Mrs. Rainwater's nemesis, the "degraded dilettante" Tisdale, suggests Carl Van Vechten, a progenitor of the white "Negro fever" or "Harlemania" that surged and eddied over the black capital in the 1920s and early '30s. As for Chief High, he has an intuitive grasp of certain commuters' personalities, whims, and routines—attributes inherent in the real Chief Williams.

It was Williams's well-known promotion of racial uplift that had inspired Reverend Bolden to launch his Harlem profile series, and Williams's scores of Red Caps seemed to attest to the job's value. The journalist and politician Earl Brown, an alum of both the Grand Central University and the actual Harvard University, would later recall, "Only because the Chief had a big heart and was proud of his race were hundreds of young colored men able to go through college."[33]

◈

In January 1935, the film critic Archer Winsten wrote about famous people of the race who had lived, or still lived, in the Dunbar Apartments.[34] Dr. Du Bois, then heading Atlanta University's sociology department, lived in a fifth-floor walk-up apartment with his wife, daughter, and granddaughter, the same apartment he had moved into when Rockefeller opened the project. Bill Robinson lived there with his wife, Fannie, purportedly "one of the cleverest women in Harlem, financially speaking." Matthew A. Henson, a U.S. Customs House official, was most famous as the black explorer who twenty-six years before had trekked with Admiral Peary—"He walked while Peary, on account of amputated toes, rode"—to discover the North Pole.

Lester Walton lived there, of course. So did twenty-eight-year-old E. Simms Campbell, the rare black cartoonist and illustrator for *Esquire*, *The New Yorker*, and other slick magazines. In a photograph, he nestled cozily on his pale green leather couch among his "folding bar and severely modern furniture," looking every bit the picture of rising success. His hilarious, recently published "Night-Club Map of Harlem" was almost instantly iconic. His artistic forte was in the genre of "good girl art," as he adhered to the magazine world's requirement of drawing skimpily clad white women. Yet, Campbell was said to have insisted upon giving work to black models; one wonders how readily white models would have availed themselves as subjects for a black artist. And in yet another celebrity apartment, Winsten noted Chief Williams of the Grand Central Red Caps and father of Wesley Williams, "the only Negro fire captain in New York."

The Dunbar's attentively tidy inner court exuded a pride of place with horticultural touches "ranging from big bushes to little trees." Parents could mind their kids in a central playground and nursery. "There are no benches where people might sit and mar the effect," Winsten wrote. But the inner court, if rarified, likely felt reassuring to Williams and his neighbors during Harlem's sudden turmoil a couple of months later.

The housing market's downward spiral into the sinkhole of the Great Depression precipitated Harlem's decline. A volatile climate arose that exploded into the Harlem Riot of 1935. On March 19, 1935, a rumor spread that employees at S. H. Kress, a five-and-dime store on 125th Street, had killed a boy for shoplifting a penknife or a bag of jelly beans. The rumor was potent enough to set people off. The riot involved 3,000 to 5,000 people. For about twelve hours, police wove through the district in radio cars, and emergency trucks emerged with riot guns, gear and tear gas. Harlem appeared to be a battlefield. Whatever the Harlem Renaissance had promised, the unrest seemed a manifestation of its deferral.

But the rumor that had set off the riot was unfounded: "A colored boy, a nickel penknife and a screaming woman were no more the cause of the Harlem uprising in 1935, than was a shipload of tea in the Boston harbor, in 1773, the cause of the Revolutionary War," wrote educator and activist Nannie Burroughs in the *Baltimore Afro-American*. "An unknown boy was simply the match," while "a frightened woman's screams lighted it and threw it into the magazine of powder, and Harlem blew up."[35]

To investigate the cause of the Harlem riot, Mayor Fiorello La Guardia appointed a biracial commission—whose members included the Chief's acquaintances, Dr. Charles H. Roberts and attorney Eunice Hunton Carter. The unprecedented commission pointed out underlying social and economic conditions, urging that racial discrimination in jobs, education, recreation, and hospital staffing be outlawed. It advocated reforms in the processing of citizens' complaints against police. But charges that La Guardia suppressed his own commission's analysis—which surfaced when the *Amsterdam News* published the report more than a year later—compounded public frustration.[36]

The Rev. Adam Clayton Powell, of Abyssinian Baptist Church, identified the fundamental cause of the riot as the continued exploitation of blacks "as regards wages, jobs, working conditions." "Think of all the milk used in Harlem, yet not one bottle of it is delivered by Negroes," he said. "We see our boys and girls come out of college, well-trained, compelled to go on relief or work as red caps." The pastor's comment was particularly apt: almost a decade and a half earlier, Williams had hired Adam Clayton Powell, Jr., as a Red Cap.[37]

After much pain and ruin, the Harlem Riot of 1935 did lead to something optimistic. In 1937 the Harlem River Houses were constructed a block from the Dunbar Apartments at West 151st Street, the country's first federally funded housing project. From an old wound had come the promise of a new deal.

Barely was the year 1935 under way than far-flung conflicts addled the local mood. Chief Williams's friend, the blues singer Alberta Hunter, back home from a tour in Europe, warned fellow black performers that Hitlerite sentiments were feverishly agitating race prejudice abroad.[38] And under dictator Benito Mussolini, fascist Italy was poised to invade the black Ethiopian kingdom, fueling whatever latent spark of American black-versus-white animus that was still left to ignite. Under these circumstances, Black America longed for another Jack Johnson, for a new hero. It seemed to find one in Joe Louis, "Black Dynamite," a rising Negro boxing star who was training for a much-anticipated match against the Italian boxer Primo Carnera, conveniently derided as "Mussolini's Boy."

On May 15, 1935, two days after his twenty-first birthday, Joe Louis arrived from Detroit at Grand Central, "totally unprepared for the admiration of the colored red caps who clustered about him," NAACP leader Roy Wilkins would later recall.[39] He stepped off the train sharply dressed in a three-piece suit, necktie, overcoat, and fedora. No sooner did he appear than a dozen of Williams's porters rushed him and exuberantly raised him aloft to their shoulders. Once they set him back down, he gamely swapped his fedora for a crimson cap, then heaved his bulging leather suitcase to his shoulder. The crowd cheered as he "smashed his own baggage" for press photographers. The good fun warmed up onlookers for the coming battle, which would ultimately benefit the New York Milk Fund, a charity established by Mrs. William Randolph Hearst.

On June 25 at Yankee Stadium, Louis's powerful right knocked out Carnera in the sixth round, making him the new heavyweight champion of the world. As Louis subsequently became a frequent commuter on the *20th Century Limited*, his friendship with Chief Williams blossomed.

On May 15, 1935, Red Caps exuberantly lifted twenty-one-year-old Joe Louis aloft as he detrained at Grand Central, and the prizefighter gamely effected the role of a Red Cap "smashing his own baggage." *Bettman Archives/Getty Images; ACME Press Photo.*

Unlike Joe Louis, the Chief encountered other heroes who were less inspiring than intriguing. After Booker T. Washington died in 1915, Robert R. Moton took up the reins of the Tuskegee Institute in Alabama and served as president until his retirement in 1935. On April 7 the school's trustees elected his successor, Dr. Frederick Douglass Patterson, dean of the agriculture department. His installation was a double ceremony: Tuskegee's new head also married the president emeritus's daughter.[40]

But during that transition, a certain Red Cap at New York's Grand Central Terminal suddenly felt "imbued with the spirit of the founder of Tuskegee" and claimed to newspapers to be the school's new leader. He even presented a business card: "Tuskegee Institute, Tuskegee, Alabama; EUGENE H. MOORMAN, President."[41]

At first no one questioned Moorman's claim. After all, Red Cap porters were often remarked to be deceptively worldly in light of their humble vocation—one from Penn Station had recently won a New York Assembly seat. Or perhaps Moorman's claim was so quintessentially American in its improbability—like something out of Horatio Alger, or akin to Booker T's own *Up from Slavery* saga—as to make it worth egging on to pass the time. When informed of the fact that Tuskegee had just installed its new director, Moorman was magnanimous: Dr. Patterson should carry on as acting president until he was "able to go down and take over my new duties."

By reputation, Chief Williams did not suffer fools gladly, but neither was he likely to turn one out to starve. Just how to confront Moorman gave him reasonable cause for concern. How had he not sensed that this young fellow was odd and a potential source of trouble? Papers often reiterated Williams's words that a Red Cap needed a résumé five years deep to get hired. Would being too harsh on Moorman throw his own judgment into a bad light? Some co-workers described Moorman as "nice . . . studious, but a little queer." Checking the reckless behavior of someone who knew better was one thing, but Moorman seemed bona-fide touched. The Chief could picture his name on the silver Williams Cup tennis trophy—of which Tuskegee was the first guardian—tarnishing like copper. In the end, the Chief dismissed the eccentric Red Cap genially as "harmless, but something of a nut."[42]

In mid-summer, President Patterson wrote to Dr. Du Bois to assure him that Moorman, who had written to the latter, was "a mental defective."[43] That became the official consensus when Moorman, en route to his imagined presidential errand, was confined to a mental hospital in Baltimore. In the end neither Dr. Patterson nor Chief Williams was much affected, though Moorman's fixation wavered little over the passing decades. In 1967 his enduring fidelity to Booker T. Washington prompted his avowal in a letter to the *Baltimore Sun*, "I shall make an effort to revive a great educator's dream of peace and harmony between the races."[44] Which actually was one of the more wholesome delusions of the time.

In light of the Moorman distraction, Chief Williams had a number of family concerns that demanded his attention. On a sad note, on April 23, 1935, his son James Leroy, or Roy, died—his granddaughter Gloria's father. The nature of their relationship is not clear, nor how he learned the news of the thirty-three-year-old's death. But his son was still working for the railroad, most recently as a car cleaner, and whether it was at Grand Central or Penn Station, any news of import would likely reach the Chief in a timely manner. Roy was also buried at Woodlawn in the Bronx, though not with his forsaken wife, Lula.

Nearly two years earlier, in June 1933, the Chief changed his apartment at the Dunbar for another one, due to Lucy's death.[45] And by summer of this year, he finally sold his house on Strivers' Row. The house, valued at $30,000 five years before, was now "assessed at $12,800" when he sold it to the Harlem Center of the Rosicrucian Anthroposophical League, a spiritual group founded in 1932 by astrologer and occultist Samuel Richard Parchment.[46]

A few months later Chief Williams acquired a son-in-law: on July 29, 1935, his daughter Gertrude married Leroi T. Jennings.[47]

The newlyweds—she a manicurist, he a government employee—were celebrated with a modest dinner party in the home of Harlem friends. Some surely wondered if Gertrude—given her beauty, charm, influential connections, and performing skills—hadn't missed her calling. Chief Williams himself might have wondered if he had not missed his own.

PART V

ECLIPSE

CHAPTER 12

Organized Labor Pains

People will never know the troubles of a red cap unless they grab a bag and carry it themselves.

—WILLARD S. TOWNSEND, 1939[1]

On June 15, 1938, the New York Central inaugurated a faster, sixteen-hour run from New York to Chicago. At six p.m., movie star James Cagney and other passengers boarded the new streamlined *20th Century Limited* from Tracks 36 and 37, as the Chief's twelve-piece Grand Central Red Cap Orchestra performed a swing fanfare to set the tone of their grand departure.[2] The Red Cap musicians continued to have a palpable impact on the traveling experience. Perhaps even informing white musician Mary Lee Read's regular live organ performances in the terminal: "What they will play on that Grand Central Terminal organ is troubling the program makers," Franklin P. Adams, a humorist of the storied Algonquin Round Table, quipped. "Well, there might be . . . 'When That Midnight Choo-Choo Leaves for South Norwalk' . . . and 'I've Been Riding' on the Railroad.' Not to add, 'The Pullman Porters' Ball.'"[3]

On the morning of May 11, 1938, Williams met the *20th Century Limited* as usual. It was one of his routine formalities, as there were almost always celebrities or VIPs arriving—some regular, some new. Back in February, he had made a bit of small talk on the platform with Paul Whiteman and his wife, Margaret; the tall bandleader likely knew of the Chief's enthusiasm for music, as Whiteman's band and the Red Cap Orchestra or Quartet often appeared in the same radio columns. That same week a rising teenage singing star stepped off the *Century* as if the terminal were a Hollywood movie set: a baby grand and an accompanist materialized, not to mention half a dozen of the Chief's porters who knew a thing or two about spontaneous jam sessions. Fifteen-year-old Judy Garland sat atop that piano, flanked by a melodious Red Cap chorus, to the delight of lucky passersby.

But on this day, Chief Williams beamed as his friend Joe Louis, the world heavyweight boxing champ, once again appeared in the *Century*'s door and stepped across the gap from the train. This time he was dressed casually in sports clothes and cap.[4] He locked the

On February 2, 1938, Chief Williams greeted bandleader Paul Whiteman and his wife, Margaret, detraining from the *20th Century Limited*—the same radio columns encapsulated the two men's shared musical interests. *AP Photo Archives.*

On February 7, 1938, a feat of pretended spontaneity treated Grand Central passersby to Hollywood starlet Judy Garland jamming with half a dozen singing Red Caps. *Bettman Archives/Getty Images.*

Chief's handshake. The two men were well acquainted by now, their friendship plain as they walked the length of the red and gray carpet together. Louis chatted loosely about being back in New York to sign up to fight Max Schmeling at Yankee Stadium on June 22.

For his part, the Chief effused about Wesley's promotion to fire department battalion chief, the first Negro of that rank in the country. Though Louis had probably already heard about Wesley's promotion—newspapers across the country had been reporting it for weeks—Williams surely relished sharing the news with the boxer firsthand.

Wesley may have been the one to cinch his father's easy rapport with Louis, in the three years since the boxer's 1935 Carnera fight. Although Wesley was nearly seventeen years Louis's senior, his civil service uniform concealed a kinetic athlete's body. As a rookie fireman in the 1920s, he had won numerous municipal boxing tournaments, including the amateurs' heavyweight championship title two years in a row. Even now, in his early thirties, Wesley had recently impressed crowds at a Harlem Y weightlifting exhibition as "the man whose physique is the wonder and admiration of the whole metropolis."[5] The Chief's years were advancing—he was almost sixty—but Wesley's avid athletic interests naturally gave him and Joe Louis some common ground for conversation.

Other news the Chief had to share with Louis was about their mutual friend, the dancer Bill Robinson. It's not clear to what degree Williams and Robinson socialized with each other, but they both lived in the Dunbar, and Robinson's brother Percy was one of the principal Red Cap musicians.

The Chief's news was that Robinson had opened an exclusive members-only supper club, with bandleader Don Redman and others. The Mimo Professional Club was in the basement of the old Lafayette Theatre on Seventh Avenue, but it was no dive: it was

By May 11, 1938, Chief Williams and Joe Louis had become close when the *20th Century Limited* brought the heavyweight champ to New York to sign up for an imminent bout with Max Schmeling. *AP Photo Archives.*

$40,000 worth of members-only swank. Williams could have described for Louis how, in an anteroom two flights down, a steward checked membership cards, or letters of recommendation, before granting admission. When you stepped into the hall, the walls and ceilings exploded into florid accents of silver and gold against buff backgrounds. The menu offered Chinese as well as American food, from eleven o'clock at night until four in the morning. There was a central dance floor, but this was no cabaret, with floor shows and featured vocalists: members themselves provided the music, impromptu, "usually the work of some nimble-fingered piano playing guest."[6]

The Chief was a member and a fairly regular fixture at the Mimo, often at the center of the club's vibrant social scene: "After work each day he arrives at the Club Mimo about 5, lingers through the dinner hour and talks with the manager, Mal Frazier. Everybody knows [Chief Williams], so he is constantly speaking to patrons coming and going. Sometimes part of his large family joins him at dinner."[7]

Inasmuch as Joe Louis had come to feel like family, it would have been no surprise if the Chief indulged a meddlesome notion of the boxer as a son-in-law—a match for his beloved Kay. Since 1935 Chief Williams's daughter Kay, his youngest child, had been involved in an on-again off-again relationship with a fellow named Harold Bundick. It was highly publicized: gossip columns would report on rumors of his infidelity, then announce the couple's engagement, then announce their separation weeks later. But finally on Sunday, July 10, 1938, Kay and Harold were married at St. Mark's Methodist Episcopal Church. Williams greeted the guests, a moderate gathering of immediate family members and close friends from both sides. Kay was lovely, sporting an informal white afternoon dress with a gathered waist that buttoned primly below her throat, delicate white gloves, and a giant flower corsage. A wide-brimmed hat haloed her bright face. Her sister Gertrude was her matron of honor, complementing her in a pale blue dress, gloves, and smart disk of a hat. Harold, the groom, and Ballard Swann, his best man (and a Red Cap), wore dark suits. No doubt to Kay's disappointment, Wesley was absent—her celebrity big brother was slated to be promoted to battalion chief—but a wedding announcement noted her sister-in-law Margaret. Chief Williams's older brother Charles and his wife Jennie came.[8] The Chief looked dapper in a light double-breasted suit, his usual pocket square and boutonniere, and a straw hat. His left arm bore a mourning band.

The couple's wedded bliss was short-lived. "By now Harold Bundick and Kay Williams must be used to being 'Mr. and Mrs.,'" an item read less than a month after their wedding. "Just heard about a very fine friend of ours being on the 'Y' boat ride with someone other than the wife." Apparently, they reconciled, but two years later he was living at the 135th Street YMCA. "And have you heard of the rift between the Hal (Kay Williams) Bundicks," the columnist asked rhetorically, "which by the way reminds us that Kay came to the affair Friday night accompanied by A—— T——."[9] Alas, prying eyes were relentless.

On July 28, 1938, Chief Williams went downtown to attend Wesley's promotion ceremony. In the Municipal Building, at 1 Centre Street, near City Hall, his son made history by being installed as battalion chief—the first and only black officer of any rank on the force. The new position came with a healthy annual salary of $5,300 (or about $95,000 in 2018). But the ceremony was also bittersweet. This honored occasion for the Chief, a moniker that his son now rightly owned as well, must surely have turned his thoughts to his own father. John Wesley Williams, who had proudly stood beside Mayor John Hylan when his grandson was commended at City Hall some years before, was now slowing down at eighty-seven. One can only surmise the Chief's happiness that his father got to see his grandson Wesley make history again, to see his granddaughter Kay married, and to see their cousin Lloyd, Ella's boy, become the first black teacher hired by the Detroit public school system.

Exactly five years to the day after his mother Lucy's death, the

On July 28, 1938, the Chief saw his son Wesley become the first black officer promoted to Battalion Chief of New York City's Fire Department. *Press photo.*

Chief's father went under a doctor's care. He underwent prostatic surgery and endured a monthlong illness, then on December 19, 1938, he succumbed. He died at the Colored Mission across the street, which Williams's sisters Ella and Lena still ran. Though the Chief had long been the family figurehead, he knew his place as he looked now upon his lifeless father, who had once extracted himself from bondage by his own volition, then wove his own inextricable lineage into the world. John Wesley Williams, the patriarch of five generations of Williamses, was surrounded by his family, who would bear him to rejoin his Lucy at the Evergreens in Brooklyn.

◈

The advance of the Great Depression through the 1930s steadily polarized labor and management. The desperate economic times fueled union consciousness, notably among railroad workers. A decade earlier A. Philip Randolph had organized the Brotherhood of Sleeping Car Porters, affiliated with the American Federation of Labor (AFL). In 1937 Chicagoan Willard S. Townsend similarly founded the International Brotherhood of Red Caps (IBRC), as labor tensions increased among the station porters across the country. Early the following year a bellicose letter from an anonymous "Negro Red Cap, at the Grand Central Station," railed about wages and working conditions: "Together with the Red Caps throughout the country we have planned to hold a Red Caps' Convention in Chicago," he wrote to the *Daily Worker*, a Communist Party newspaper. "And we plan to come out of that Convention in a two-fisted fighting mood."[10] Similarly echoing the critical articles in *The Messenger* a decade earlier, the angry missive neither named nor alluded to Chief Williams, who did not respond to it—at least not directly.

About a week later, on January 28, Chief Williams typed a letter to Eleanor Roosevelt, reminding her of a conversation in which she had promised to send him an autographed photo of President Roosevelt. Williams had known Mrs. Roosevelt for years as a stalwart New Yorker, with an admirable aplomb at dodging her irksome security. Five years earlier, when no one had met the first-lady-to-be returning to Grand Central Terminal from Chicago, Mrs. Roosevelt simply "gave her small overnight bag to a red cap like any other passenger, walked through the station," and went home in a taxi.[11]

Now Mrs. Roosevelt's private secretary "Tommy" (Malvina Thompson Schneider) handled Chief Williams's letter, to which she hurriedly attached her own note—penciled on an upside-down slip of White House letterhead—to forward to FDR's private secretary: "Miss [Marguerite] LeHand, This man is head porter at Grand Central Station—always meets Mrs R + knows the President. Mrs R promised him a photo from the President + herself! MTS." Mrs. Roosevelt intercepted the letter from Tommy; to ensure that the message would be seen to, she penciled across Williams's letterhead in the upper left corner: "Missy, Tell FDR old head porter," she instructed LeHand. "I know he will do. ER."[12]

Chief Williams's letter might have been a straightforward request for a presidential souvenir, but it seems just as likely a politic ruse to draw Mrs. Roosevelt's attention. While he could speak freely about some things, his position required that he broach

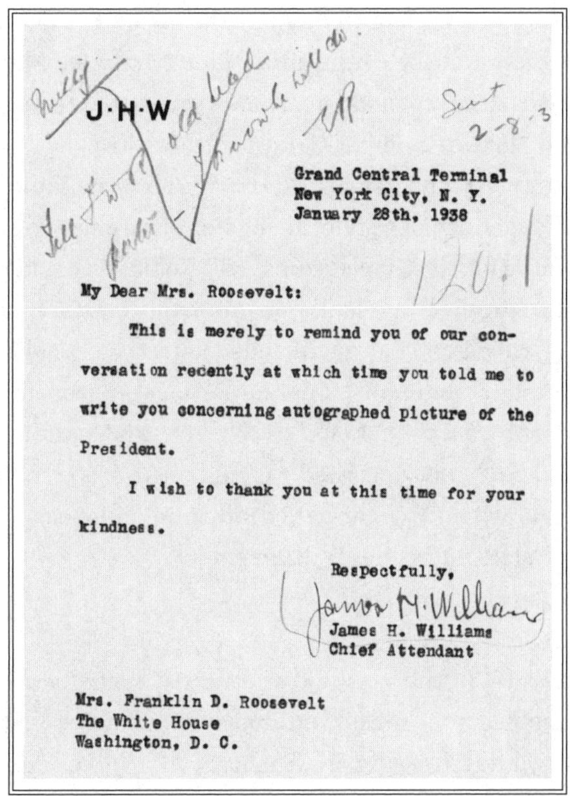

J·H·W

Grand Central Terminal
New York City, N. Y.
January 28th, 1938

My Dear Mrs. Roosevelt:

This is merely to remind you of our conversation recently at which time you told me to write you concerning autographed picture of the President.

I wish to thank you at this time for your kindness.

Respectfully,

James H. Williams
Chief Attendant

Mrs. Franklin D. Roosevelt
The White House
Washington, D. C.

In 1938, First Lady Eleanor Roosevelt intercepted Chief Williams's letter from her secretary to give it her personal attention. *Franklin D. Roosevelt Presidential Library.*

certain subjects—such as the increasingly volatile labor disputes—with circumspection and tact. Whether their tacit correspondence amounted to anything or nothing, both the Chief and the First Lady would have known that the International Brotherhood of Red Caps, led by Townsend, had just opened its office headquarters in the capital and was mobilizing for a wage war against the railroad companies.[13]

As the Chief's union men were preparing for battle, his boxing friend was ceremoniously taking off his mitts. In the spring of 1939,

Joe Louis wanted to celebrate his twenty-fifth birthday in Harlem, so Chief Williams booked himself at Club Mimo for May 13. That Saturday a varied cast of adoring friends turned out to fete the boxer, their beloved "Brown Bomber." Manager Mal Frazier arranged the Mimo's sumptuous and starry affair: Wilhelmina Adams hosted, and Ralph Cooper of the Apollo, as master of ceremonies, read aloud all the incoming felicitous telegrams. Bill Robinson could not attend, but his wife Fannie Clay spoke on his behalf. Other notables on hand to toast the young champ included actresses Ethel Waters and Fredi Washington; journalist Thelma Berlack Boozer; Roy Wilkins; Harlem Hospital surgeon Louis T. Wright; and bandleader Duke Ellington. Though not recorded, a published roster of the young boxer's friends whom Cooper called up to make speeches included Lieutenant Battle and Chief Williams.[14]

In early July 1939, the issue of whether tips legally compensated Red Caps instead of a minimum hourly wage drew station attendants to a two-day hearing in Washington. Workers came to testify from Philadelphia, Boston, Harrisburg, Jacksonville, St. Louis, Cleveland, Kansas City and New York.

A wage-hour bill had been enacted whereby railroads and terminal companies required Red Caps to sign individual contracts guaranteeing them twenty-five cents an hour. But every Red Cap was required to report his tips, which were to be considered wages. The agreement stipulated that a Red Cap receiving two dollars in tips for an eight-hour day would earn no wage for that day's work, and that if he made less, the railroad company would make up the difference.

By and large, the hearing revealed, Red Caps were afraid to report less: they daily turned in their obligatory receipts from the tipping public, reporting their two-dollar take whether they made it that day or not for fear of reprisals if they dared ask the railroad for money. Conversely, as John Lee, a thirty-year veteran of Grand Central's Vanderbilt Avenue entrance, testified. "I have a very advantageous location at Grand Central Station," he said. "I've been there so long people know me by name. Their ego wouldn't allow them to reduce their tips."[15]

In Grand Central's early years, Chief Williams had effectively organized and inspirited his men through numerous mutual benefit and philanthropic enterprises, but many pundits regarded the Red Caps as impervious to unionization. As a labor force that needed no particular skill set, as compared to Pullman porters or waiters, workers with grievances had "virtually no leverage vis-à-vis railroad station management," as a historian later noted.[16] Chief Williams had notably populated Grand Central's crew of menial laborers with college students, some of Harlem's most ambitious young men. He took great pride in being able "to help the young man who is trying to help himself," and he pointed constantly to the many erstwhile Red Caps who had made careers or had expertise in law, medicine, and almost every field imaginable. He claimed that the Red Cap sector supported more college-going men than any other terminal department. "This year we employed 101 college men," he told Abram Hill in 1939, "25 of them graduates."[17]

Why did college graduates stay on afterward? It's understandable that young men might tolerate such grunt work to defray their college expenses. But what kept some redcapping after graduating—even after establishing businesses? The rude awakening for many was that a diploma did not ensure the ability to break through certain prevailing Jim Crow barriers. Redcapping, however taxing, was at least a viable moonlighting occupation.

One of the station captains acknowledged that the Chief carried out a trying job admirably, which perhaps made their own not only bearable but purposeful. Indeed, whether every Red Cap loved him or not, "he is deeply respected by everyone."[18] Their high esteem for Chief Williams personally did not invalidate the Red Caps' occupational dissatisfaction—which grew more acute. But even during the most heated arguments on Red Cap labor issues, personal censure of the Chief was indeed rare.

During their efforts to form a labor union, Chief Williams was conspicuously silent. The columnist James Hogans noted: "There is one subject . . . on which Jim will not commit himself: this is, the union movement among redcaps. What his opinion is about the matter he discreetly keeps to himself." Hogans posited that Williams's decades-long tenure as Chief was likely due to his "ability to keep his own counsel and not speak out of turn."[19] Perhaps Hogans was damning the Chief with faint praise by noting his silence. On the other hand, Hogans was more cognizant than most of the delicate balance, and leverage, of Williams's position. Conceivably Hogans considered the Chief's avowed neutrality as a tactical gambit: railroad executive antagonists of the Red Caps' union might rest assured that their sole Negro manager was loyal. In the black press, Williams was a visible supporter of labor-strong social organizations, and of labor-friendly political candidates like Herbert H. Lehman, who was then campaigning for governor.

In September 1939, as the unionization effort gained more heat, the *Age* ran a flintier headline: "'Chief' Williams Remains Silent as Grand Central Terminal Holds Labor Representations." The Red Caps had won legal clarification of their job status. The rail transport lines had tried to block their petition, contending that Red Caps were merely "privileged trespassers" or "concessionaires." But the Interstate Commerce Commission overruled them, deeming porters to indeed be railroad company employees.

On the day when the National Mediation Board was supervising a labor election for the terminal's Red Caps to vote on the question of union representation, Williams was again taciturn, but explicitly so. "Do not ask me to say anything," he said. He'd lowered his signal whistle from his lips only to eschew a reporter's questions. "I am not allowed to discuss it," he explained, because of his supervisory position.[20] Yet with a courtesy worthy of a stage whisper, played for an audience, the Chief gratuitously clued in the reporter as to which union point persons he should talk to who were monitoring the voting in the terminal: There was John A. Bowers, vice president of the International Brotherhood of Reds Caps (IBRC); and there was

John R. Lee, the driving force and president of the New York system's brotherhood.

The wheels of Grand Central's labor relations may have seemed to Williams—who was once their principal impetus—to be turning now of their own volition. If his position enjoined him from demonstrably revealing either his solidarity with or his disdain for this change, no one appears to have measured his silence ponderously. As his men cast their votes in favor of representation by the IBRC, his signal whistle resumed its intermittent chirrs that echoed through the great marble concourse.

In January 1940 the second annual International Brotherhood of Red Caps convention was held in New York at the YWCA's Emma Ransom House (at 137th Street and Seventh Avenue) in Harlem. Being management, Williams did not attend the convention, though shop talk, neighborhood social gatherings, and newspapers readily informed him of its proceedings. Several notable labor leaders and politicians sent greetings to the convention, including officers of the International Ladies Garment Workers Union and the National Women's Trade Union League of America; New York City mayor Fiorello La Guardia and New York governor Herbert Lehman; educator Mary McLeod Bethune; *Chicago Defender* publisher Robert Sengstacke Abbott; and Abyssinian Baptist Church pastor Adam Clayton Powell, Jr. (who had succeeded his father).

Red Cap John Lee, the union shop steward, had been at Grand Central about as long as Williams, since they were young neighbors on 134th Street. As chairman, he called the three-day convention to order, and IBRC president Willard Townsend presided. During the Great War, Townsend had been briefly married to Williams's friend Alberta Hunter, whose father had been a Pullman porter. Townsend introduced A. Philip Randolph, of the Brotherhood of Sleeping Car Porters, who addressed the convention.

The Red Cap workforce fell under the jurisdiction of the Union of Baggage Clerks and Carriers, whose membership was white and which "withheld . . . benefits and opportunities from the Red Caps over whom they claim jurisdiction," including salary, voting and seniority rights for jobs. The Pullman porters and Red Cap porters—both predominantly black railroad workforces—might have united in a formidable alliance against the Baggage Clerks and Carriers Union. However the Red Cap union, opting for autonomy, voted not to affiliate with the Brotherhood of Sleeping Car Porters. It also changed its name from the International Brotherhood of Red Caps to the United Transport Service Employees of America (UTSEA).

One adopted resolution complained that "the Pullman porters publicly criticize the red caps in the presence of passengers as being lazy and no good" and formally requested that Randolph instruct all Pullman porters to cease such behavior.

But more broadly, the Red Cap membership voted to immediately start organizing red caps and porters beyond railway stations, in bus terminals, airports, and docks, and to include cleaners, sweepers, janitors, and elevator operators nationwide.

They voted to support Black American Sugar Cane workers who were currently protesting the importation of offshore refined sugar. In light of the recent outbreak of a second European war, the convention pledged to cooperate with the Keep America Out of War Congress and the Labor Anti-War Council.

The shortest resolution required no preamble: the convention endorsed the New York Democratic representative Joseph Gavagan's Anti-Lynching Bill, which was then before Congress. The House of Representatives had passed the bill in 1937, but a number of Southern lawmakers were determined to hold on to white supremacy in the Senate. "Some of the southerners, of course, are not charming," the *Crisis* had written two years before, "but many of them are reasonable men—except on the Negro. By that reasoning peculiar to some sections of the South, they argued that passage of an anti-lynching bill would be a signal for the wholesale raping of their wives, daughters and mothers by 'black brutes.'"[21]

After heated discussion, the members voted to grant honorary life memberships to three men for their financial and moral support: Julian D. Steele, a black settlement house director and a rising star in Boston area social work; Alfred Baker Lewis, a white union organizer and NAACP member; and Henry Longfellow Wadsworth Dana, a white labor activist and Harvard professor.

Chairman John Lee bade the convention to stand in a moment of silence for American Newspaper Guild founder Heywood Broun, a staunch friend of the union, who had died a month earlier. Broun had sat on the advisory board since the IBRC's first convention in Chicago the previous year, and his columns were occasionally reprinted in the Red Cap industry monthly, *Bags and Baggage*. Broun had been the first columnist to champion the organizing efforts of the Pullman porters back in 1925; James Hogans asserted that "his writings had much to do with molding public sentiment in their behalf."[22]

Williams knew personally many of the public figures who were present. And a few of them, like Reverend Powell Jr. and Lester B. Granger, he had hired nearly twenty years earlier as Red Caps. Notably Granger, who Williams once caught wooing his daughter Gertrude on work time, was now assistant executive secretary of the National Urban League, whose mission was to desegregate racist trade unions.

By and large, the convention was a triumph. By month's end the New York Central Railroad, the Grand Central Terminal Company, the Michigan Central Railroad, the Cleveland Union Terminal, and the Red Caps' UTSEA signed an agreement covering some seven hundred station Red Caps and corollary workers.[23]

But formidable opposition to UTSEA's efforts predictably came from George M. Harrison, president of the Brotherhood of Railway Clerks, which constitutionally banned all but white men. Negro railway clerks could join only "auxiliary locals," which required them to pay membership dues but barred them from policy-making conventions. "Harrison was like the dog and the bone," Hogans later wrote. "He didn't want the Negro Red Caps himself, but he didn't want anyone else to organize them."[24] Harrison's efforts to derail and co-opt the new Red Cap union helped Townsend and others to engage the invaluable media and legal resources of the Urban League and the NAACP. A few months after the Red Cap convention, Townsend met at the 135th Street Y with representatives of several New York Central locals to consider proposed revisions to the UTSEA contract, soon to be presented to the railroad company management.[25]

In June, Grand Central converted the women's room on the lower concourse into a Red Cap check room, an overdue improvement for workers.

Being a major transit hub, Grand Central had ample distractions from labor tensions. On March 16, 1940, at about one o'clock in the afternoon, Chief Williams was passing through the terminal in his civilian clothes, a plump green carnation in his lapel marking the eve of St. Patrick's. An odd sound halted the Chief as he neared the baggage room. "I heard a zip like a skyrocket," he told police detectives afterward, and an audibly crackling blaze prompted him to blow his whistle. The baggage room counterman, a nearby clerk and Red Cap, and he himself emptied "eight or ten" extinguishers to put the flames out. A low level time bomb was found attached to two wristwatches set for nine o'clock. Police suspected the detonation was intended for another time, possibly another location, an isolated incident. Yet a bit of press was perhaps wryly telling: "The chief attendant is the father of Battalion Chief Wesley Williams, only Negro of that rank in the [fire] department," the *Times* wrote,[26] unwittingly revealing the increasing eclipse of Chief Williams's fame by his son.

On June 1, 1940, New York's Grand Central, 125th Street, and Pennsylvania stations joined several other northeastern stations in putting into place a uniform, universal tipping system that was to become effective countrywide. In adherence with new National Labor Relations Board's minimum wage requirements, the railroad company would pay Red Cap porters thirty cents an hour—or $2.40

a day—in addition to a fixed tip amount of ten cents per bag. The policy was advertised "to improve and standardize Red Cap porter service to the public."[27] Indeed, many Red Caps initially regarded the establishment of the system as a victory, as it would now guarantee them a calculable salary.

But the new rate met with strong objection from Red Caps in New York. While the measure ensured the traveling public uniformity, it threatened to diminish a Red Caps' opportunities to potentially earn more, or the ability to make a decent living. Under the old system, a passenger might hand a Red Cap his five bags with a twenty-five- or thirty-cent tip. "Two of the bags might be large, the other three small," John Lee, a Grand Central Red Cap and UTSEA officer, explained. "Now the passenger carries the three small bags himself and gives the red cap 20 cents."[28] Red Caps soured over the restrictive policy during the next year.

"There's no more sugar on Sugar Hill," Samuel H. Boyd, a Red Cap captain, testified at City Hall. On August 7, 1941, the U.S. Labor Department was hearing New York workers' testimonies about the new system. The gray-haired Boyd had long supervised the terminal's Vanderbilt Avenue entrance, nicknamed for Harlem's distinctly affluent enclave. He had been at Grand Central since 1905, almost as long as the Chief, and the two men were brothers in Elkdom as well as Harlem and Williamsbridge neighbors. Boyd now asserted to the department's Wages and Hours division representative, Thomas Holland, that the Vanderbilt Avenue Red Caps felt that they were making less under the new ten-cent-per-bag policy than before: "There used to be a lot of sugar there, but there's none anymore," he said frankly. "So you were pretty happy under the old tipping system?" Holland pressed for clarification. "I would not say I was happy," Boyd responded. "But I did do better under the [old] tipping system."[29]

The Red Caps' issues were complex. They wrestled for months to clarify the essential question of whether they worked for the railroads that hired them or for the public they depended on—to no wholly satisfying resolution. Even First Lady Eleanor Roosevelt questioned whether Red Caps' tips ought to be considered as wages. At a National Urban League gathering in New York, she had addressed the conundrum: should the expense for carrying handbags rightly be borne by their owners, or by the porters, or by those who run the railroads? She posited that the question was one of national import, revealing "what we in our country want for the people who perform services which are worthy of pay."

> Do we want in our country to have something we know of as tips considered a living wage? I don't think we do . . . but in any case I think it is an obligation . . . for every citizen in a democracy to think about such questions.[30]

For Chief Williams and the Red Caps, these and all manner of other questions about their democratic standing would soon be abundantly forthcoming.

CHAPTER 13

"Things Reiterated as the American Way"

Soon I shall be a soldier fighting for those things that are constantly being reiterated as the American way.

—LEN BATES, 1943

On June 26, 1941, the New York parks department held its sixth annual barbershop quartet contest. About fifteen thousand people gathered at the Naumburg Bandshell on the Central Park Mall to listen to eighteen a cappella singing groups perform. The contest judges included the parks commissioner Robert Moses, former New York governor Alfred E. Smith, and Mayor Fiorello La Guardia, who in the promotional brochure had personally invited "all harmonizers" to participate. The winning group would go on to St. Louis to compete at the finals, held by the Society for the Preservation and Encouragement of Barber Shop Quartet Singing in America, or SPEBSQSA.

At least since the 1870s, African Americans had fostered a popular close-harmony singing style for four unaccompanied voices. In 1879 the white Massachusetts abolitionist William Lloyd Garrison's funeral featured "a colored quartet, and the musical selections . . . designated by [the deceased] before his death." Similarly, in Washington, D.C., James Garfield and Chester A. Arthur's 1880 presidential ticket got a boost from black journalist John Edward Bruce's four-man Black Republican Glee Club. Though steeped in black spirituals, the quartet style also lent itself well to popular ballads. As white singers adopted the quartet's economy of voices—and adapted its repertoire and image—the performance style quickly flourished in social, music hall, and recording settings as "barbershop quartet," a rubric of musical Americana that excited widespread competition.

For the Grand Central Red Cap Quartet the singing challenge in Central Park must have been irresistible. Perhaps ex-governor Smith, an enthusiast and contest official, had encouraged his friend the Chief to get the quartet to compete. In any case, they entered the contest and sang two numbers from the approved list of barbershop ballads. One of the singers was sick, so a fourteen-year-old relation stuck on a fake handlebar mustache and stood in for him at the last minute—and still they won.

Despite the group's name, the Grand Central Red Cap Quartet that won the New York City competition was not the same as the one Robert Cloud formed under Chief Williams around 1930. This new incarnation consisted of Owen Ward, second tenor; his brother Robert Ward, baritone; their nephew Jack Ward (a tenor substitute); and William Bostic, bass. The group originated as a family act called the Four Southern Singers or sometimes the Southern Singers Jug Band, which included James Hornsby "Jim" Ward, bass, and his wife Annie Laurie Ward, singing tenor. By 1933 the quartet had recorded "Be Ready" and "Old Man Harlem" and appeared to be doing well enough that Owen Ward's manager gave him a new alligator-skin violin case.[1] When the group broke up, Chief Williams gave the men work. The former Southern Singers soon regrouped and could be heard singing together during spare hours at the terminal.

Being familiar voices from radio, and likely aided by the Chief's introductions, they gained entrée to entertain railroad officials and to appear as featured guests on broadcasts like Major Bowes' Amateur Hour. Of course, now performing as the Grand Central Red Cap Quartet, the contest win in Central Park was a big deal for the singers and the Red Caps corps collectively.

But even city officials had been excited by the prospect of winning since the previous year. On July 15, 1940, New York had lavishly

In the summer of 1941, the Barbershop Harmony Society barred the Grand Central Red Cap Quartet from its national competition in St. Louis, Missouri, due to race, prompting resignations from two New York officers, parks commissioner Robert Moses, and former governor Alfred E. Smith. *New York City Parks Photo Archive.*

hosted SPEBSQSA's second national convention and competition at the 1939 World's Fair, which was in its second year. Spearheaded by Parks Commissioner Robert Moses, Mayor Fiorello La Guardia, and former governor Alfred E. Smith—all of whom were judges, then and in 1941—New York had outbid several other major cities vying to host the 1,800-member society's event.

SPEBSQSA's convention happened to coincide with the fair's "Negro Week," which Mayor La Guardia kicked off by opening a literary exhibit from the Schomburg Collection in the American Common:

> Show me in the records of history any race anywhere that in our generations have contributed to science, the arts, government itself and have above all attained a position of dignity to fight for their own people than what has been accomplished by Negroes of America, and you will defy history itself.[2]

An ongoing production at the fair called "Railroads on Parade"—a pageant set to music by Kurt Weill—included a dozen black WPA actors portraying Red Caps, Pullman porters, and other essential workers in American railroad history. Across the fairgrounds, on the plaza in front of the New York City Building, ex-governor and contest judge Smith, wearing a brown derby, led the audience and other judges in a round of "East Side, West Side." The quartets' participation in the 1940 fair had clearly won over New York City's officials, who were gung-ho about the present victory of the Grand Central Red Cap Quartet.

On June 27, the day after the 1941 quartet competition, Parks Commissioner Moses notified SPEBSQSA that New York would be sending the winning Grand Central Red Cap Quartet to compete in the finals in St. Louis. But O. C. Cash of SPEBSQSA, who received the telegram, was not in harmony with New York's results: the society had a whites-only policy. The previous year, at the World's Fair, SPEBSQSA had recognized the Southerners, a black male NBC Radio quartet, as "honorary members."[3] But no black quartet had ever won a regional competition before, qualifying it to show up in person to the nationals. And as if the Red Cap Quartet's victory didn't beat all, New York's second-place winner was also a Negro team: the Harlem YMCA Quartet.

Cash wrote back to New York, explaining that SPEBSQSA had often discussed whether to allow colored singers to compete "with others," and that "last year the board came to the conclusion that to keep down any embarrassment we ought not to permit colored people to participate." He did not wish to offend the organization's expansive membership base in the South, "where the race question is rather a touchy subject." Assuring the New Yorkers that he and the Society's president were not "narrow about such matters," they nevertheless did not want to broach "a question of this kind." With that awkwardness aside, he added, "I hope you will be in St. Louis with the other quartets."[4]

Upon receipt of this letter, Parks Commissioner Moses and ex-governor Smith, both of whom were vice-presidents of SPEBSQSA, quit. Moses railed at Cash's and the organization's absurd bias in a letter that he shared with the press:

> *The first and second quartets were composed of colored men. The judges took their duties seriously and even insisted that the four leading quartets sing a second time before the final decision was reached.*
>
> *We are now informed by your recent letter and telegram that colored quartets may not compete in the National Finals in St. Louis. If we had known this before we should immediately have dropped out of the national organization, a step which we are now compelled to take.*
>
> *It is difficult for me to see any difference between your national ballad contest and a national track meet in which colored men run in relays or compete individually. This is not a social event, but a competition, which should be open to everybody.*
>
> *Let me add that if American ballads of Negro origin are to be ruled out of barber shop singing, most of the best songs we have will be blacklisted. There was a man named Stephen Foster who never hesitated to acknowledge his debt to the Negroes for the best of his songs. Along with many others [who] found pleasure in the harmless amusement of American ballad contests, I am very sorry that this sour note has marred our pleasant harmonies.*

Ironically, Moses' demonstrable racial solidarity here appeared at odds with his own vexing flights of prejudice—but it was affecting. Smith also lambasted the board of directors in St. Louis for ruling out the winning singers "because they are colored men," as he, too, resigned from the society: "I assume that the New York State organization will go on independently of the international organization."[5]

Back at Grand Central, the mood in the Red Cap Check Room was a mix of resignation and triumph. "You know how a man feels about a thing like that," said Robert Ward, the quartet's manager. "It's their policy—that's all there is to it."[6] The men had worked hard to win first place, and were of course disappointed to miss boarding a train in Grand Central as regular passengers.

But they were not overly discouraged. They surely did not miss having to find hospitality when traveling in inhospitable places. Chief Williams had already approved their time off, and their fellow porters lavished them with gifts for their prospective trip. The quartet was soon fulfilling requests for public appearances all over the city, occasionally at the behest and in the company of Commissioner Moses.[7]

By 1943, numerous railroad stations across the country had their respective "Red Cap" musical aggregations. But one particular singing group emerged with the moniker that had no connection to the railroad. In the midst of the 1942–44 American Federation of Musicians' strike, a rhythm and blues quartet called the Four Toppers, like scores of other artists, sought an unobtrusive way to get around the union's recording ban. Dubbing itself the Five Red Caps (with an extra member), the group likely maintained its marketing appeal to black audiences by evoking the iconic railway station baggage handlers. The quintet even recorded a peppy ditty titled "Grand Central Station," which enjoyed much commercial success.

A few weeks after the barbershop quartet fiasco, but unrelated to the competition, ex-governor Smith heard from Wesley Williams on another matter. After more than twenty years in lower Manhattan, Wesley wanted to transfer to an assignment closer to home, specifically on White Plains Avenue in the Bronx. On August 18, 1941, he wrote with hopes that Smith might intercede on his behalf: "May I be allowed to take advantage of your long years of friendship with my father by requesting a favor of you?" Smith's response is not known, but the younger Chief Williams got his transfer.[8]

◈

On December 7, 1941, the Japanese bombed the American naval base at Pearl Harbor, an attack that triggered a congressional declaration of war. Though black citizens had thrown themselves valiantly into every conflict of American history, their efforts had been constantly rejected or subject to some arbitrary policy. The very morning the Japanese bombs rained down on American warships, Jim Crow proved to be alive and well. Dorie Miller, a black messman, rushed up from the ship's galley and flew into action. He had no training in navy guns, and military regulations put them off limits to him. Nevertheless he seized an unmanned machine gun and emptied its fire on the enemy. Afterward Miller climbed back down to the mess galley, "where, because he is a black American, he must remain—in spite of heroism, ability, or the need of the Navy for first-class fighting men."[9]

Earl Brown, the Chief's former Red Cap who was now a prominent journalist, reported this story, which made headlines in the black press nationwide. Writing in *Harper's*, Brown articulated the widespread black disaffection with the war. "Because he must fight discrimination to fight for his country and to earn a living," Brown wrote, "the Negro to-day is angry, resentful and utterly apathetic about the war." Mrs. Roosevelt had expressed a similar sentiment in a recent speech: "The nation cannot expect colored people to feel that the United States is worth defending if the Negro continues to be treated as he is now."[10]

A few days later, and thousands of miles away in New York, workers at Grand Central Terminal mounted an enormous fifty-ton photo mural on the east balcony to promote the sale of defense bonds and stamps. The mural—stretching 110 feet high by 118 feet wide—was said to be the world's largest. Certainly no one entering the station could fail to notice the montage of images of servicemen, children and laborers—all of whom were white. Williams and the Red Caps surely saw it as a reminder that complexions still outranked qualifications.

The onset of another world war must have struck Williams as eerily familiar. Countless Red Caps had served as officers and soldiers in the 369th "Hellfighter" and 367th "Buffalo" regiments. And when those who survived had returned after the war, he had given work to dozens of veterans. They were retired now, visibly gray and wizened in their whipcord coats and red caps. One might bet they could tell you about the Great War "over there." And why they might be skeptical about this one. But when as always Negroes went to the country's defense after Pearl Harbor, the Chief sometimes patched vacancies in the staff by calling back these "outside men."

One of the young fellows over there now had been a Red Cap back in the '20s, and who the Chief and some of the older men perhaps recalled, was Joseph L. Washington. They knew Joe's father better: back in 1895 Thomas Washington had started as a Pullman porter down south before he moved north in 1907 to work for the New York Central. The public often commonly pegged Williams and Washington as "porters to Presidents," the Chief inside the terminal and his Pullman counterpart aboard the *Empire State Express*. Though Pullman rules forced Washington to retire at seventy in 1929—he rode between Grand Central Station and Buffalo for more than twenty years—his income had afforded academic opportunities to his ten children, especially his son Joseph. In 1920 young Joe, a student at Erasmus Hall High School, became captain of the football team; won the school's "highest honor possible" in athletics, its prestigious John R. McGlue Trophy for the best all-around record; was athletics editor of Erasmus's yearbook, the *Flying Dutchman*; and almost won the student government presidency. Washington's athletic excellence gained him a scholarship to New York University—and to Chief Williams's university of Grand Central.

During Joe Washington's three years at NYU, he became secretary of the student body and distinguished himself on the school's baseball and football teams. He then went to Colby College in Maine, where he graduated with a bachelor of science in the class of 1927, eager to enter medical school. Several leading U.S. colleges reportedly accepted him, then rejected him due to clerical errors when he showed up Negro, so he applied internationally. Hearing nothing for months about a particular application, "he hopped a steamer, worked his way across the Atlantic and reported to the University of Edinburgh," where the Scottish school apparently had no issues with accepting him.

Back home, the Chief and all the Red Caps and Pullmans keenly awaited news from Tom Washington's boy, who had become one of their own. On December 10, 1927, the *Age* reprinted part of a letter from Joe to his father: "Father, it's all like a dream to me to be here and find the place and people so congenial. It's the best treat you've given me in my life. I hope never to forget it, and will do my utmost to make good in appreciation of it. I pray to God that I'll be a success."[11]

But Joe's road to success soon came to an impasse. Despite his high marks, his finances were dwindling, and students at Edinburgh were not allowed to work. Worse, an official suggested he quit. "Universities should be attended only by those who have the means," he told Washington. "You do not have the means."

Joe Washington ignored the advice, eked through, and earned his medical degree from Edinburgh. But a medical school graduate required a license to practice legally, and obstacles thwarted his every effort. In 1938, as tensions threatened to draw Britain into the war, Washington was unable to attend his father's funeral back in the States. After the war began in 1939, dogfights ignited the English skies, and for months Washington treated the wounded in a small hospital in Lancashire. He subsequently toured in Africa and other countries, earned the rank of captain in the Royal Army Medical Corps, and married a local girl in Scotland. There he made his home as a contract physician, still struggling to get a license.[12]

Even as an officer, gaining a bona-fide license might not have solved Joe's problems back in his home country. Maj. Ralph B. Teabeau, a star player on Howard University's baseball team and a member of the Grand Central "nine," was an enlisted officer in both world wars. He ranked Lieutenant in the first, and Major in the second. In 1942 he headed the U.S. Army's dental unit of the "all-Negro setup" at Fort Huachuca, Arizona, but was demoted so the military could install white officers in the infirmary instead.[13]

In 1941, up in Harlem, A. Philip Randolph was organizing a

March on Washington movement. The apt slogan on its flyers read: "Winning Democracy for the Negro Is Winning the War for Democracy." Chief Williams could attest to the U.S. Army's caprices at Grand Central, as one of his student Red Caps, Leonard Bates, tried to move up in the ranks to a gateman's position. In the fall of 1940, Bates had gained national headlines as a preeminent NYU football star. When the NYU team was scheduled to play the University of Missouri team, the Missouri officials objected to any Negro playing on their field, a reference to Bates, the NYU team's only black player and its star fullback. NYU officials capitulated, agreeing in writing to uphold the color line by signing a "mutual pact." Students were outraged. Dozens of student groups rallied in solidarity with the wronged athlete—fraternities, the American Students Union, drama clubs and others—to protest NYU's decision. "Bates must play or the game be canceled," the student chairman Guy A. Stoute wrote to Walter White at the NAACP. "Students have already signed over 2,000 statements in protest against this discrimination." NYU turned a deaf ear to them and upheld its agreement to bench Bates. He did not board the train bound for Columbia, Missouri, with his white teammates.[14]

Bates focused instead on maintaining a good academic average, redcapping as he earned his sociology degree. When war came, Bates and his wife were newlyweds and had a child on the way. He wisely decided to try to move up in the ranks at Grand Central and become a gateman, controlling platform access to ticket-holding passengers—a job with a higher pay grade. Having helped enough "green" gatemen decipher train schedules, he knew the terminal was in short supply of men and had become lax in training them.

But the New York Central turned him down. A terminal manager admitted the company had never hired a colored gateman; perhaps none before Bates had had the temerity to apply. L. W. Horning, New York Central's labor relations president, denied color had anything to do with it. Rather, every contract had a "scope rule" describing the positions in the department covered in the agreement. "You just can't move men from one class to another without fouling these scope rules," he claimed. If redcapping didn't satisfy Bates anymore, Horning asked, would he prefer to apply for a mail-and-baggage porter's job?

In the spring of 1943, Bates earned his degree in sociology. He doffed his red cap to don the army's khaki, but not before first mailing a letter of protest to New York Central, and sending a copy to the federal Fair Employment Practices Committee. A few newspapers printed some of the former athletic star's righteous complaint:

> *Just a short time ago I applied at your office [of the stationmaster] for a job as gateman. First I was told that the Brotherhood [of Railroad Clerks] did not employ colored persons. When I pointed out that the Brotherhood had nothing to do with the hiring of gatemen, I was told that the job "was all filled."*
>
> *When I disputed this, I was finally told that the NYCRR did not employ colored persons in this capacity. Your company should be proud of this record [wherein] it proclaims even in posters and signs that it is all-out for the war; that all kinds of records are being broken.*
>
> *There is just one area in which it remains constant: it still does not think that the colored person fits into the general scheme of things. His is a different world. He must remain menial. Be polite and know his place. This has got to change.*
>
> *You have tyrannized, intimidated, and plagued the colored worker. . . .*
>
> *Soon I shall be a soldier fighting for those things that are constantly being reiterated as the American way. I want to be a good and efficient soldier. I want to draw my inspiration for killing the fascists I face on the front from those I have known at home.*

Bates signed the letter "your fellow American," adding as a postscript: "I shall save this for my boy when he becomes of age. This will be his first lesson in American History."[15]

Williams's own son, Wesley, was fighting the war at home. In the mid-1940s, nearly a quarter-century after he entered the force in 1919, he was still the only black officer in the whole New York City fire department. While the war raged abroad, he and other black firemen were waging a war against discriminatory practices at home. The black firemen's grievances included a medical plan that used a code indicating they were "to be first referred to Negro physicians"; their being bypassed for assignments to fireboats, rescue companies, the band and company baseball teams; their difficulty in obtaining transfers to companies where no other blacks were assigned; and the fire department's tabulation of Negroes as "the only personnel list kept on a racial basis," whereas it kept no similar list for other ethnicities. One officer of the Vulcan Society, the fraternity of black firemen that Wesley recently co-founded, cited the absurdity of this sort of list, "for there are Negroes whose names do not appear because they are not obviously Negroes and in one instance a man who insists he is not a Negro is listed."

Another grievance was that the fire department routinely reduced the seniority of black firemen in order to promote their white counterparts as officers. This was particularly galling since departmental orders explicitly mandated preferences for particularly qualified members for certain assignments. "In one company," Wesley's group pointed out, "the only college graduate is a Negro. Yet when the Department order was received, specifically stating that men with the best educational background should be given preference, in making the assignments as Red Cross Instructors and Auxiliary Speakers, we find that the Negro man was passed over constantly."[16]

Perhaps the most egregious offenses were the segregated sleeping arrangements, often painstakingly arranged. Wesley followed his father's example by writing to Judge Hubert T. Delany and others to ask for their help in ending Jim Crow beds in New York station houses. At his behest, Walter White wrote Mayor La Guardia. Wesley also helped orchestrate City Council hearings on the matter. He admitted wryly at one meeting that conditions had improved to some degree since he started twenty-five years before, when he was assigned to sleep in the cellar. "The Captain said he thought I would be more comfortable there," Wesley, now a battalion chief, said. "But we didn't agree on that point so I was given a bed by the toilet."[17]

Back at Grand Central, despite their myriad reasons for disillusionment, Chief Williams's Red Caps nevertheless answered their country's call to help the war effort. A number of them responded to the nation's heightened anxiety and alertness by establishing an emergency medical corps in the terminal.

A registered nurse observed how inconspicuous, well-equipped hospitals attended to the traveling public in New York's railroad stations:

> At the Grand Central, five doctors serve the hospital, one of them always on call nearby at night. Registered nurses of wide experience . . . are on duty every day, two at the Grand Central, and one at the Pennsylvania, with extra nurses for emergencies and holidays. . . . A knowledge of community resources both within the station and outside is important.[18]

Chief Williams knew his Red Caps were just such a community resource: when one of the men wanted to organize a Red Cap first aid unit, he green-lighted it. Jonah R. Davis was on the scene when a traveler had had an accident, and he was able to apply his own training to help. Convinced of Davis's knowledge, Williams vouched for the terminal to commission the young man to organize a first-aid class: Davis oversaw a number of station volunteers including other Red Caps, policemen, gatemen, and the stationmaster's force. The encouragement and hands-on opportunity no doubt gave Davis an incentive to continue his medical studies that led to his career in dentistry.[19]

"Grand Central Terminal is a parish. A big one and a mighty good one," said Ralston Crosbie Young, officially Red Cap no. 42 but better known as the Red Cap Preacher. During the war, every Monday, Wednesday, and Friday at noon, he stole away from Grand Central's congested concourse and passed through the archway of Track 13. A little farther within, in the hush of an idle railroad coach, the Red Cap Preacher conducted prayer services for a microcosm of the station's disparate sea of humanity. Though some of his coworkers ribbed him, Young's unassuming evangelism gave solace to anxious commuters, soldiers, businessmen, merchant seamen, and lonely hearts. It also garnered him invitations to speak at far-flung churches and colleges, and flurries of press for many years. "I wouldn't trade my job here for any in the world," he said. Then, having done with his ethereal errand, he resumed his earthly duties of trucking luggage.[20]

Chief Williams unavoidably witnessed the ominous specter of war as it penetrated the terminal in even mundane ways. Upon the shallow landing high up on the south wall, workmen darted about at the curved base of the magnificent zodiac ceiling. Their almost inconspicuous silhouettes carried out some daily task as casually as when they had hung the great photo mural. Way up there, they moved along the line of five half-moon sidelights: from these windows, the bright midday beams shot through daily like searchlights, lazily sweeping the marble concourse floor. One can't say what nostalgia, or disquiet, stirred the Chief to look up at the workmen: assigned to dull the terminal's visibility in case of an air raid, they systematically blinded every window, one by one, with black paint. But the iconic clock kept time all the while.

CHAPTER 14

A Second Marriage

No, sir, that's not the quickest way to the restaurant.
I know all the short cuts.
Ought to. I've been here thirty-seven years.

—HILDEGARDE HOYT SWIFT, 1947

Williams's relations with the management of the Dunbar Apartments remained civil under pressure, despite occasional annoyances. In 1934, his apartment had been damaged when the building underwent renovations. At the time Frank Staley, an agent from Rockefeller's office, wrote to the complex's manager, "I went through Chief Williams's apartment this morning and was very much upset about the way in which we have had to tear it up in order to make our improvements in the 'M' apartments. . . . I feel that it is no more than fair that we should not charge the Chief any rent for the month of November."[1] Williams had undertaken costly repairs and improvements on his own—combining his own apartment 3M with 3L, tiling both baths, and installing parquet floors and French doors throughout—appreciably increasing its value.

In 1937 Rockefeller sold the Dunbar complex; it had been Williams's understanding that the "unpaid balance of $78.66" reflected in his account would be nullified at the time of the sale.[2] To the Chief's exasperation, the charge had not been canceled.

On the morning of January 5, 1942, he ran into Frank Staley passing through Grand Central Terminal. The Chief broached the issue with him, and Staley was sympathetic. Williams followed up in a letter to Staley that afternoon: "It is not my reputation to have indebtedness, and the constant letters from the office relative to this matter are of further annoyance."[3]

Staley duly forwarded Williams's typed letter with his own scribbled approval on it to Philip F. Keebler, Rockefeller's accountant: "Phil—I would be in favor of this—he was put to a terrible inconvenience for a period of 7 months. . . . Please let me know." The next day Keebler told Elias C. Stuckless, the Dunbar's subsequent realtor, that "Mr. Staley and I have decided to cancel the balance due by Mr. Williams, and I suggest that you advise Mr. Coleman [the Dunbar's manager] of our decision."[4]

The Chief's encounter with Staley in Grand Central was not only fortunate but timely: at the end of that year, yet a new landlord entered the picture, as the $3,000,000 Dunbar Apartments were deeded to the Missionary Society of the Methodist Church.[5]

Williams's uncharacteristic testiness might have been due to a change in his domestic life. The Chief had "been vacationing week ends at Oak Bluffs, Mass.," James Hogans mentioned toward summer's end.[6] For Williams, the exclusive colony on Martha's Vineyard—"Negro Newport," some dubbed it—was more than a seaside getaway. Apparently, the Chief was courting.

"I am a widower, and you can say I will not marry again," Williams had told an interviewer a few years before, adding facetiously, "unless I get some nice lady with a lot of money."[7] His sense of resignation was understandable: Lucy, his wife of thirty-five years, was still only six years gone. But in 1942 he was romantically involved once again. Martha Armstrong Robbins was a few years widowed like himself. Like Lucy, she was a New England gal, originally from Roxbury, Massachusetts. In 1908 Martha, a manicurist, had married Charles Henry Robbins, the official stenographer at Suffolk Superior Court in Boston, assigned to cases in the Massachusetts counties of Barnstable, Dukes, Nantucket, and notably in Plymouth, where he recorded the testimony during the controversial Sacco-Vanzetti trial in 1921.

In the 1920s Martha served as treasurer of the League of Women for Community Service in Boston, foreshadowing her later career. Charles died in 1937, whereupon she quit Massachusetts to become the secretary for the Phyllis Wheatley Home in Ohio. The facility at 4450 Cedar Avenue in Cleveland had been founded in 1927 as a refuge for single Negro women from teens to late middle age; Martha resided as well as worked there. But despite her relocation to Cleveland, she maintained her New England roots, returning summers to her old house at Oak Bluffs on the Vineyard.[8]

It's unclear how Williams and Martha met. In 1929 their mutual friends included Lottie Williams, Bert Williams's widow, whose funeral Martha and her first husband had attended from Boston. In any case, on February 19, 1943, James and Martha married. Officiating at the ceremony at the Abyssinian Baptist Church was Reverend Adam Clayton Powell, Jr., one of Martha's old friends from the Vineyard as well as a former Red Cap.[9]

On May 25, 1944, an important social event took place a block from Grand Central in the grand ballroom of the Hotel Roosevelt on Madison Avenue and 43rd Street. The Scottish-American educator William Allan Neilson, president emeritus of Smith College, had founded a "Committee of 100" as a corollary of the NAACP, appealing to Americans to secure equality for "our Negro fellow citizens." The diverse membership included Helen Keller, Alain Locke, Reinhold Niebuhr, and A. Philip Randolph. To raise $100,000 for the NAACP's Legal Defense Fund, headed by Thurgood Marshall, the committee organized a testimonial dinner. It would coincide with Walter White's return from fifteen weeks overseas visiting black American troops stationed in Europe and North Africa, as well as White's twenty-fifth anniversary with the NAACP. The banquet's keynote speakers included First Lady Eleanor Roosevelt, lawyer Wendell Willkie (who made the largest personal contribution of $5,000), and Carl Van Vechten. Duke Ellington's Orchestra provided the music; the "Father of the Blues" W. C. Handy and William Grant Still gave testimonials—the entertainment alone making it an affair not to be missed.

But the Chief missed it. Martha Robbins Williams sat at table three, a big banquet round, fairly front and center to the dais, with IRS collector James Johnson and his wife and a few others. However, she was without her husband that evening.

Considering his wife's attendance, what could account for Chief Williams's absence? An admittedly conjectured clue may be found in a later profile, whose interviewer wrote: "Jimmy bowed again; then for the first time smiled. It was a broad, quiet smile. But it was sudden and, in a way, disconcerting. Jimmy, apparently, had been having a bout with the dentist lately—for the smile was toothless."[10] If Williams was self-conscious, he was unlikely to risk making a toothless greeting to Mrs. Roosevelt and the countless others he knew among the thousand guests. And though alone, Martha may well have brought her own connections to the table.

There was also a considerable chance Chief Williams, while no doubt also invited to attend the Walter White Testimonial, had other personal misgivings. Businessman Harry H. Pace, Williams's Elk brother and former Strivers' Row neighbor, had once been active with the NAACP'S New York branch, but he now felt undeservedly slighted by it. The organization was not infallible—Thurgood Marshall once remarked that "there was a redcap at Grand Central Station who brought more than three hundred members into the organization. Somebody proposed that he be put on the executive board. The other board members were horrified. A *redcap!* . . . 'What college did this person attend? Who are his family?'"[11]

Marshall's aside was unspecific (and numerous Red Caps had worked assiduously for NAACP initiatives). But the remark was telling, especially if that unsuccessful nomination to the executive board was Chief Williams's.

◈

The yuletide week of 1947 was seasonably white but not festive. On December 26 a twelve-hour storm blanketed the city under more than two feet of snow and caused over two dozen deaths.

By 1940, Chief James H. Williams, sixty-one, had worked for thirty-seven years at Grand Central Terminal. With his iconic whistle, he directed some 500 black Red Caps, "who handle 85,000 pieces of baggage each month," throughout the forty-eight-acre gateway to a continent. *ACME Press Photo.*

Days into the new year, the record-breaking snowfall—which, except for mortalities, had surpassed the three-day Blizzard of 1888 of Williams's childhood—was still keeping emergency crews deployed. Grand Central was normally deserted after midnight but was now a nexus of irritated travelers, the snowbound delays having made the main concourse "a Stalingrad of desolate refugees," as journalist Alistair Cooke described it. Sixty-nine-year-old Chief Williams hustled to coordinate the Red Caps, conceding the congestion was the worst he'd seen in more than forty years at the station.

"I just stand there blowing my whistle and answering questions," he had said with good-natured modesty not so long before. "And sort of checking up on the boys, too. . . . I can close my eyes and tell from the sound how many bags are on their trucks."[12] He confessed he was looking forward to retiring at seventy, but he was summoned from his job prematurely.

On May 4, 1948, Grand Central awakened to a chilly but clear morning. Red Cap porters rushed to and from the platforms as usual, heaving luggage through the station with commuters in tow. They bustled through the station's ramps and halls to the taxis pulling up at "Sugar Hill" on Vanderbilt Avenue, on Lexington Avenue, and on 42nd Street. At about 11:10 a.m., several miles uptown in the Bronx, Chief Williams died quietly at Morrisania Hospital, where he had been for five days.

Wesley made the funeral arrangements for his father through the undertaking firm of Levy and Delany, co-owned by a family friend, Samuel R. Delany, who had been one of his father's station captains. The funeral took place at Grace Congregational Church in Harlem. The Chief's surviving family included his second wife, Martha; his three brothers, Charles, Francis, and Richard; his two sisters, Ella and Lena, both still running the Colored Mission on West 131st Street; his two surviving sons, Wesley and Pierre; and his two daughters, Gertrude and Katherine. Neither of his daughters had had children, but his sons had sired several.

Wesley arranged for a multiple plot at Woodlawn Cemetery in the Bronx. Buried there, James H. Williams was reunited with his first wife, Lucy; their son James Leroy "Roy" Williams; and Wesley's first wife, Margaret. Williams's older brother, Charles Wesley Williams, would die just a few months later, in November 1948, and be buried at Woodlawn with his wife, Jennie. Wesley himself, when he died, would be cremated and interred nearby with his soulmate Francine Musorofiti, whom he had met while assigned on Broome Street in Little Italy. Though Woodlawn Cemetery was geographically convenient to both Harlem and the Bronx, a good number of the immediate family were buried at the Evergreens Cemetery in Brooklyn. A single marker locates the latter plot, inscribed "To My Beloved Husband Lloyd M. Cofer Jr., aged 21 years, from Ella W. Cofer 1881–1967." Williams's sister had never remarried.

In the wake of Williams's death, several obituaries remembered him principally for his giving jobs to college-going young men.

Though he was not the first Red Cap porter, he broke the color barrier at the world's most prominent railway station. His hiring signaled an inflection point for the burgeoning black middle class in urban centers connected by trains. His promotion in 1909 to chief attendant positioned him as the preeminent Red Cap in the country—a position that he undertook as a calling. "If an institution is the shadow of a man," an editorial read, "Mr. Williams cast a shadow of his personality over the Red Caps he carefully selected, trained and supervised."[13] For almost half a century, he encouraged hundreds of young black men to work their way through college as Red Caps. Not a few of them came to personify the professional diversity that was at the heart of Williams's mission: to foster the growth of successful African-American men in New York and beyond.

In the first quarter of the twentieth century, anticipating the emergence of a formal railroad labor union, he was a principal organizer, protagonist, and arbiter of black railroad workers. As Grand Central was a city within the city, he was the architect of redcapping that black college students came to regard as an institution within an institution. Abram Hill noted the Chief's great pride that his department was a higher employer of college men than any other in Grand Central.

Many in Harlem regarded Chief Williams as a community hero. Born to parents who were themselves born in slavery, he was one of the last graduates of New York City's race-based Colored School system, whose teachers strove to inculcate their pupils with a moral purpose to uplift the race from systemic adversity. He numbered in the first manifest wave of African-American residents to Harlem. He was one of the earliest officers of Manhattan Lodge no. 45, the largest black fraternal lodge in the country of the Colored Elks, and one of the founding signatories of its newly chartered body. He was among the first black residents to buy a home in Strivers' Row, and a principal notable of Celebrity House, as Rockefeller's experimental Paul Laurence Dunbar Apartments were colloquially known.

It was no small matter of pride to Chief Williams that his assistant chief, Jesse Battle—a cherished friend of the entire Williams family—became New York City's first African-American police officer. Bolstered by Battle's example, his son Wesley would become Manhattan's first black fireman and the city's first black fire department officer. Williams's often-cited intimate connection with these two historic figures, who broke the glass ceiling of the city's racially restrictive hiring and promotion practices, inspired numerous young black students countrywide. Many of these young men were students, for whom inhospitable college dormitories made the Williams's home a vitally welcoming refuge.

Socially, Chief Williams cultivated personal relations with the societal and artistic elite both white and black. The press often reflected esteem for his diligent activism and philanthropy, notably on behalf of the NAACP, the Urban League, and his diligent support for black soldiers during two world wars.

Chief Williams played a conspicuous role in recreation and athletics. In the 1910s, his Grand Central Terminal Baseball Club made him a key participant in the evolution of the competitive "black nines" of semiprofessional Negro League baseball, as it did similarly in the 1920s, with his "black fives" team of professional basketball. Despite having created Red Cap baseball, basketball, and bridge teams under Grand Central Terminal's banner, Williams doesn't appear to have organized a tennis team, an activity where he nevertheless made an outstanding impact with the eponymous Williams Cup. Sponsored by the Grand Central Red Caps, the silver Tiffany trophy was awarded by the American Tennis Association, the country's oldest active historically black athletic organization, as one of its highest honors for three decades. Though its potency lessened as black professional tennis stars, such as Althea Gibson and Arthur Ashe, broke through the sport's racial barriers, the prize nevertheless enriched the legacy of black American tennis history.

Williams had established and promoted the Grand Central Red Cap Orchestra, two Grand Central Red Cap Quartets, and a choir, all of which were influential in public social life within and beyond

Harlem through live, recorded, and radio broadcast performances. The artistic integrity of the orchestra and quartet also contributed to making Grand Central an uplifting holiday destination where New York locals and tourists enjoyed caroling for years.

As a public figure, Williams promoted enterprises that fostered race pride, and that also influenced interracial alliances to affect social reform. Through his position, he created a gateway that produced such agents of social change as Lester Granger of the Urban League, the activist and performer Paul Robeson, the pastor and U.S. congressman Adam Clayton Powell, Jr., the civil rights leader and jurist Raymond Pace Alexander, the journalist and politician Earl Brown, and the Broadway star and booking agent Richard Huey.

In the travel industry, his famously disciplined Red Cap porters imbued a distinct humanity to the American experience of railroad travel. "We can't run Grand Central without the Chief," the supervisor of the station's Travelers Aid Society had said some years prior to Williams's death. "He's as much a part of the place as the *20th Century*."[14] Her comparison of the Chief to one of the world's most famous railroad trains was apt, evoking how essential the system of Red Cap porters were to the function and experience of the Terminal City and of railroad travel itself in the first half of the twentieth century.

In the mid-1940s, the Red Caps at Grand Central numbered about three hundred. In his book about the terminal, David Marshall disabused readers of "the minstrel-show dialect imputed to them" quite unfairly in the press. "Their grammar is not too bad; for New York, it's better than average," he wrote. "Their diction is good, sound, working-class diction."[15] Marshall also admitted "that the red cap is a trained manager who takes you in charge as well as your luggage; who steers you the right way by every possible short cut, and gets you through the gate before the gateman slams it shut; who talks as well as any gentleman's gentleman should; who cheers you with a flashing smile, bows like a nobleman, and—pays you the tribute of overestimating your importance."[16]

In 1952, fourteen years after Chief Williams's death, former New York State governor Herbert H. Lehman wrote a letter of regard to Wesley Williams, on Wesley's retirement from the fire department: "I had the privilege of your father's friendship for a great many years, and I know that I first met you through him when he introduced us at the Grand Central Station just before you were appointed as Battalion Chief. He, too, was a very fine man."[17]

In popular culture, countless film, stage, and literary works reflect the legacy of Williams. Whether they appear incidentally or are featured prominently, black Red Cap porters are ubiquitous in depictions of American railroad stations. They populate scenes of diverse cinematic fare that either employ or evoke Grand Central Terminal. In Roy Mack's 1932 musical short *Smash Your Baggage*, dancers from Harlem's Small's Paradise nightclub portray travelers and porters in breathless abandon at Grand Central. Raoul Walsh's *Going Hollywood*, a big-budget, feature-length 1933 musical starring Marion Davies and Bing Crosby, features a large dance number at the terminal.

We see Red Caps or the terminal in *The Band Wagon* (1953), starring Fred Astaire, and even in Alfred Hitchcock's suspense thrillers *Strangers on a Train* (1951) and *North by Northwest* (1959). In 1932 the dramatists Ben Hecht (who later collaborated with Louis Armstrong on the song "Red Cap") and Charles MacArthur wrote a hit Broadway farce, *Twentieth Century*. In creating a character of the chief of ten Grand Central Red Caps, played by actor Frank Badham, they evoked Williams.

In 1978, thirty years after Chief Williams's death, a musical version of the Hecht/MacArthur play, *On the Twentieth Century*, afforded an ensemble of four black Red Cap porters a nightly Broadway showstopper called "Life Is Like a Train." Joseph Wise, one of the ensemble, understood the palpable connection of American railroad history to his own African-American heritage. He knew the Red Cap occupation once gave manifold opportunities to African

Americans, and now it gave ineffable opportunities to four aspiring black performers within the narrow casting parameters of a period theater piece. Ironically, the show's nontraditional casting of the porters extended less liberally to other principal roles. In February 2015 the musical was revived, and a promotional poster portrayed the Red Caps as three whites—a fourth one in the cast, who was black, was not shown. The omission was telling. "I think it is a missed opportunity," Wise wrote in a blog at the time. Indeed, it was telling of how much Chief Williams's mission to eradicate the color bar remains ongoing.

By the time Williams died in 1948, his moniker "Chief Williams" had been eclipsed by his son, Wesley, who had become Battalion Chief Williams of the fire department ten years earlier. But the railroad itself was losing purchase in the modern age as well. Travelers increasingly preferred the romantic expediency of flying, or surrendered to the lure of highways and automobiles. And as they did, the pulse of the great railroad station gradually and naturally waned.

The Red Caps have disappeared from Grand Central Terminal, although they exist in some railroad stations elsewhere in the country with greatly modified job descriptions. From our twenty-first-century perspective, we cherish the grand Beaux-Arts complex as an architectural achievement, its preservation championed by such celebrities as the late Jacqueline Kennedy Onassis. But the intersecting narratives of Grand Central and Harlem's vibrant African-American community are woefully incomplete without attention to the contribution of James H. Williams. He had a keen vantage point of the proverbial passing parade, maintaining a sure footing in the antipodes of downtown Grand Central Terminal and uptown Harlem. More than just witnessing history, Williams had direct agency in the unfolding histories of each, and to both he demonstrated lifelong constancy.

James H. Williams's story is especially significant today, as the challenge of acknowledging and mending America's racially divided past often triggers defensiveness or engenders bitterness. His life chronicles how a representative body of African-American workers proactively countered Jim Crow, which pervaded even the most resplendent public halls of the nation's most enlightened modern city. Not through brawn and stamina alone, but rather with persistent fellowship, ingenuity, and grace, Williams and his men remained determined to attain their North Star in even a painted-on vault of heaven.

ACKNOWLEDGMENTS

This biography began as a little online article in February 2013 to celebrate the centennial of New York City's Grand Central Terminal, which, in a timely way, coincided with Black History Month. But no sooner had the project taken on the life of James H. Williams, than it took on a life of its own, with countless past lives jumping aboard. I have many to thank who aided me in making the acquaintance of so many disparate people, places, and events that comprised my journey with this book.

Columbia University's Community Scholars Program was indispensable, as it afforded me access to the school's vast historic newspaper and journal databases. These resources were crucial in discovering Chief Williams, a most elusive public figure. I thank the helpful staff of the Rare Books and Manuscripts Library: Sean Quimby, Thai Jones, Jennifer B. Lee, and Meredith Self. I'm also grateful for the fellowship of the Community Scholars Program administrators and staff: Maxine Griffith, Karen Jewitt, Kevin Brannon, Bashar Makhay; trustee and biographer A'Lelia Bundles, who also contributed from her own Madam Walker Family Archives to my book; and George Calderaro, director of Community Relations. I thank professors Matthew Sandler (American Studies) and Kimberly Johnson (Urban Studies), who graciously allowed me to audit and participate in their classes. The disparate interests of my fellow community scholars was an inspiration—Cohort I: Mariama C. Keita, Paula Kimper, Vivian Nixon, Steven A. Watkins, and my ever simpatico colleague John Reddick; Cohort II: Adarsh Alphons,

Sheila Anderson, and Martha Diaz; Cohort III: Mable Haddock, Kanene Holder, Lisa Jones, and Rodney Trapp; Cohort IV: Renee L. Hill, Regan Sommer McCoy, Peter Noel, Lil Nickelson, and Vivian Williams-Kurutz; Cohort IV: Nancy Dorsinville, Keisha Sutton-James, April Tyler, and Michele Y. Washington; Cohort V: Debra Ann Byrd, Karioki Crosby, Debbie Meyer, and Chris Pellettieri, and especially Melanie Edwards, a constant resource and champion for years. My deep appreciation goes to the many referees for my program application: Yuien Chin, Ethan P. Cohen, Vivian Ducat, Alana Farkas, Pamela Gillespie, Gillian G. Hannum, Kathleen Hulser, David King, Earl Kooperkamp, Dan Levatino, Bruce Morrow, Vic Puccio, Nan Rothschild, Mark Schoofs, E. R. Shipp, Linda Villarosa, Barbara Wilks, and Jonathan R. Wynn.

My profound gratitude goes to the Leon Levy Center for Biography, at the City University of New York Graduate Center, whose fellowship enabled me to dive into the basic research to put this book on track. I'm so indebted to the guidance of Gary Giddins, Annalyn Swan, and Michael Gately; and to the talented company of my co-biography fellows Colin Asher, Blake Gopnik, and Gordana-Dana Grozdanić, along with dissertation fellows Jennifer Chancellor and Daron Jabari Howard; as well as previous fellows Pamela Newkirk and James Davis. My heartfelt thanks goes to those who wrote support letters for my application: David Freeland, Kathleen Hulser, Retha Powers, Linda Villarosa, Jonathan R. Wynn, and Mark Schoofs.

I'm profoundly thankful to the Museum of Fine Arts Houston and Brown Foundation for my residency at Dora Maar House/Maison Dora Maar in Ménerbes, France, to work on this project. I thank director Gwen Strauss for her railway pickups and drop-offs, food runs, and general acclimations. I was most fortunate to have shared the house with Darragh McKeon, Marysia Lewandowska, and Elisabeth Frost; as well as former Fellow Mary Flanagan. And what an honor to meet local photographer Brice Toul, who shot my book cover profile.

Essential were the rich collections and helpful staff at the Schomburg Center for Research in Black Culture of the New York Public Library: Mary Yearwood, Steven Fullwood, Maira Liriano, Michael Mery, Tom Lisanti, and scholar emeritus Chris Moore, who were invaluable pilots as I navigated the myriad resources of this indispensable archive.

I particularly thank the Municipal Art Society of New York for recruiting me to give the tours of Grand Central Terminal that introduced me to my unsung subject, Williams, and the station's former Red Cap porters. I thank MAS's successive program directors Alana Farkas and Ted Mineau for engaging my docent talks and public tours, allowing me to introduce others to the Terminal and Harlem's connective history. Thanks to MAS docent Fred Fischer, whose Grand Central walk I learned much from.

I'm sincerely thankful to Ginger Adams Otis for enhancing my appreciation of pioneer African-American New York City fireman Wesley Williams while researching her own book, *Firefight*; her subject turned out to be Chief Williams's son. Moreover, I am grateful to Ginger for introducing me to Wesley's grandson, Charles. I also thank historian Gary Urbanowicz of the New York City Fire Museum for his guidance in locating resources about Wesley Williams, and to the New York City Police Museum for those pertaining to Samuel J. "Jesse" Battle.

Of course I am deeply grateful to Charles Ford Williams, great-grandson of James H. Williams, who generously made available his abundant collection of Williams family photographs, and who shared personal anecdotes and insights from his own book, *The Chief*, about his grandfather, Fire Battalion Chief Wesley Williams. That Charles and I discovered we were exactly the same age, born a week apart, surely added to our simpatico vibe. I also thank Michael DiPrima, for his own personal recollections of Wesley Williams and his son James.

I was fortunate to have the aid of Susan Olsen at the Bronx's Woodlawn Cemetery, and Helen Thurston and Eva Bowerman at Brooklyn's Evergreens Cemetery. I thank them for locating records whose details helped to revivify voices of permanent residents from both Williams family members and their contemporaries. Additional thanks to the Municipal Archives and Municipal Research and Reference Library: Kenneth Cobb, for stewarding a trove of vital records and tax photos, and the always helpful staff. My thanks also to Carey Stumm at the New York City Transit Museum Archives.

The Rockefeller Archive Center in Sleepy Hollow, New York, provided a trove of documents on Harlem's Paul Laurence Dunbar Apartments and the Dunbar National Bank—as well as a wonderful researchers' lunch! My thanks to the helpful staff: Bob Clark, Bethany Antos, Tom Rosenbaum, Michele Hiltzik Beckerman, and especially former archivist Nancy Adgent, who had just retired, but was ever resourceful. I'm very grateful to the staff at the Franklin D. Roosevelt Presidential Library: Kirsten Carter and William Baehr, for correspondence between James H. Williams and Eleanor Roosevelt. Thanks to the David Rumsey Map Collection: David Rumsey and Brandon Rumsey. And to the David Graham Du Bois Trust: Odell Murray and Frederick T. Courtright, for documents related to W.E.B. Du Bois, the NAACP, and Grand Central. Thanks also to the Molly Rea/Molly Rea Trust, Christie Fernandez, and Marie Noehren, for permission to use the Rea Irvin *New Yorker* magazine cover.

I thank the staff of many academic institutions, including the Yale Beineke Library: Danijela Matković; Haverford College: Mary Crauderueff, curator of Quaker Collections; Tuskegee Institute: Cheryl Ferguson, archival assistant; Hampton University: Donzella Maupin, archives manager; Cornell University's *New York Amsterdam News* Photo Archives, Division of Rare and Manuscript Collections: Hilary Dorsch Wong, reference coordinator, and staffers Weston Tate, Eisha Neely, and Cheryl Rowland for their assistance. Princeton University, Mudd Manuscript Library: special collection archivist Sara Logue, and at Firestone Library: AnnaLee Pauls. Colby College, Miller Library: April Paul, coordinator. University of Massachusetts Amherst Libraries: Blake Spitz, Special Collections and University Archives. St. Bonaventure University: Dennis Frank, archivist; and Emory University's Manuscript, Archives, and Rare Book Library: Courtney Chartier, head of research services, for leading me to the Langmuir Photograph Collection. I thank AP Images: Maria Schiff; and Getty Images: Christiana Newton, Daniel Romo, and Donna Daley.

I could go on singing my gratitude to the New York City Parks Photo Archive: Jonathan Kuhn and Rebekah Burgess provided me a plum Red Cap Barbershop Quartet image. Trinity Wall Street: Anne Petrimoulx and Joe Lapinski, archivists. Independent photographic researchers: Denise Bethel and Chris Mahoney, who fielded my questions about the Otto Sarony Studio. Frederick Ely Williamson Library: Michael Vitiello and the New York Railroad Enthusiasts, for access to Grand Central Terminal's hidden repository. Illuminating guidance came from the Greenwich Village Society for Historic Preservation: Andrew Berman and Sarah Bean Apmann, who gave me a clearer picture of John Wesley Williams's first New York City neighborhood in the 1870s. My appreciation to the Tiffany & Co. Archives Department: Cristina Vignone, assistant archivist. Thanks to Herb Boyd's encouragement at the *New York Amsterdam News*. And thanks to Tricia Vita for her tweets from the Coney Island History Project.

I'm grateful for occasions to engage students with my still unfolding research on Chief Williams's Harlem. I thank various professors at the City College of New York: Dave Davison, who invited me as guest lecturer at his MFA Film Program class; Grazyna Drabik, with her Macaulay Honors Class students; Joshua Cohen, with his African Art History class; and visiting Fisk University students of the Fisk Jubilee Singers, sponsored by the Harry T. Burleigh Society. I also thank New York University professors Robin Nagle and Olivier Berthe, whose students I was able to show the Chief's Grand Central. My sincere appreciation to others who afforded me opportunities to preview my biography project in various development stages goes to Thomas Allen Harris, for his online Digital Diaspora Family Reunion Project; Medgar Evers College Library Conference; the Institute for the Exploration of Seneca Village History; Harlem One Stop; the Harlem Chamber Players; and the Guides Association of New York City (GANYC).

Such a project, of course, bites off more material than it can reasonably digest. I thank many who generously offered photo or anecdotal images that were inevitably compressed out of the narrative. I thank Linda Kenney Miller, whose amiable conversation—and her book, *Beacon on the Hill*—deepened my appreciation of Dr. John A. Kenney and his sister-in-law Martha Robbins Williams. And I thank James H. Johnston, whose book, *From Slave Ship to Harvard*, introduced me to Robert Turner Ford; and to Ford's daughter Alice Truiett for his photograph. Thanks to quilt artist extraordinaire Michael Cummings, my friend and neighbor, for his photo showing Richard Huey's Harlem restaurant, Aunt Dinah's Kitchen. And also to Jacqueline Jones Compaore, at Francis Marion University, for locating an old *Tattler* news photo for me.

My gratitude goes to Wendy Johnson, whose father Howard "Stretch" Johnson's memoir, which she completed, *Dancer in the Revolution*, led me to a rare photo of Chief Williams's Grand Central Terminal Red Cap Baseball team; and to Dr. Bennett Rosner, for his photo of the Brooklyn Royal Giants, which he graciously allowed me to scan at his home in Yonkers. I'm fortunate to have had the encouragement of various experts in particular fields: Harlem historian and W.E.B. Du Bois biographer David Levering Lewis; Grand Central Terminal historian Anthony W. Robins; labor historian Daniel Levinson Wilk; music historian Elliott Hurwitt; and tour guide extraordinaire Justin Ferate.

Author Samuel R. "Chip" Delany, a son and grandson of Grand Central Red Caps, graciously shared his memories in a phone interview. I also appreciate my acquaintance with a couple of Australian Harlemites: biographer Bill Egan, for his inexhaustible knowledge of Florence Mills; and historian Clare Corbould of Deakin University, for expanding my awareness of Maurice Hunter. Thanks to the Hotel Employees and Restaurant Employees/Local 6: John Turchiano; Barbershop Harmony Society: Neal Siegal; and the New York Academy of Medicine: Arlene Shaner. I'm also beholden to the sustenance of dinners, coffees, emails, and Instagrams from David Silverman, Kevin McGruder, Steven Watson, Michael F. Moore, Daniel

Atkinson, Richard Myers, Adrienne Ingrum, and Monique Lewis. Of course I can't imagine accomplishing this project without the patience, and foodstuffs, of my partner, James "Anton" McDermott.

I extend my warmest gratitude to my dear brilliant agent, Faith Childs, a constant source of wisdom and encouragement—who found this project a great home.

I'm indebted to Bob Weil and everyone on the Liveright team of miracle-workers who helped me to realize this book. It was such a pleasure to work with the astonishingly insightful associate editor Marie Pantojan. I also thank my copy editor Janet Biehl, and project editor Dassi Zeidel. Thank you also, Peter Miller, director of publicity, and Gabe Kachuck, editorial and publicity assistant. I am appreciatively speechless for my wonderfully evocative book cover from graphic designing wizard Steve Attardo.

NOTES

Introduction

1. New York City Landmarks Preservation Commission Designation Report, Pershing Square Viaduct (Park Avenue Viaduct), September 23, 1980.
2. E. B. White, "Notes and Comment," *New Yorker*, March 19, 1949.
3. "'Chief' James H. Williams," *New York Herald Tribune,* May 6, 1948.
4. "The Red Cap Tells the World," *Elks*, June 1927.
5. Earl Brown, "Timely Topics," *New York Amsterdam News*, May 15, 1948.

Chapter 1: "To Hustle While You're Waiting"

1. Johnson, *Autobiography.*
2. James H. Hogans, "America's No. 1 Redcap," *Baltimore Afro-American*, August 27,1938.
3. Reginald A. Johnson, "Red Caps Seek A Living Wage," *Opportunity*, April 1, 1939.
4. "First Redcap Will See Son Made Battalion Fire Chief," *Baltimore Afro-American*, March 26, 1938.
5. "How Come, 'Strivers Row'?" *Amsterdam News*, November 9, 1940.
6. "Strivers Row—A Satire by Abram Hill," Proscenium Theater, Cleveland, Ohio, 1976.
7. Richard Wright was later cited as author of the uncredited "Portrait of Harlem" chapter.
8. "Criticizes 'Portrait of Harlem' in Guidebook," *New York Age*, September 24, 1938.
9. James Williams, interview by Abram Hill, August 29-30, 1939, Federal Writers' Project.
10. "For Grant, Enthusiastic Meeting of the Colored General Committee," *New York Times*, May 28, 1880. As an officer of the Colored Republican General Commit-

tee, George F. Mack championed an unsuccessful campaign to secure the party's presidential nomination to President Ulysses S. Grant for a third term.

11. Freedmen's Savings and Trust Company (aka Freedmen's Bank) account records, 1872–73.
12. *African Repository*, the report of the colored population estimate continued to enumerate 150 whitewashers, 80 coachmen, 64 cooks, 48 barbers, 182 laborers, and 124 sailors; also 183 washerwomen, 214 widows without occupation. It noted, "Colored professional and tradesmen are few, viz: 2 farmers, 1 broker, 3 printers, 6 physicians, 7 teachers, 18 priests, and 1 ventriloquist." May 1, 1859.
13. Freedmen's Bank.
14. "The Pastime Literary Club," *New York Clipper*, November 27, 1875. The reviewer claimed that this was "the first amateur dramatic society of colored men that was ever organized in this city," but he overlooked William Alexander Brown's famous, if short-lived, African Grove Theater, founded more than half a century earlier in 1821.
15. "Negro Waiters . . . Fashionable Parisiennes at Their Receptions," *Graphic*, January 25, 1879.
16. "Hotel Drouot in America," *Art Amateur Monthly*, January 1880.
17. "Terry Lodge History," *Pacific Appeal*, March 13, 1875. John Wesley Williams was associated with Terry Lodge in his later years, but when he joined is not known.
18. "New York and Vicinity," *Commercial Advertiser*, August 14, 1866; David P. Thelen and Leslie H. Fishel, Jr., "Reconstruction in the North: The World Looks at New York's Negroes, March 16, 1867," *New York History* 49, no. 4 (October 1968): 404–40.
19. "Personal," *Elevator*, November 15, 1873.
20. "The Colored People—Extension of the Franchise—A New County Organization," *Frederick Douglass' Paper*, September 21, 1855.
21. Philip Hone, *The Diary of Philip Hone, 1828–1851*. The former mayor acknowledged the African-American caterer Thomas Downing's role in the famous "Boz Ball," New York City's extravagant welcome to English novelist Charles Dickens, which took place at the Park Theater on February 14, 1842, noting: "This branch of the business was farmed out to Downing, the great man of oysters, who received $2,200."
22. J.W.C. Pennington's *The Origin and History of the Colored People* (1841) is generally regarded as the first book-length history of African Americans.
23. "Another Outrage Upon the Eighth Avenue Railroad," *Liberator*, December 26, 1856.
24. "Public Meetings. A Colored Anniversary," *New York Morning Express*, February 24, 1858.
25. "Outrage Upon a Colored Gentleman," *New York Daily Tribune*, August 11, 1859.

26. "Riding in City Cars," *New Orleans Tribune*, July 26, 1864.
27. "Presentation," *Elevator*, December 20, 1867. Upon Porter's death in 1884, the *New York Times* obituary recalled his prominence as the "Railroad Champion for Equal Rights."
28. A deed filed at the New York City Register's office shows that Peter S. and Maria A. Porter sold their property in 1877 to a Jacob G. Fundis for $13,200 (which was a bit of a loss), yet stayed on in the townhouse until his death in 1884.
29. "Metropolitan Items," *New-York Evening Post*, November 21, 1871.
30. Regardless of this publicized opening, the eponymously named Porter's Mansion repeatedly advertised its establishment since "1853." Did this curious date allude to a previous haven Porter had maintained before the Civil War? Indeed, some of his past abolitionist friends still gratefully recall instances of his determined, if necessarily elusive, hospitality.
31. "Ex-Gov. Pinchback," *New York Times*, August 26, 1873.
32. M. F. Armstrong and Helen W. Ludlow, *Hampton and Its Students* (New York, G.P. Putnam's Sons, 1874).
33. Fletcher, *100 Years of the Negro.*
34. *Liberator*, February 2, 1849.
35. "An Undoubted Right," *Harper's Weekly*, May 30, 1874; and "Condition of the South," *New York Times*, December 8, 1874.
36. Johnson, *Autobiography.*

Chapter 2: "A Gilded, but Gritty Age"

1. U.S. Federal Census, 1880.
2. "Marshal Douglass Denies," *Washington Post*, April 30, 1880; "Fred Douglass on Chastine Cox," *Chicago Tribune*, May 1, 1880.
3. "Ashton's Exhibition," *Brooklyn Daily Eagle*, October 9, 1879.
4. "Chastine Cox's Funeral," *New York Sun*, July 17, 1880.
5. Berlin and Harris, *Slavery in New York*; "Will of Lieutenant Governor Colden," New York Genealogical and Biographical Society, 1873.
6. Trotter, *Music and Some Highly Musical.*
7. "Walter F. Craig Dead," *New York Age*, February 4, 1933.
8. "Sarah J. Smith Tompkins Garnet," entry in James, James, and Boyer, *Notable American Women,* vol. 2. Garnet served as school principal from "her appointment, Apr. 30, 1863, to the date of her retirement, Sept. 10, 1900."
9. "At a Mass Meeting," *New York Evangelist*, February 22, 1883.
10. "Pupils in City Schools," *New York Times*, July 2, 1884.
11. Grover Cleveland to Charles L. Bartlett, March 14, 1904, in Cleveland, *Letters and Addresses.*
12. "Fifteenth Amendment Celebrated," *New York Times*, March 31, 1887.

13. "Owing to the Colored Children," *New York Herald*, May 6, 1888.
14. Help Wanted, *New York Herald*, December 4, 1887.
15. *New York Herald* and other papers featured the gift of "handsome bouquets for the ladies from Thorley's greenhouses" in regular advertisements for Tony Pastor's Fourteenth Street Theater in the early 1880s.
16. "Sales at Auction," *New York Herald*, February 3, 1883.
17. "How Did You Get Your First Job?" *New York Herald*, July 17, 1910.
18. "Orchids for Market-flowers," *Garden and Forest*, December 13, 1893.
19. Sewall Read, "Fin de Siecle" (poem), *Life*, February 23, 1893.
20. "Song Publishers Branching Out," *Broadway Magazine*, December 1898.
21. "Of Interest to Women," *Illustrated American*, November 3, 1894.
22. "Neck or Nothing," *Brother Jonathan*, April 9, 1842.
23. "Coaches for Mexico," *Troy Daily Whig*, March 4, 1844.
24. "Omnibus Driving," *New York Tribune*, May 23, 1844.
25. "What Shall Be Done?" *Commercial Advertiser*, July 8, 1844.
26. U.S. Federal Census of Defective Cases, 1880.
27. Edwards, *Words Made Flesh*.
28. Annual Report of New York Society for the Deaf, 1856.
29. Edwards, *Words Made Flesh*.
30. "The 'Girl in the Pie' at the Three Thousand Five Hundred Dollar Dinner at the Artist Breese's New York Studio," *New York World*, October 13, 1895.
31. "Attendants at the Grand Central to Assist Passengers," *Baltimore Sun*, March 5, 1895.
32. Ibid.
33. "New York Central's New Feature," *Daily Inter Ocean*, March 3, 1895.
34. "Attendants at the Grand Central to Assist Passengers," *Baltimore Sun*, March 5, 1895.
35. Ibid.
36. "In the Grand Central Station at New York City," *Railroad Gazette*, March 8, 1895.
37. "To Greet Travelers," *New York Herald*, February 27, 1895.
38. "Have You Seen the Red Headed Men," *New York Herald*, September 1, 1895.
39. "Boy Baggage Smashers," *Washington Post*, April 2, 1905.
40. "Free Attendant Service, Grand Central Station," *Nashville American*, March 20, 1896.
41. "Known by Their Clothes," *New York Tribune*, October 4, 1896.
42. Lisa Elsroad, "Tenderloin," in Jackson, *Encyclopedia of New York City*.
43. "Map Showing Proximity of Evil to Schools and Churches," illustration, *New York Press*, May 18, 1890.
44. "Summary of the News," *New York Herald*, May 17, 1894.
45. St. Chrysostom's Chapel, Guild of St. Cyprian, Year Book and Register of Trin-

ity Church 1884. The guild, organized in 1883, was "a Mutual Benefit Society for colored men and women, providing for its sick, and burying its dead. Initiation Fee, $1; Monthly Dues, 25 cents."

46. Tom Miller, "The Lost St. Chrysostom's Chapel," *Daytonian in Manhattan*, July 6, 2015, quoting *New-York Tribune*, September 8, 1884.
47. Vital Records, Municipal Archives of New York City.

Chapter 3: "If We Cannot Go Forward, Let Us Mark Time"

1. "New-York Negroes: They Are Moving Uptown—Entering the Professions," *New-York Tribune*, April 1, 1900.
2. Ibid.
3. "Pointed Paragraphs—In the Death of Charles Thorley, Millionaire Florist," *New York Age*, November 24, 1923.
4. "The Pan-African Conference," *Manchester Guardian*, July 25, 1900.
5. "Harris Trial Testimony," *New York Evening Post*, October 26, 1900.
6. Citizens' Protective League, *Story of the Riot,* pamphlet, September 1900.
7. "More Rioting in New York," *San Francisco Chronicle*," August 17, 1900.
8. "Quieter on West Side," *New York Tribune*, August 17, 1900.
9. "The New York Riots," *Cleveland Gazette*, September 1, 1900.
10. "English Subjects Clubbed," *Iowa State Bystander*, August 24, 1900.
11. "West Side Race Riot," *New York Tribune*, August 16, 1900. Numerous papers across the country carried the story of Walker's and Logan's abduction and drubbing by the mob. Trainor's Hotel was located at 1291 Broadway, just south of Herald Square. Other sources for this same year cite Clarence Logan as having been both Williams's and Walker's private secretary for four years, then a shortstop on the W&W Co.'s baseball team and a family friend to both. Logan was also the business manager for a road company of J. Leubrie Hill's *Darktown Follies* in 1914.
12. "The New York Riots," *Sun*, August 17, 1900.
13. "Negro Pastor Defies Police to Answer," *New York Times*, August 27, 1900.
14. "N. H. Hashim Arrives" and "Negro Seriously Stabbed," *New York Times*, August 21, 1900.
15. "Chief Devery Denounced," *New York Times*, August 25, 1900.
16. "Negroes Demand Justice," *New York Tribune*, September 13, 1900.
17. "One Effect of Race Riots," *New York Tribune*, September 17, 1900.
18. "Change in White House Servants," *Washington Post*, March 25, 1889; "White House Help," *St. Louis Post-Dispatch*, March 26, 1889.
19. "White House Scenes," *Chicago Daily Tribune*, November 30, 1890.
20. Zeisloft, New Metropolis.
21. "White or Colored Servants," *Austin Daily Statesman*, April 26, 1901; "Colored

Waiters Are Grateful," *New York Tribune*, April 27, 1901; "Help Issue Rends Union League," *New York Tribune*, May 11, 1901.

22. Russell Spaulding, president of the Elblight Company, in "Display Lighting, Signs and Decorations," read at the National Electric Light Association Convention, in 1902.
23. National Souvenir of Prince Henry's Visit to the United States, 1902.
24. "Prince Henry of Germany Is Billed," *Broad Ax*, February 22, 1902.
25. "Prince Henry Should Be Given," *Topeka Plain Dealer*, March 7, 1902.
26. "Prince Henry Is Here To-Day," *Nashville American*, March 2, 1902.
27. Robley D. Evans, "Prince Henry's American Impressions," *McClure's Magazine*, May 1902.
28. "Prince Henry Is Here To-Day," *Nashville American*, March 2, 1902; "All Who Read the Dailies Will Remember," *Colored American*, March 22, 1902.
29. Evans, "Prince Henry's Impressions."
30. "A Bit of Biography," *New York Age*, October 9, 1913.
31. Estimated currency inflation from 1902 to 2018: $700 ($19,000); $6,000 ($161,000).
32. "Ship to Be a Garden of Flowers," *New York World*, March 8, 1902; "Flowers for the Prince," *New York Times*, March 8, 1902; "Prince Henry Gave Him a Watch," *New York Herald*, April 12, 1902; "A Negro Floral Decorator Enjoyed Prince's Hospitality," *New York Sun*, April 12, 1902; and "In the Death of Charles Thorley," *New York Age*, November 24, 1923.
33. "Says They Beg Too Much—Urges Negroes to Amass Property," *New York Tribune*, May 2, 1903.
34. "Rev. Dr. W. H. Brooks Suggest 'Jim-Crow' Commonwealth," *Baltimore Sun*, March 22, 1904.
35. Philip A. Payton, Jr., "Afro-American Realty Company," *Colored American*, November 1904.
36. Williams may have been unaware of the building's earlier distinction: according to various newspaper items, the address in 1898 was home to Dr. Jin Fuey Moy, a prominent New Yorker during the fraught era of the country's Chinese Exclusion Act.
37. Sylvester Russell, "A Quiet Evening with Jesse Shipp," *Washington Freeman*, September 16, 1905.

Chapter 4: Fraternity and Ascendancy

1. *Railroad Gazette* (citing a letter quoted in the *Four-Track News*), October 25, 1901.
2. "The Colored Girl Here—Race Prejudice Bars Her," *New York Tribune*, August 6, 1904.
3. Ibid.

4. "Says They Beg Too Much—Urges Negroes to Amass Property," *New York Tribune*, May 2, 1903.
5. "Must Live By Tips," *New York Globe and Commercial Advertiser*, May 18, 1904.
6. Samuel J. Battle Oral History, Columbia University, 1960. Estimated currency inflation from 1902 to 2018: $32 ($855); $300 ($8,012).
7. T.H.A. MacDonald, "Fifty-fourth Street and Third Avenue, Brooklyn, advises . . . ," The Pharmaceutical Era, July 20, 1905.
8. "Gossip of the Art World," *Brooklyn Standard Union*, October 15, 1905; "Negroes Show Pictures of Their Own Painting," *Brooklyn Daily Eagle*, October 17, 1905; and Harry Roseland, "Notes of Brooklyn Artists," *Brooklyn Daily Eagle*, August 11, 1929. The artist William Ernest Braxton, later associated with the bibliophile Arturo "Arthur" Schomburg, was identified at the time of the Brooklyn exhibition as Ernest W. Braxton.
9. "Lady Betty Goes to Newport," *Ladies' Home Journal*, December 1905.
10. The photographer Otto Sarony (1850–1903) was the son of French-Canadian-born Napoleon Sarony (1821–96), a renowned celebrity portrait photographer, especially of the late nineteenth-century American theater. Thorley had occasion to work with both father and son. Various photographers operated out of the late Sarony studio for some years.
11. "Ivanhoe Commandery Holds Re-Union Picnic," *New York Age*, July 26, 1906.
12. J. E. Robinson, "James H. Williams and His Success at Grand Central Terminal," *Colored American*, August 1, 1909.
13. "Elkdom Locally and Otherwise," *Colored American*, September 1, 1907.
14. "At the Academy of Music," *Turf, Field and Farm*, June 9, 1868. The euphemistic word *ethiopian* was a common exoticization for black Americans.
15. On November 2, 1904, the Brooklyn Lodge no. 32 and Progressive Lodge no. 35 of Jersey City "set up on Manhattan Island the first Elk lodge, Manhattan Lodge no. 45, with thirty-two members enrolled." For a historical overview of New York City's secret orders of Masons, Elks, Odd Fellows, Knights, and the female branches, see Charles T. McGill, "Do You Know the Password?," *New York Amsterdam News*, December 18, 1929.
16. "(I.)B.P.O.E.(W.) a Winner," *New York Age*, June 20, 1906; and "Negro Elks Win Court Decision," *Atlanta Constitution*, June 20, 1906.
17. "Elks Ready for Meeting," *New York Age*, August 9, 1906.
18. Although usually printed in later years as Samuel J. Battle, his name often appeared in earlier years as Jesse S. Battle and J. S. Battle. Close acquaintances often called him Jesse, which I've chosen to use for consistency.
19. "First Annual Picnic and Summernight's Festival," advertisement, *New York Age*, May 24, 1906.
20. "Howard Will Be Deposed," *New York Age*, August 2, 1906; and "The Elks' Convention in Brooklyn," *Colored American*, October 1, 1906.

21. "The Elks' Convention in Brooklyn," *Colored American*, October 1, 1906.
22. "First N.Y. Lodge Set Apart in 1904," *Colored American*, August 23, 1927.
23. "Elkdom Locally and Otherwise," *Colored American*, August 1, 1907.
24. "New York Elks' Memorial," *New York Age*, December 5, 1907.
25. "Fever-Mad, Leaps from Hospital Window to Death," *New York Evening Telegram*, August 29, 1906; and Mary White Ovington, "A Life of Service," *Colored American*, November 1906.
26. *The Negro in the Cities of the North* (New York: Charity Organization Society, 1905).
27. Burial record, Evergreens Cemetery—Mt. Seir, Lot 821, Owner: John W. Williams and Lucy E., deed no. [unclear], Brooklyn, New York. John W. Williams, Jr.'s, death certificate gives his date of decease as April 28, 1908, due to "phthisis pulmonalis asthenia." Vital Records, Municipal Archives of New York City.
28. Grand Central Terminal timeline, compiled November 26, 1940, Metropolitan Transportation Authority (MTA) Archives. Running between New York and Chicago, the famous high-speed and luxurious *20th Century Limited* debuted on June 15, 1902. It entered and left Grand Central on electric power but switched to steam power at Croton-Harmon Terminal in Westchester, New York.
29. "Mr. J. H. Williams Promoted—After Seven Years of Faithful Service Appointed Chief Attendant of the 'Red Cap' Employees," unattributed news clipping, possibly *Colored American*, May 1909.
30. J. E. Robinson, "James H. Williams and His Success at Grand Central Terminal," *Colored American*, August 1, 1909.
31. "Porter Killed by a Train," *Brooklyn Daily Eagle*, August 18, 1909; "Funeral of Louis H. Blackwell," *New York Age*, August 26, 1909; and "Judgments," *Eastern State Journal* (White Plains, N.Y.), December 14, 1912. Five hundred dollars in 1912 is equal to about $12,000 in 2018 currency.
32. Certificate and Record of Death of Dorothy Williams, September 24, 1909, State of New York.
33. "Red Caps Organize," *New York Age*, September 23, 1909; and "R.R. Attendants Organize," *New York Age*, July 21, 1910.
34. "Red Cap Benefit By Sissle & Blake and Chocolate Dandies," *New York Age*, November 15, 1924.
35. "Removal of General Offices New York Central Lines to Grand Central Terminal," advertisement, *New York Tribune*, March 31, 1910. The ad noted that the new terminal, when completed, would have an entrance at Lexington Avenue and Forty-fifth Street, three blocks north of its main 42nd Street entrance.

Chapter 5: Harlem Exodus to the Bronx and to the Sea

1. "Live Tips from Reno Camps," *Columbus Enquirer-Sun*, July 3, 1910; "Poolselling on the Sabbath," *New York Sun*, July 4, 1910; and "When Johnson Beat Jeffries in Reno," *New York Evening Telegram*, November 6, 1921.
2. "Send Johnson $20,000," *New York Age*, June 9, 1910.
3. "Big Reception for Johnson," *New York Age*, July 7, 1910.
4. "Wild Scramble over Johnson," *Baltimore American*, July 12, 1910.
5. "Harlem Property Owners Discuss Negro Problem," *Harlem Home News*, April 7, 1911, July 31, August 28, 1913, cited in Osofsky, *Harlem*.
6. "20,000 to Keep Negroes Out," *New York Times*, December 8, 1910; "Negroes Given Clean Sweep," *Baltimore Sun*, December 21, 1910.
7. "Leroy's Formally Opened," *New York Age*, November 17, 1910.
8. "Banded Against Negro," *Baltimore Sun*, December 8, 1910; and "Negro Saloon Driven Out," *Baltimore Sun*, December 9, 1910.
9. "First Sale in Restricted Harlem District," *New York Times*, February 22, 1911.
10. "Break Covenant in 136th Street," *New York Age*, April 25, 1912; and "Negroes in 130th St. House," *New York Times*, June 29, 1912.
11. Edwin B. Henderson and William A. Joiner, eds., *Official Handbook, Interscholastic Athletic Association of Middle Atlantic States* (New York: American Sports Publishing, 1911).
12. Fifty-Ninth Annual Report of the Young Men's Christian Association of the City of New York, May 1911.
13. "At a meeting of the Williamsbridge Colored," *New York Age*, October 6, 1910.
14. Real estate advertisement, *New York Age*, March 7, 1912.
15. "Jacob Charles Canty," obituary, *New York Age*, October 22, 1932.
16. "Overheard on the Avenue," *New York Age*, August 20, 1908.
17. "Negroes Cause Trouble," *New York Tribune*, August 31, 1913.
18. "Situations Wanted," *Daily Argus*, February 3, 1914.
19. "Women of Williams Bridge, New York City," *Chicago Defender*, July 20, 1918.
20. "Amateur Actors of Butler Church Present Two Plays," *Daily Argus*, June 12, 1916.
21. Record of Marriage, State of New York, no. 18254, November 6, 1915, Municipal Archives of New York City.
22. "At the Summer Resorts," *New York Age*, August 14, 1913, p. 5.
23. "Arverne Fears Negroes," *New York Tribune*, June 28, 1904; and "Arverne's Boardwalk Row," *New York Times*, June 28, 1904.
24. "To Starve Negroes Out," *New York Tribune*, June 5, 1905.
25. "Ball at Arverne," *New York Times*, July 15, 1906.
26. "Asks Work for Negroes," *New York Tribune*, June 5, 1908.

27. "At Seaside: Arverne-by-the-Sea," *New York Age,* July 30, 1908; and "Dressmakers' Assoc'n Gives Fashion Show," *New York Age,* November 5, 1921.
28. "Spend your 4th at the Hotel Lincoln," advertisement, *New York Age,* July 3, 1913.
29. "Drawing the Color Line . . . Asbury Park," *New York Times,* July 19, 1885.
30. Paulsson, *Social Anxieties.*
31. "Going Out With the Tide," *Colored American,* September 3, 1898; "Will Open at the Same Old Stand," *Colored American,* June 29, 1901; "Atlantic City No Longer Dry," *Washington Bee,* July 20, 1901; "Lawsuit Threatens Negro Bath House in Atlantic City," *New York Press,* July 13, 1913; "Walls' Bath Houses," advertisement, Official Souvenir Program Fourteenth Annual Convention IBPO Elks of the World (Lighthouse Lodge, no. 9), August 26 to 29, 1913; "Efforts to Oust Walls," *New York Age,* September 28, 1916; and "George Walls' Bath House . . . Passes," *Pittsburgh Courier,* August 8, 1925.
32. Advertisement for Walls' Bath Houses in Atlantic City, N.J., 1913.
33. "The Adirondacks and How to Reach Them," *Four-Track Series,* no. 20 (Summer 1903).
34. The August 18, 1910, issue of the *New York Age* mistakenly reported Williams's departure "for a stay in camp in the Adirondack Mountains . . . the guest of former Governor Smith of Montreal." The camp, called Madawaska, was also the name of a sizable pond in New York's Adirondack region. But the Smith family's camp of the same name was located farther north, in Ontario. Edward C. Smith served as governor of Vermont from 1898 to 1900.

Chapter 6: War at Home and Abroad

1. Parkhurst Whitney, "The Table d'Hote Hounds," *New York Tribune,* October 29, 1916.
2. New York Transit Museum; Robins and Leighton, *Grand Central Terminal.*
3. "The New Grand Central Terminal," *Town & Country,* July 8, 1911.
4. Lester Walton, "The Star Among Stars," *New York Age,* July 6, 1911. The New York Theater roof (also known as the Jardin de Paris) proscribed African Americans from the audience, so for his column, he aggregated a few select reviews from other newspapers "touching upon Mr. Williams' appearance in the *Follies of 1911.*
5. "Big Crowds Visit the New Terminal," *New York Tribune,* February 3, 1913.
6. Ibid.
7. "City Folks Crowd New Grand Central," *New York Times,* February 3, 1913.
8. "Full Dress Reception and Ball," advertisement, *New York Age,* November 16, 1911; "Amalgamated Railroad Employees Association," *New York Age,* August 15, 1912; and "The Red Caps Have Opened a Social Club," *New York Age,* January 2, 1913.

9. "Red Cap Is Linguist of First Class," *Chicago Defender*, October 7, 1922.
10. Irving Putnam, "Foreigners at Grand Central," and Edward Witkowski, "Interpreters at Grand Central," Letters to the Editor, *New York Times*, October 9 and 15, 1913.
11. "Red Capped Porter Was Emperor Menelik's Subject," *New York Sun*, January 23, 1914.
12. Zoe Beckley, "Porter Speaks 18 Languages," *Baltimore Afro-American* (from the *New York Evening Mail*), January 15, 1916.
13. In 1920 Gabriel's first U.S. passport identified his occupation as "interpreter," but it's possible that Grand Central Terminal did not immediately recognize him in that capacity.
14. Gabriel died in Buffalo on May 14, 1957, soon after his retirement from the railroad.
15. Kelly Miller, "The Harvest of Race Prejudice," *New York Amsterdam News*, March 25, 1925.
16. "Red Caps to Have Fine Ball Team," *New York Age*, March 2, 1918; and "Webster Accepts Terms," *Chicago Defender*, March 30, 1918.
17. "With Amateur and Semi-Pro Ball Tossers in 'Met' District," *New York Sun*, May 12, 1918.
18. "To Break Nat Strong in Baseball," *Baltimore Afro-American*, February 11, 1921. See Michael E. Lomax, *Black Baseball Entrepreneurs, 1902–1931: The Negro National and Eastern Colored Leagues* (Syracuse, N.Y.: Syracuse University Press, 1914).
19. Lester Walton, "Square Deal for Red Caps," *New York Age*, June 8, 1918.
20. Lester Walton, "Nat Strong Gives His Side of Controversy," *New York Age*, June 29, 1918.
21. "White Men the Boss—Why?" *Chicago Defender*, May 10, 1919.
22. "An Everyday Church and Its Pastor," *Rainbow*, October 23, 1919.
23. "College Men's Round Table," *Chicago Defender*, May 19, 1917; and Minutes of the Meeting of the Board of Directors, *Chicago Defender*, May 14, 1917.
24. "15,000 Negroes in Anti-Riot Parade," *New York Sun*, July 29, 1917; Lester Walton, "Nearly Ten Thousand Take Part in Big Silent Protest Parade Down Fifth Avenue," *New York Age*, August 2, 1917.
25. "Raise $40,931.32 Subscriptions," *New York Age*, November 27, 1913.
26. "'Red Caps' Are Saving 5 Cents a Day for Fund," *New York Age*, April 27, 1916; and "'Red Caps' Give $250 to the Memorial Fund," *New York Age*, July 13, 1916.
27. "The 'Red Cap' and the 'Big Negro'," *New York Age*, July 13, 1916.
28. "Vast Number of $50 Subscriptions," *Railway Age Gazette*, June 22, 1917.
29. "Fewer Red Caps at the Grand Central Station," *Chicago Defender*, July 20, 1918.
30. "Red Caps at Grand Central Subscribe $20,000," *New York Age*, October 26. 1918.

31. "New Canteen Is Opened in Harlem"; and "Tells of the Employment of Negro Troops by French," *New York Age*, August 10, 1918.
32. "Progress of Grand Central Red Caps," *New York Age*, July 6, 1918.
33. "Members of Old 15th Enjoy Eating Candy," *New York Age*, June 15, 1918. Wilson was indeed spared on the battlefields. He was honorably discharged on February 24, 1919, and later became treasurer of the Tarrytown, New York, school board.
34. Alice Dunbar-Nelson, "Negro Women in War Work," in Scott, *Official History*, chap. 27.
35. Irvin S. Cobb, "Young Black Joe," *Saturday Evening Post*, August 24, 1918.
36. "Roosevelt Gives Peace Prize to War," *New York Times*, April 26, 1918.
37. Theodore Roosevelt Center at Dickinson State University blog.
38. "War Correspondent Lauds Negro Soldier Fighting in France," *New York Age*, November 2, 1918; and Theodore Roosevelt, "Remarks at Meeting held under the auspices of the Circle for Negro War Relief, Carnegie Hall," November 2, 1918, Digital Library, Theodore Roosevelt Center, Dickinson State University.
39. "John W. and James H. Williams I, II and III, New York City," group photo, *Crisis*, October 1918.The "II" in the photo is Wesley, and the "III" is Wesley's infant son, James II.
40. "Grand Central Red Caps in Bridgeport," *New York Age*, May 10, 1919.
41. "Marking the End of War's Long Debauch," *Marcellus Observer*, May 18, 1932.
42. "Dinner for Old 15th to Follow Parade Monday," *New York Tribune*, February 15, 1919, p. 18.
43. "Black Paris and Its Critics," *Rainbow*, October 30, 1919.
44. "Acts Opening at Paris Alhambra" and "Paris Casino Opening Delayed," *Variety*, December 5, 1918.

Chapter 7: "A Sweet Spot in Harlem Known as Strivers' Row"

1. On Wesley's exam result, see "Chief Williams on Vacation" and "Williamsbridge Breezes," *Chicago Defender*, August 17, 1918; and "Bronx Youth Passes Examination for Fire Dept, Is 100 Percent Physically Perfect" [undated clipping], *Bronx Home News*, c.1918.
2. James W. Johnson, "Views and Reviews—John Henry Woodson," *New York Age*, July 19, 1917.
3. Wesley Williams, interview by John Ruffins, FDNY firefighter and Vulcan Society historian, private collection, 1980.
4. John H. Woodson to Wesley Williams, January 6, 1919, Williams Family Collection.
5. Williams interview.
6. Ibid.
7. Ibid.

8. Ibid. Examples of Wesley's reading matter were mentioned in "Negroes in Uniformed Service," *New York Age,* October 27, 1927.
9. Articles on Dr. Chas. H. Roberts's run for alderman in *New York Age*, August 2 and 23, and December 13 and 27, 1919.
10. Certificate and Record of Marriage, September 3, 1919, State of New York.
11. "French Now Want Colored Musicians from United States," *New York Age*, February 8, 1919.
12. Ibid.
13. Tom Lemonier, "Lemonier's Letter," *Chicago Defender*, June 21, 1919.
14. "The First Guests of the Rose's New Hotel," *New York Age*, October 18, 1919.
15. "Urban League Staff Dined by Officers," *New York Age*, January 17, 1920.
16. "Women Police Honor Miss S. E. Frazier," *New York Age*, February 21, 1920.
17. "Aurora Saturday Evening Dances," *Chicago Defender*, May 8, 1920; "New York City Briefs," *Chicago Defender*, September 11, 1920; and "Lucille Hegamin Story," interview by Dinosaur Discs, *Record Research*, November 1961.
18. "300 Red Caps Employed at Grand Central R.R. Station Serve Thousands Each Day," *New York Age*, July 21, 1923.
19. "Unique Exercises Attended by 5,000 in Grand Central Terminal," *New York Times*, August 11, 1923; and "Harding's Creed One of Love," *New York Tribune*, August 11, 1923.
20. "Red Caps Open Season," *Chicago Defender*, December 8, 1923.
21. "Central Red Caps Will Be Represented in Basketball," *New York Amsterdam News*, July 18, 1923.
22. For an overview of African Americans in basketball, see the Black Fives Foundation website, founded and curated by Claude Johnson, http://www.blackfives.org.
23. "Professional Basketball Is Magnet for Many New Aggregations in Harlem," *New York Age*, November 17, 1923.
24. W. Rollo Wilson, in *Pittsburgh Courier*, December 15, 1923.
25. "Red Caps Defeated," *New York Age*, December 29, 1923. The Commonwealth Casino was located at 135th Street and Madison Avenue.
26. "Professional Basketball Is Magnet," *New York Age*, November 17, 1923.
27. "Basketball in the Spot-Light," *Pittsburgh Courier*, March 15, 1924.
28. "Mae Walker with Bridesmaids and Flower Girls at Villa Lewaro on November 24, 1923," photo, Madam Walker Family Archives/A'Lelia Bundles.
29. "Campaign Committee for N.Y. Urban League Drive," *New York Age*, November 23, 1923.
30. "'Houn' Dogs' Arrive Eager To Be Shown," *New York Post*, June 21, 1924.
31. "20,000 Jeer Smith in Rally of N.J. Klan," *New York Herald*, July 5, 1924.
32. "Red Caps' Club News," *Broad Axe*, August 9, 1924.
33. "New York Society," *Chicago Defender*, August 16, 1924.

34. "Ethiopian Art Theater School in Premier Dance Exhibition," *New York Age,* June 28, 1924.
35. "Laster Cottage," *New York Age*, August 9, 1924.
36. Dr. Fred Palmer's Skin Whitener, advertisement, *Pittsburgh Courier*, February 23, 1929.
37. "At the Seashore," *Pittsburgh Courier*, July 11, 1925.
38. "At the Seashore," *Pittsburgh Courier*, September 12, 1925.
39. "Gertrude E. Williams," photo, *Pittsburgh Courier*, November 6, 1926.
40. Romeo Dougherty, "About Things Theatrical," *New York Amsterdam News*, December 8, 1926.
41. "New York Daily Uses Pretty Picture," *Pittsburgh Courier*, December 18, 1926.
42. "New York Fireman Lauded for Rescue," *New York Age,* June 21, 1924.
43. "Firemen Save Five Clinging to Ledges," *New York Times*, October 20, 1924.
44. "Wesley was named after the son of a man who was greatly respected by my father, his supervisor, Chief Williams, when he was a 'red cap' at Grand Central Terminal." Johnson and Johnson, *Dancer*, p. 15. Johnson, aka "Stretch," was the son of Monk Johnson.
45. Williams interview.
46. One of the fire chiefs recounted the story to Wesley when they returned. Ibid.
47. "200 Invited to Wedding of Miss Stillman and Henry P. Davison," *Daily Argus*, October 18, 1924.
48. "Stillman's Invite 'George,'" *New York Post*, October 18, 1924.
49. "Pullman Porters Ask Why George Is Popular Name," *Buffalo Courier*, September 9, 1923.
50. "The Porters in the Pennsylvania Station," *Variety*, October 7, 1925.

Chapter 8: The Black Decade

1. Eden Bliss, "This Harlem," *Baltimore Afro-American*, October 9, 1926.
2. "Colored Law Student at Columbia University Is Object of Ku Klux Ire," *New York Age*, April 12, 1924.
3. William Pickens, "Columbia University Begins Dormitory Segregation," *Baltimore Afro-American*, August 29, 1925.
4. Thelma E. Berlack Boozer, "Chatter and Chimes," *Pittsburgh Courier*, February 28, 1925 (on Omega Psi Phi) and May 30, 1925 (on Semper Fidelis); on Gertrude Williams, see Mrs. H. Binga Dismond, "New York Society," *Pittsburgh Courier*, November 14, 1925; and "Alice Davis and Gertrude Williams Represent New York at Football Classic," *New York Age*, November 28, 1925.
5. "Many of Grand Central's 'Red Caps' Are College Students," *New York Evening Post*, October 30, 1926.
6. Arthur P. Davis, "With a Grain of Salt—Recollections of the Harlem of the Era

of 1925 Stirred by the Death of Claud McKay," *New Journal and Guide*, June 5, 1948.

7. "Crooks Get Summer Savings," *New York Age,* October 4, 1924.
8. Ralph Matthews, "Red Cap University," *Baltimore Afro-American*, July 30, 1927.
9. "Walter A. Dawkins, a Former Porter," *New York Age,* October 5, 1929.
10. Lester B. Granger, undated clipping.
11. Grand Central School of Art to Frank Smalls, September 29, 1925; Smalls to W.E.B. Du Bois, October 3, 1925; Du Bois to Smalls, October 7, 1925, all in W.E.B. Du Bois Papers, University of Massachusetts, Amherst; and "Two Art Students Face Negro Quota," *New York Amsterdam News*, September 30, 1931.
12. W.E.B. Du Bois for Richard Huey, letter of recommendation, October 15, 1925, W.E.B. Du Bois Papers, University of Massachusetts, Amherst. Huey's Los Angeles friends, John and Vada Watson Somerville, were the first black graduates from the University of Southern California School of Dentistry in Los Angeles—who would also build that city's famous Dunbar Hotel for an African-American clientele.
13. Floyd Calvin, "Richard Huey Has Made Fine Record with Broadway Shows," *Pittsburgh Courier*, April 18, 1931.
14. Charles E. Searle, "American Livery, Well Defined Styles Now in Vogue: The Original Reason for Livery and How This Same Idea Is Now Applied," *Clothier and Furnisher*, May 1914.
15. Lester Walton, "Morris Hunter Is Most Sought After of Race by Artists," *Pittsburgh Courier*, reprinted from *New York World*, January 1, 1927. The misspelling of Hunter's first name, as "Morris," suggests the model, who was a native of Guyana, might have used the common British pronunciation.
16. "What Price Glory? Asks Super Model," *Brooklyn Daily Eagle*, February 28, 1932. Historian Clare Corbould shared her invaluable expertise on the career of Maurice Hunter.
17. Ibid.
18. Ibid.
19. Franklin Snow, "A Day at Grand Central Terminal," *New York Central Lines*, January 1929.
20. Fannie Hurst, *Star-Dust: The Story of an American Girl* (New York: Harper & Brothers, 1921).
21. Burton Rascoe, "Daybook of a New Yorker," *Poughkeepsie Eagle*, March 29, 1927.
22. Mrs. S. R. Kaufman to A. H. Smith, letter in *New York Central Lines*, February 1924.
23. Allen Churchill, *The Year the World Went Mad* (New York: Crowell, 1960), p. 36.
24. "Picked Up Here and There," *New York Age*, November 20, 1926.
25. James H. Hogans, "Things Seen, Heard and Done Among Pullman Employees" and "A Suggestion to Committee C and to Head of the G. C. Red Caps," *New York Age*, November 2, 1929.

26. "Big Boss," *Chicago Defender*, September 24, 1927.
27. John R. Tunis, "The Red Cap Tells the World," *Elks Magazine*, June 1927.
28. Ibid.
29. Edward M. Swift, M.D., and Charles S. Boyd, M.D., "The Pullman Porter Looks at Life," *Psychoanalytic Review*, January 1, 1928. The authors note that, for simplicity, their collaborative essay uses the singular term "I" throughout, instead of the plural "We."
30. "Red Cap Captain Friend of Presidents," *Summit Herald*, July 13, 1928.
31. Earl Brown, "Timely Topics," *New York Amsterdam News*, May 15, 1948.
32. James H. Hogans, "Things Seen, Heard and Done Among Pullman Employees" and "A Suggestion to Committee C and to Head of the G. C. Red Caps," *New York Age*, November 2, 1929.
33. Allan Macdonald, "Up from Slavery: Four Generations of the Williams Family," *New York World*, March 27, 1927.
34. Allan S. A. Titley, "Slaves of Grand Central Terminal," *Messenger*, October 1927.

Chapter 9: Testaments in Transit

1. "Negroes in Uniformed Service," *New York Age* (from the *New York Sun*), October 27, 1927.
2. Wesley Williams to *New York Age*, August 8, 1925, Wesley Williams Papers, Schomburg Center/NYPL.
3. "Negro Fireman To Be Promoted to Lieutenant," *New York Herald Tribune*, September 15, 1927.
4. Wesley Williams to Robert F. Wagner, Jr., November 17, 1962, Wesley Williams Papers, Schomburg Center/NYPL.
5. James H. Williams to Patrick Cardinal Hayes, September 9, 1927, Wesley Williams Papers, ibid.
6. "A Group of Harlem Gentlemen," *Inter-State Tattler*, February 3, 1928.
7. "Tiffany Watch Given Lieut. Williams at Testimonial Dinner," *New York Age*, February 4, 1928.
8. "A Group of Harlem Gentlemen," *Inter-State Tattler*, February 3, 1928.
9. Tiffany & Co. watch sale records show that on January 26, 1928, J. H. Williams of Grand Central Terminal purchased a watch for $225. The reported value differential might include the added cost of the watch chain and/or the "small gold knife," for which no record was found.
10. *New York Extracted Death Index* gives June's birthdate about 1925; age given as nine months at time of death, on February 1, 1926. The New York census dated June 1, 1925, records the family living in Manhattan at 108 West 141st Street: Lula Williams, 19; James L. Williams, 23; Gloria Williams, 1 year 6 months; and June Williams maybe three weeks, but it's unclear.

11. The word *creole* was a frequent marketing term to promote usually light-skinned black acts.
12. "Chorister's Salaries," *Baltimore Afro-American*, February 20, 1926.
13. "Calvin's Diary of the New York Show World," *Pittsburgh Courier*, July 3, 1926.
14. "Known for Personality Plus," *Pittsburgh Courier*, April 30, 1927.
15. "Alabam Revue Closes," *Baltimore Afro-American*, May 28, 1927.
16. Bessye J. Bearden, "Tid-Bits of New York Society," *Chicago Defender*, June 11, 1927.
17. "Chorus Girls in New York City at a Premium," *Baltimore Afro-American*, May 26, 1922; and "Colored Chorus in 'Follies,'" *Billboard*, May 27, 1922. A subsequent item in "Dancer Out of 'Follies,'" *Billboard*, June 17, 1922, reported the black cast never saw opening night: "The sixteen Negro chorus girls who were to have appeared in the show also were eliminated in rehearsals. There is a number in the show, sung by Gilda Gray, called 'It's Getting Dark on Old Broadway', and it was figured that the idea of this ditty, which tells of the recent 'invasion' of the cabaret field by the colored performer, would not jibe with chorus girls of that type in the show. They were given two weeks' salary and dismissed, tho it was intimated to them that they might be put in the show later to take the place of one of the inevitable elisions in the piece."
18. "'Showboat' Chorus Girl Kills Herself," *New York Amsterdam News*, July 25, 1928; and "Popular 'Show Boat' Beauty a Suicide by Gas," *Inter-State Tattler*, July 27, 1928.
19. "Red Cap Commits Suicide," *Chicago Defender*, September 8, 1923.
20. "Lindy of the Ground Rides Motorcycle Around the World," *Philadelphia Tribune*, January 19, 1933.
21. Romeo Dougherty, in *New York Amsterdam News*, June 13, 1928. The sports editor quoted from a 1927 article by R. D. Pepin in *American Motorcyclist* (date of issue not given). On the history of racial prejudice in organized motorcycle culture, see Ed Youngblood, "Moving Beyond Prejudice," *American Motorcyclist*, March 1995.
22. William T. Davis, "A $2,000.00 Motorcycle Trip Around the World," *New Journal and Guide*, January 21, 1933; as well as numerous newspaper articles on Davis's career and world trip, 1926–35.
23. "Making Trip Around the World," *Chicago Defender*, June 29, 1929.
24. William T. Davis to sports editor Romeo Dougherty, *New York Amsterdam News*, May 7, 1930.
25. Romeo L. Dougherty, "'Lindy of the Ground' to Hit the Trail Again the Coming Sunday Morning," *New York Amsterdam News*, June 13, 1928.
26. "Why Not Call Lindy 'Davis of the Air'?" *Philadelphia Tribune*, February 2, 1933.

Chapter 10: Bandwidths

1. *Louis Armstrong and His Orchestra,* Decca Records, 1347B, 1937.
2. James Weldon Johnson to James H. Williams, March 13, 1929, in NAACP Papers, Women's Auxiliary to the NAACP, January 3 to May 3, 1929, Manuscripts Division, Library of Congress.
3. "N.A.A.C.P. Dance Promises To Be Gala Affair," *New York Age*, March 16, 1929; "Rid-Bits of New York Society," *Chicago Defender*, March 23, 1929.
4. "Anniversary Dinner to 'Blackbirds' Co. Season's Outstanding Social Event," *New York Amsterdam News*, May 15, 1929.
5. Dave Peyton, the music columnist, cites these artists in explaining the importance of music arrangers. "The Musical Bunch—Our Fine Arrangers," *Chicago Defender*, May 5, 1928.
6. Geraldyn Dismond, "Social Snapshots" *Inter-State Tattler*, July 5, 1929.
7. Advertised program calendar, *New York Amsterdam News*, October 2, 1929.
8. "Old-Time Barnum Clown Reincarnating Showman," *Brooklyn Daily Eagle*, December 21, 1929.
9. "Raps Amos 'n Andy," *Pittsburgh Courier*, July 24 or 25 [unclear], 1930.
10. "Amos 'n' Andy Mobbed," *Brooklyn Eagle*, January 22, 1930.
11. "Brooklyn News," *New York Amsterdam News*, July 30, 1930, Performing Arts database, Library of Congress.
12. Ibid.
13. "Among the pre-Lenten Affairs," *Inter-State Tattler*, December 27, 1929.
14. "Mere Male Blossoms Out in Garb of Milady," *New York Amsterdam News*, February 19, 1930; "Men Tenors, Women Wear Tuxedos at Costume Ball," *Baltimore Afro-American*, February 22, 1930; Edward G. Perry, obituary, *Jet*, February 10, 1955.
15. "New York—Jimmy and His Gang," *Baltimore Afro-American*, March 1, 1930. In 1919 singer Alberta Hunter married future Red Caps union founder Willard S. Townsend in Kentucky; they divorced in 1923. Hunter was still living at 133 West 138th Street, apartment 5E, which she'd bought through noted Harlem realtor John E. Nail, at the time of "Jimmy's" party at the nearby Renaissance Casino.
16. "Jimmy and the Gang Hosts," *Baltimore Afro-American*, July 26, 1930.
17. "Wooding Being Kept Very Busy," *New York Amsterdam News*, September 18, 1929. See also Percival Outram, "Activities Among Union Musicians," *New York Age*, November 8, 1930.
18. Handy, *Father of the Blues.*
19. "Stage All Set for Big Midnight Benefit," *New York Amsterdam News*, November 19, 1930.
20. Ibid.

21. Romeo L. Dougherty, "Lafayette Midnight Show Among the Best of Its Kind Ever," *New York Amsterdam News*, November 26, 1930.
22. Cora Gary Illidge, "Red Caps Are Musical," *New York Amsterdam News*, December 24, 1930. Illidge refers to Herbert Johnson as the orchestra's business manager, who "discusses terms only in accordance with the Musicians' Union, of which it is a member." An article in the *Pittsburgh Courier*, January 9, 1932, refers to Percy Robinson as "one of the best drummers in the country" and "a Red Cap at Grand Central Terminal and the business manager of the Red Cap Band."
23. "Yuletide Dance To Be Joyous Event" and "Yuletide Dance Is Highly Successful," *Rhinebeck Gazette and Red Hook Times*, December 13, 1930, and January 3, 1931.
24. Mark Miller and John Wilby, "The Story of Robert H. Cloud," compact disk liner notes, *Florida Rhythm*, 1999.
25. J. A. Jackson's notes, *Billboard*, August 30, 1924.
26. "Recommended Disk Records," *Variety*, November 30, 1927.
27. "Robert Cloud," photo, *Inter-State Tattler*, August 9, 1929; "Constance Perdue Now Leading the Tattler's Big $1,000.00 Contest," *Inter-State Tattler*, August 16 and (advertisement) 17, 1929.
28. Cora Gary Illidge, "Red Caps Are Musical," *New York Amsterdam News*, December 24, 1930.
29. "At the Lafayette," *New York Age*, January 3 and 10, 1931.
30. Ibid.
31. "'The Gang' Entertains," *Baltimore Afro-American*, February 28, 1931.
32. NAACP minutes Committee on Administration, February 24, 1931, W.E.B. Du Bois Papers, University of Massachusetts, Amherst. Col. The next year Miles Bronson retired as manager of Grand Central Terminal after thirty-five years of railroad service. Circumstances suggest that Chief Williams likely broached the idea of the Red Cap Orchestra to Bronson, then brokered the subsequent introductions of Marsh and Wooding, in order for Bronson to sign off on their compensations.
33. Walter White to W.E.B. Du Bois, February 25, 1931, NAACP Papers, Manuscripts Division, Library of Congress.
34. Daisy Wilson to Walter White, February 27, 1931, W.E.B. Du Bois Papers, University of Massachusetts, Amherst.
35. Walter White to Miguel Covarrubias, March 2, 1931, NAACP Papers, Manuscripts Division, Library of Congress.
36. Walter White to Eunice Hunton Carter, March 13, 1931, NAACP Papers, ibid.
37. "Four Orchestras to Play at N.A.A.C.P. Dance in Harlem," *Topeka Plain Dealer*, March 13, 1931.
38. "N.A.A.C.P. Dance," *Baltimore Afro-American*, March 28, 1931.

39. "Four Orchestras to Play at N.A.A.C.P. Dance in Harlem," *Topeka Plain Dealer*, March 13, 1931.
40. "Red-Caps' Orchestra Is Heard," *New York Herald Tribune*, March 17, 1931.
41. "N.A.A.C.P. Dance," *Baltimore Afro-American*, March 28, 1931.
42. "Mrs. Mary E. Downs Old Washingtonian Dies in New York," *New York Age*, March 28, 1931.
43. "Former Gov. Smith to Speak at Harlem Unemployment Meeting," *New York Age*, January 17, 1931; "Ticket Selling Drive for Costume Charity Ball at 369th Armory," *New York Age*, April 11, 1931; Bessye J. Bearden, "New York Society," *Chicago Defender*, May 9, 1931; and "Biographical/Historical Information," finding aid, Wilhelmina F. Adams Papers, NYPL Archives & Manuscripts, processed by S. M. Howard and S. E. Davis, May 9, 1979.
44. Directory of American Historical Recordings (DAHR), online database.
45. "So That the Nation May Hear Them," photo, *Philadelphia Tribune*, June 4, 1931.
46. "Wooding to Form 'Red Cap' Band," *Pittsburgh Courier*, June 13, 1931. This item, reported from Camden, New Jersey, where the RCA Victor recording studio was located, carried no byline. However, on June 30, the Virginia paper *New Journal and Guide* ran the article verbatim with the heading "Wooding With Red Cap Band," under the byline of E. E. Obersteen [*sic*]. Eli E. Oberstein, a noted music producer, supervised the Red Cap Orchestra's RCA Victor studio session.
47. *New York Central Lines*, photo, November 1931.
48. Percival Outram, "Activities Among Union Musicians," *New York Age*, July 18, 1931.
49. "'Red Cap' Choir Featured on Phillips Lord Air Program," *Pittsburgh Courier*, December 12, 1936.
50. Alice Hughes, "A Woman's New York," *Buffalo Courier-Express*, December 24, 1940.
51. Directory of American Historical Recordings (DAHR), online database; "Lone Star State Girl Stops Big R.K.O. Show," *Pittsburgh Courier*, January 10, 1931.
52. Robert Cloud to Walter White, August 17, 1931, NAACP Papers, Manuscripts Division, Library of Congress.
53. Cited from the *Register-Herald* (Pine Plains, N.Y.), March 29, 1934.
54. Walter Winchell, "On Broadway," *Philadelphia Inquirer*, July 3, 1933, p. 7.
55. "Jim McCloud" [*sic*], *Baltimore Afro-American*, March 11, 1934. This article appears to be about Robert Cloud, with subject's name reported incorrectly.
56. Outram, *New York Age*, May 30, 1931.
57. *Princeton Alumni Weekly*, May 6 and July 2, 1932.
58. Helen Worden, *The Real New York* (Indianapolis: Bobbs-Merrill, 1932).
59. "Sidelights of New York," *Saratogian*, September 28, 1932.
60. James Aswell, "My New York," *Berkshire Daily Gazette*, January 17, 1934.

61. Robert W. Bagnall to Edward B. Moss, protesting the barring of black tennis players from the U.S. Lawn Tennis Association national tournament, December 24, 1929, NAACP Papers, Manuscripts Division, Library of Congress.
62. Edward B. Moss to Robert W. Bagnall, December 26, 1929, NAACP Papers, ibid.
63. "Tennis," *Pittsburgh Courier*, August 16, 1930.
64. The first organization would later change its name to the Central Intercollegiate Athletic Association. The second, whose name was identical to a white organization established in 1894, would become the Southern Intercollegiate Athletic Conference.
65. A. E. Francis, "Tennis," *New York Amsterdam News*, August 19, 1931.
66. A. E. Francis, "Tennis," *New York Amsterdam News*, September 23, 1931.
67. "National Tourney Opens Monday," *New Journal and Guide*, August 12, 1933.
68. "Dunbar Players Win 2 Contests" and "Dunbar Players Win in Contest," *New York Amsterdam News*, June 15 and 29, 1932.
69. "Mr. Ely Culbertson," British Pathé newsreel, 1932.
70. "Mu-So-Lit Club Enters Team in National Bridge Tourney," *Baltimore Afro-American*, September 24, 1932.
71. "Culbertson Gives Indorsement to American Bridge Asso.," *Philadelphia Tribune*, July 27, 1933.
72. Ibid.
73. "Officers Revealed," *New York Amsterdam News*, August 30, 1933.

Chapter 11: Moving to the Dunbar

1. George S. Schuyler, "Views and Reviews," *Pittsburgh Courier*, February 14, 1931.
2. Walter Stabler to John D. Rockefeller, June 9, 1926, Rockefeller Archives.
3. John D. Rockefeller, "Memorandum for Mr. C. O. Heydt—Naming the Project," July 25, 1927, Rockefeller Archives.
4. "Rockefeller Builds Houses for the Negro Colony in Harlem," *Boston Sunday Globe*, April 22, 1928.
5. "Kute Kommend by Komic," *New York Amsterdam News*, February 22, 1928.
6. "Rockefeller Apts. Business Success," *Pittsburgh Courier*, September 6, 1930. Notwithstanding the financial crisis, a 1930 report showed the Dunbar accumulated a $31,500 surplus.
7. "Frolich and Epstein Pharmacy," advertisement, *New York Amsterdam News*, April 11, 1928; "Mme. C. J. Walker Beauty Shoppes," *Pittsburgh Courier*, August 18, 1928.
8. A. A. Schomburg to Mr. Henderson, April 12, 1928, Rockefeller Archives.
9. "Harlem Shadows," *Pittsburgh Courier*, January 17, 1931.
10. "Dunbar Apts. Will Go to Methodists," *Baltimore Afro-American*, December 12, 1942.

11. The primary cause of death given as "cerebral Hemorrhage non-traumatic, arteriosclorotic in origin; secondary contributory as Pulmonary Edema." Certificate of Death, October 2, 1932.
12. "Dies Suddenly at Home in Dunbar," *New York Amsterdam News*, October 5, 1932; and "Mrs. Lucy Williams Dies Suddenly," *New York Age*, October 8, 1932.
13. Bishop William J. Walls, *The African American Episcopal Zion Church* (Charlotte, N.C., 1974).
14. "Rev. R. M. Bolden Begins Series of Articles on Harlem Characters," *New York Age*, December 10, 1932.
15. Ibid.
16. Samuel J. Battle to Wesley Williams, September 6, 1933, Wesley Williams Papers, Schomburg Center/NYPL.
17. Dr. T. W. Kilmer to Chief Williams, telegram, June 1, 1934, Wesley Williams Papers, ibid.
18. "Harlem Healer," in T. R. Poston, "Harlem Shadows," *Pittsburgh Courier*, January 24, 1931.
19. Walter White to Chief Williams, October 16, 1933, NAACP Papers, Manuscripts Division, Library of Congress.
20. William Pickens to Chief Williams, October 21, 1933, NAACP Papers, ibid.
21. William Pickens to Rudolph Foster, October 27, 1933, NAACP Papers, ibid.
22. William Pickens to Chief Williams, February 25, 1934, NAACP Papers, ibid.
23. Karl K. Kitchen, "The Red Cap Guild," *Cleveland Plain-Dealer*, June 24, 1921.
24. Wesley Williams to W. W. Atterbury, July 9, 1934, Wesley Williams Papers, Schomburg Center/NYPL. This collection contains additional correspondence from Pennsylvania Railroad Company and station officials.
25. James Williams, interview by Abram Hill, August 29–30, 1939, Federal Writers' Project.
26. "Sugar Hill," *New Yorker*, December 10, 1927.
27. Dorothy West, "Cocktail Party" narrative, Folklore Project, Life Histories, 1939, U.S. Works Projects Administration, Federal Writers' Project, Library of Congress.
28. "Ph.D. Carries Your Bags," *Ken*, August 11, 1938.
29. Karl K. Kitchen, "The Red Cap Guild," *Cleveland Plain-Dealer*, June 24, 1921.
30. George S. Schuyler, "Views and Reviews," *Pittsburgh Courier*, February 14, 1931.
31. Williams interview.
32. Arna Bontemps, "A Woman with a Mission," in *The Old South* (New York: Dodd, Mead, 1973),
33. Earl Brown, "Timely Topics," *New York Amsterdam News*, May 15, 1948.
34. Archer Winsten, "Harlem Garden Spot, Rockefeller Endowed, Nurtures Variegated Culture," *New York Post*, January 14, 1935.

35. Nannie H. Burroughs, "Declaration of 1776 Cause of Harlem Riot," *Baltimore Afro-American*, April 13, 1935.
36. "Complete Riot Report Bared," *Amsterdam News*, July 18, 1936.
37. "Race Exploitation Hinted as Cause of N.Y. Riot," *Pittsburgh Courier*, March 30, 1935.
38. "Singer Warns Against Nazis," *New York Amsterdam News*, February 9, 1935.
39. "Brown Kings of the Ring," *Tops*, December 21, 1938.
40. "Weds Educator," *New York Amsterdam News*, June 15, 1935.
41. "Is This a Joke?" *Baltimore Afro-American*, June 15, 1935.
42. "Red Cap Thinks He's Tuskegee's President, But Chief Williams Thinks He Is Queer," *New York Amsterdam News*, June 15, 1935.
43. Frederick D. Patterson, Tuskegee Institute president to W.E.B. Du Bois, August 3, 1935, W.E.B. Du Bois Papers, University of Massachusetts, Amherst.
44. "Negro Educator's Dream," *Baltimore Sun*, August 24, 1967.
45. Index to correspondence for "Williams, James H. (Chief)," letter not found, June 27, 1933, Rockefeller Archives.
46. "Operators Buy Apartments in Dyckman Area," *New York Herald Tribune*, July12, 1935; New York Office of the City Register, various records of deeds and conveyances for Block 2023/Lot 48.
47. "Manicurist Weds," *New York Amsterdam News*, August 3, 1935.

Chapter 12: Organized Labor Pains

1. "Red Caps Bare Evil of 'Tip System' at Hearing," *Pittsburgh Courier*, July 8, 1939.
2. "Two Railroads Start 16-Hour Runs to Chicago," *New York Herald Tribune*, June 16, 1938.
3. Franklin P. Adams, "The Conning Tower," *New York Herald Tribune*, February 20, 1936.
4. "Brown Kings of the Ring," *Tops*, December 21, 1938.
5. "Y.M.C.A. Notes," *New York Age,* October 10, 1931.
6. "Courier Cameraman Goes to Harlem Parties," *Pittsburgh Courier*, March 26, 1938; and "You Gotta Be 'Right' to Get into Harlem's Swanky 'Mimo' Club," *Pittsburgh Courier*, August 20, 1938.
7. "Boss of the Bag Toters," *Baltimore Afro-American*, November 26, 1938.
8. "Weddings: Bundick–Williams," *New York Amsterdam News*, July 16, 1938.
9. "Jamaica Journal," *New York Age*, April 16, 1938, August 6, 1938, and May 4, 1940.
10. "Reveals Conditions of Negro Red Caps," *Daily Worker*, January 15, 1938.
11. "Mrs. Roosevelt Is Home After Trip to Chicago," *Chicago Tribune*, January 23, 1933.

12. James H. Williams to Mrs. Roosevelt, January 28, 1938, ALS; Williams letter tacked with note from Malvina Thompson "Tommy" Schneider to Marguerite "Missy" LeHand with penciled message from Eleanor Roosevelt, February 8, 1938.
13. "Red Caps Entrench at Capital for Wage War," *Chicago Defender*, February 11, 1939.
14. "Celebs Help Louis Celebrate Here—Guest Speakers List at Party," *New York Amsterdam News*, May 20, 1939.
15. "Red Caps Bare Evil of 'Tip System' at Hearing," *Pittsburgh Courier*, July 8, 1939.
16. Arnesen, Brotherhoods of Color.
17. James Williams, interview by Abram Hill, August 29–30, 1939, Federal Writers' Project.
18. James H. Hogans, "America's No. 1 Redcap," *Baltimore Afro-American*, August 27, 1938.
19. Ibid.
20. "'Chief' Williams Remains Silent as Grand Central Red Caps Hold Labor Representation Elections," *New York Age*, September 16, 1939.
21. Editorial, *Crisis*, May 1937.
22. "Heywood Broun," *Baltimore Afro-American*, December 30, 1939.
23. "Red Caps Broth'rhood Signs Agreement with N.Y. Central Railroad," *New York Age*, February 3, 1940.
24. James H. Hogans, "Along the Railroads," *New York Age*, April 16, 1949.
25. "New York Central Red Caps Propose Contract Changes," *Bags & Baggage*, April 1941.
26. "Low-Power Bomb Sets Off a Blaze in Check Room in Grand Central," *New York Times*, March 17, 1940.
27. "Uniform Charge for Red Cap Porter Service," advertisement, *New York Age*, June 1, 1940. The new system first went into effect at the Cincinnati terminal on February 1, 1940, and the Illinois Central line followed on April 1. On April 28 New England stations in Connecticut, Massachusetts, and Rhode Island adopted the policy, as did the New York stations on June 1.
28. "Red Caps in N.Y. Object to New Rate," *Chicago Defender*, May 18, 1940.
29. "Red Caps Say There's No More Sugar Hill," *Daily Worker*, August 8, 1941.
30. Eleanor Roosevelt, speech to the thirtieth anniversary dinner of the National Urban League, November 8, 1940, excerpted as "Mrs. Roosevelt Asks For Support of Red Caps Fight for a Living Wage," *Bags and Baggage*, December 1940.

Chapter 13: "Things Reiterated as the American Way"

1. "Air Briefs," *Billboard*, June 10, 1933; "Wave Lengths," *Pittsburgh Courier*, August 5, 1933.
2. "Mayor Cites Negro Gains as Program at Fair Opens," *New York Herald Tribune*, July 24, 1940.
3. "SPEBSQSA Made Honorary Members," *Baltimore Afro-American*, August 20, 1940.
4. "Negro Singers Out, Smith, Moses Quit," *New York Times*, July 3, 1941.
5. Ibid.
6. "Negro Quartet Is Barred From Ballad Contest," *New York Herald-Tribune*, July 3, 1941.
7. "Hold Initial Water Show at Flushing Meadows Park," *Brooklyn Eagle*, August 7, 1941.
8. Chief Wesley Williams to Ex-Governor Al Smith regarding his request for assignment transfer, August 18, 1941, Wesley Williams Papers, Schomburg Center/NYPL.
9. Earl Brown, "American Negroes and the War," *Harper's Magazine*, April 1942.
10. Ibid.
11. "The Washingtons," *New York Age,* December 10, 1927.
12. "Meet Dr. Joseph L. Washington—A Fugitive from Injustice," *Baltimore Afro-American*, June 22, 1946.
13. "The Month," *Crisis*, November 1942.
14. Guy A. Stoute to Walter White, October 19, 1940, NAACP Papers, Manuscripts Division, Library of Congress.
15. "NYU Negro Star Denied Railroad Job as Gateman," *PM*, August 22, 1943; "Len Bates, Grid Star, Denied Gateman Job," *Baltimore Afro-American*, August 28, 1943; and "Len Bates in Army; Denied Gateman Job," *Chicago Defender*, September 4, 1943.
16. Correspondence related to discrimination in New York City fire department, 1942–1946, NAACP Papers, Manuscripts Division, Library of Congress.
17. "New York Firemen Fight Jim Crow Beds," *Chicago Defender*, December 16, 1944.
18. Dorothy Deming, R.N., "Serving the Traveling Public: Nursing in New York's Railroad Stations," *American Journal of Nursing* 44, no. 9 (September 1944).
19. "Grand Central Station," *Bags and Baggage*, May 1, 1942; "Grand Central Red Caps Give First Aid Demonstration," *Baltimore Afro-American,* May 9, 1942; "Grand Central Red Caps Organize to Render First Aid," *Journal and Guide*, May 9, 1942; "Pride of the Redcaps," *American Weekly*, June 16, 1946; "Gets Bachelor Degree," *New York Age,* June 14, 1947.

20. Len LeSourd, "Track Thirteen," in *Guideposts*, ed. Norman Vincent Peale (New York: Prentice-Hall, 1948).

Chapter 14: A Second Marriage

1. Frank Staley to Wilbur F. Coleman (Dunbar Apartments), November 14, 1934, Rockefeller Archives.
2. Schedule of leases and monthly tenants (without leases) at Paul Laurence Dunbar Apartments, October 1, 1937, Rockefeller Archives. On that date Williams's annual rent for his combined apartments, 3M and 3L, totaled $979.80.
3. James H. Williams to Frank S. Staley, January 5, 1942, Rockefeller Archives.
4. Philip F. Keebler to Elias C. Stuckless, with note attached from Keebler to Frank S. Staley, January 6, 1942, Rockefeller Archives.
5. "Dunbar Apts. Will Go to Methodists," *Baltimore Afro-American*, December 12, 1942.
6. James Hogans, "Among Railroad and Pullman Workers—Personals," *Baltimore Afro-American*, August 29, 1942.
7. "First Red Cap Will Soon See Son Made Battalion Fire Chief," *Baltimore Afro-American*, March 26, 1938; and "Boss of the Bag Toters," *Baltimore Afro-American*, November 26, 1938.
8. "Court Stenographers," *Boston Daily Globe*, April 11, 1909; "Final Tribute Paid Charles H. Robbins," *Boston Daily Globe*, September 26, 1937; and William Oscar Armstrong, obituary, *Boston Daily Globe*, May 23, 1932. The 1940 U.S. Census lists Martha A. Robbins among the lodgers of Phyllis Wheatley Home, where her occupation is given as "secretary" for the "Girls Home."
9. "James H. Williams Weds Boston Widow," *New York Age*, February 27, 1943.
10. Marshall, Grand Central.
11. Bernard Taper, "A Meeting in Atlanta," *New Yorker*, March 17, 1956.
12. "First Red Cap," *New York Herald Tribune*, November 3, 1946.
13. "'Chief' James H Williams," *New York Herald Tribune*, May 6, 1948.
14. "First Red Cap," *New York Herald Tribune*, November 3, 1946.
15. Marshall, *Grand Central.*
16. Ibid.
17. U.S. Senator Herbert H. Lehman to Battalion Chief Wesley Williams, April 2, 1952, Wesley Williams Papers, Schomburg Center/NYPL.

SELECTED BIBLIOGRAPHY

Arnesen, Eric. *Brotherhoods of Color: Black Railroad Workers and the Struggle for Equality*. Cambridge, Mass.: Harvard University Press, 2001.

Berlin, Ira, and Leslie M. Harris. *Slavery in New York*. New York: New Press, 2005.

Bolden, Rev. Richard Manuel. "Rev. R.M. Bolden Begins Series of Articles on Harlem Characters—Lieut. Battle and Chief Williams This Week." *New York Age,* December 10, 1932.

Bontemps, Arna. "A Woman with a Mission." In *The Old South : "A Summer Tragedy" and Other Stories of the Thirties*. New York: Dodd, Mead, 1973.

"Boss of the Bag Toters: 'Cap' Williams Heads Force of 414 at Grand Central; Friends of World's Great Men; Lives Quietly at 60." *Baltimore Afro-American*, November 26, 1938.

Burrows, Edwin G., and Mike Wallace. *Gotham: A History of New York City to 1898*. New York: Oxford University Press, 1998.

"'Chief' Williams Remains Silent as Grand Central Red Caps Hold Labor Representation Elections." *New York Age,* September 16, 1939.

Cleveland, Grover. *Letters and Addresses of Grover Cleveland*, ed. Albert Ellery Bergh. New York: Unit Book Publishing Co., 1909.

Corbould, Clare. "Race, Photography, Labor, and Entrepreneurship in the Life of Maurice Hunter, Harlem's 'Man of 1,000 Faces.'" *Radical History Review* 132 (2018): 144–71.

Drake, St. Clair, and Horace R. Cayton. *Black Metropolis: A Study of Negro Life in a Northern City*. New York: Harcourt Brace, 1945.

Edwards, R.A.R. *Words Made Flesh: Nineteenth-Century Deaf Education and the Growth of Deaf Culture*. New York: New York University Press, 2012.

Fletcher, Tom. *100 Years of the Negro in Show Business*. New York: Burdge, 1954.

Handy, W. C. *Father of the Blues: An Autobiography*. Edited by Arna Bontemps. New York: Macmillan, 1947.

Hill, Abram. "Chief James H. Williams." Federal Writers Project, August 30, 1939.

Hughes, Langston. "Radioactive Red Caps." In *The Best of Simple.* New York: Hill and Wang, 1961.

Jackson, Kenneth T., ed. *The Encyclopedia of New York City.* New Haven, Conn.: Yale University Press, 1995.

James, Edward T., Janet Wilson James, and Paul S. Boyer. *Notable American Women, 1607–1950: A Biographical Dictionary.* Cambridge, Mass.: Harvard University Press: 1971.

Johnson, Howard Eugene, and Wendy Johnson. *Dancer in the Revolution: Stretch Johnson, Harlem Communist at the Cotton Club.* New York: Fordham University Press, 2014.

Johnson, James Weldon. *Black Manhattan.* New York: Perseus, 1930.

Johnson, William Henry. *Autobiography.* Albany, N.Y.: Argus, 1900.

Macdonald, Allan. "Up from Slavery: Four Generations of the Williams Family Span the Modern History of the Republic, From Pre-War Slavery Days to the Present, Each and All Actively Exemplifying the Qualities of Loyalty and Courage." *World Magazine*, March 27, 1927.

Marshall, David. *Grand Central.* New York: Whittlesey House, 1946.

Osofsky, Gilbert, *Harlem: The Making of a Ghetto: Negro New York, 1890–1930.* New York: Harper and Row, 1966.

Paulsson, Martin. *The Social Anxieties of Progressive Reform, Atlantic City, 1854–1920.* New York: New York University Press, 1994.

"Progress of Grand Central 'Red Caps.'" *New York Age,* July 6, 1918.

Robins, Anthony W., and Maxinne Leighton. *Grand Central Terminal: 100 Years of a New York Landmark.* New York: Harry N. Abrams, 2013.

Robinson, J. E. "James H. Williams and His Success at Grand Central Terminal." *Colored American*, August 1909.

Romero, Patricia. "The Early Organization of Red Caps, 1937–1938." *Negro History Bulletin* 29, no. 5 (1966): 101–14.

"R.R. Attendants Organize." *New York Age,* July 21, 1910.

Scott, Emmett J. *Scott's Official History of the American Negro in the World War.* Chicago: Homewood Press, 1919.

"300 Red Caps Employed at Grand Central R.R. Station Serve Thousands Each Day." *New York Age,* July 21, 1923.

Trotter, James Monroe. *Music and Some Highly Musical People.* Boston: Lee and Shepard, 1878.

Tunis, John R. "The Red Cap Tells the World." *Elks Magazine*, June 1927.

Walton, Lester. "Square Deal for Red Caps." *New York Age,* June 8, 1918.

Wilk, Daniel Levinson. "The Red Cap's Gift: How Tipping Tempers the Rational Power of Money." *Enterprise and Society* 16, no. 1 (2015): 5–50.

Zeisloft, E. Idell, ed. *The New Metropolis: Memorable Events of Three Centuries, 1600–1900.* New York: D. Appleton and Co., 1899.

INDEX

Notes: Page numbers in *italics* refer to illustrations. Captions are indexed as text. Page numbers after 302 refer to Notes.